"That Was Part of Baseball Then"

ALSO BY VICTOR DEBS, JR.

*Missed It by That Much:
Baseball Players Who Challenged the Record Books*
(McFarland, 1998)

*Still Standing After All These Years:
Twelve of Baseball's Longest Standing Records*
(McFarland, 1997)

"That Was Part of Baseball Then"

Interviews with 24 Former Major League Baseball Players, Coaches and Managers

Victor Debs, Jr.

McFarland & Company, Inc., Publishers
Jefferson, North Carolina, and London

Library of Congress Cataloguing-in-Publication Data

Debs, Victor, Jr., 1949–
 "That was part of baseball then" : interviews with 24 former major league baseball players, coaches and managers / Victor Debs, Jr.
    p.   cm.
 Includes index.

 ISBN-13: 978-0-7864-1178-8
 softcover : 50# alkaline paper ∞

 1. Baseball players—United States—Interviews. 2. Major League Baseball (Organization)—Interviews. 3. Baseball—United States—History—20th century. I. Title.
 GV865.A1D3745   2002
 796.357'092'2—dc21   2002004810

British Library cataloguing data are available

©2002 Victor Debs, Jr. All rights reserved

No part of this book may be reproduced or transmitted in any form or by any means, electronic or mechanical, including photocopying or recording, or by any information storage and retrieval system, without permission in writing from the publisher.

Manufactured in the United States of America

Cover photograph © 2002 PhotoDisc

McFarland & Company, Inc., Publishers
 Box 611, Jefferson, North Carolina 28640
  www.mcfarlandpub.com

To all former major league players, coaches and managers

Acknowledgments

I want to express my gratitude to the following people for their contributions to this book:

My wife, Lola, whose work in videotaping the interviews and taking post-interview photos was invaluable, and whose companionship during our travels to meet the ballplayers made the project that much more enjoyable.

Literary agent Stephen Casari may be the world's biggest fan of former Braves slugger Eddie Mathews. It is also true that his support for this project was a steady source of encouragement.

Publicist Henry Holmes assisted in arranging the interviews with Catfish Hunter and Fred Patek.

Finally, thanks to all the former major leaguers who generously gave of their time to talk baseball. That this book would have remained a baseball fan's fantasy without their assistance and cooperation is an obvious understatement. Thanks for the memories, gentlemen!

Table of Contents

Acknowledgments vii
Introduction 1

ON THE ROAD   5

Bob Friend   7
Bobby Thomson   13
Johnny Pesky   20
Jim Kaat   28
Frank Malzone   38
Dale Berra   49
Larry Bowa   59
Gil McDougald   72
Gene Garber   85
Billy Sample   98
Nellie Briles   111
Jon Matlack   125

ON THE PHONE   145

Catfish Hunter   147
Fred Patek   151

Table of Contents

Vernon Law 156

Clem Labine 161

Virgil Trucks 166

Frank Tanana 171

Jimmy Greengrass 177

Bill Virdon 184

Sparky Anderson 189

Dick Williams 195

Hector Lopez 201

Ralph Houk 208

Index 215

Introduction

> Bliss in possession will not last;
> Remembered joys are never past.
> *British poet James Montgomery, 1925*

Every baseball fan has a favorite memory. Mine came in the nightcap of a twinbill at Yankee Stadium in late June of 1970. Having dropped the first of two to the Indians, with Sudden Sam McDowell notching the complete-game win, the Yanks were on the verge of being swept as they were one tally short in the bottom of the ninth. Cleveland closer Fred Lasher recorded the first out and faced southpaw slugger Bobby Murcer, who was experiencing his ultimate career performance that afternoon, having already connected three times; ironically, all homers came off lefty hurlers.

Lethal against righties, Lasher's right-hand deliveries were more susceptible to punishment from lefties. I was nevertheless pessimistic; Murcer had parked three and chances were slim of a record tying four-straight. When the count reached three-and-two, Lasher, to his credit or discredit depending on one's view, challenged Murcer with a knee-high strike. Bobby swung, and 17,000 roared in hopeful anticipation as the ball headed toward the right field foul pole. Plenty of distance, but would it stay fair?

The ball caromed high off the pole. After circling the bases and crossing home plate, Murcer raised his cap in salute to the crowd. Judging from the reception in the dugout and explosion from the stands, one would have thought it the victorious end to a World Series game. It amounted to as much for Yankee fans who had maintained their loyalty for five-straight frustrating seasons, an unsuccessful stretch that would endure for another five years and would rate as the worst in the proud history of the franchise. The Yanks went on to win the nightcap and I went home thoroughly satisfied with the split, knowing that my favorite Yank had etched his name in the record books.

If the Oklahoman's performance was unforgettable for spectators, it became a cherished memory for Murcer as well; as a baseball broadcaster and commentator he has more than once described his heroics of that day, albeit not always accurately. (Bobby once recalled that all the homers were hit against lefties.) It is not important that Murcer forgets the specifics, only that he recalls the ecstasy shared by player and fans that day.

All former ballplayers have unique memories. Some are more fondly recalled—the early years spent learning the game as a youngster, the first time stepping onto the field as a big leaguer, a pitcher's first strikeout, a batter's first hit. Some disappointing, even disheartening memories—the first trade, a World Series loss, a release leading to the end of a career—can still be recounted with a trace of a smile decades later.

"That Was Part of Baseball Then" focuses on the memories and opinions of two dozen old-timers. "Old-timer" refers to any former major league player, coach or manager. An attempt was made to include players spanning as many decades as possible—for example, Johnny Pesky in the forties, Frank Malzone in the fifties, Jim Kaat in the sixties, Billy Sample in the seventies, Dale Berra in the eighties.

The project began by mailing over two hundred queries requesting interviews, with about one-third positive responses received. Nothing was deduced from a player's rejection or lack of response except an unwillingness to participate. Or inability. Numerous letters were returned unopened, as old-timers had moved to unknown addresses. In a few instances, they were too busy or sick to participate, or had passed away. I recall the courteous reply sent by the daughter of former pitcher Tom Buskey indicating his tragic death at age 53 a month prior to receipt of the letter.

Arrangements were made to meet with some old-timers in person, while others agreed to telephone conversations. Whether face-to-face or on the phone, each former player proved gracious, enthusiastic and extremely generous with his time. Indeed, most conversations lasted well beyond the agreed forty-five minutes to one-hour time limit. After the interview at his Swampscott, Massachusetts home, Johnny Pesky even apologized for "talking too much," but was assured of its impossibility from the point of view of the listener.

During all conversations, a conscious attempt was made by the interviewer to *avoid* mentioning episodes that might be regarded as embarrassing or objectionable by the ballplayer. (I am reminded of a 1995 interview of Ted Williams by ESPN's Roy Firestone, who wonders about the reasons for the Hall of Famer's often-irascible attitude toward the press while an active player and for his spitting in the direction of the Fenway crowd during a 1956 game.) Unless the old-timer initiated discussion about a distasteful aspect of his career, as did Dale Berra when he talked about his substance abuse problem of the early 1980s, no such topic was broached. The book focuses on memories that are significant and unique to the old-timers, not on consequential or controversial events in baseball history.

Some will correctly detect the absence of a theme in "*That Was Part of Baseball Then*," while baseball historians might complain about the author's failure to provide ample accompanying research or "fresh insight." Readers should keep in mind the book's main purpose—to entertain more than inform; it offers more nostalgia than news. No pretense is made of its being intellectually stimulating. Just some old-timers and a longtime fan talking baseball.

Finally, throughout the conversations there was no conscious attempt by the players to hurt anyone's feelings. If, on rare occasions, they are critical of former teammates, opponents, managers, or executives, it is merely a reflection of their honesty rather than any purposeful attempt to demean. Jon Matlack probably summarized the intent of all the players when he wrote underneath his signature granting permission to use his comments, "All of the information given is based on my memory and opinion, and was given with no intention of hurting anyone or being controversial. Please keep that in mind as you proceed with your book. Thanks and good luck!"

Well put, Jon, and thank you!

ON THE ROAD

All of the dozen in-person interviews were arranged with the convenience of the ballplayers in mind, which usually meant traveling by car from Staten Island to towns as near as Watchung, New Jersey, a half-hour's drive, and as distant as Fox Chapel near Pittsburgh, a six-hour-plus journey. Most round-trips were accomplished on the same day, although Pittsburgh excursions meant staying overnight at a motel.

My wife of twenty years, Lola, accompanied me on each trip, and besides sharing driving duties in our minivan, videotaping the interviews and taking post-interview photos, she proved a delightful companion; I can honestly report our not coming close to a squabble throughout the project. It is also my belief that Lola came away from it with a better understanding of the magnitude of the task of becoming a big leaguer, the dedication required to remain a big leaguer, and the always active post-career life of a big leaguer.

"Conversation is one of the greatest pleasures in life," Somerset Maugham once wrote. Perhaps he had just finished chatting with an old-timer.

Bob Friend

"The pendulum has swung a long way in the players' direction. It needed to swing that way." Bob Friend is commenting on modern player-owner bargaining relations from his home located in a secluded cul-de-sac in Fox Chapel, Pennsylvania, just outside of Pittsburgh. "When I played, we didn't really have a union. It was a representative system, and that didn't amount to much bargaining power. We had no leverage, so we didn't really have many gripes at the time. Maybe we were concerned about scheduling, night games, meal money. It wasn't the big deal that it became."

In 1966, his final season of a 16-year major league career, Friend was the National League Player Representative and became one of four on a search committee to choose a chief spokesman for the Players Association. The list of candidates was narrowed to two. "I was kind of leaning toward Bob Cannon until I found out that he didn't really want the job." Friend corrects himself. "Well, he wanted it, but started losing interest when the players began to push for having the office in New York. Cannon was a sitting judge in Milwaukee and didn't want to move. So that's when Robin Roberts and Jim Bunning brought in Marvin Miller."

The former legal consultant for the Steelworkers Union was chosen, and today Miller is credited (or blamed) more than anyone for revolutionizing baseball's labor-management relations. Through his efforts, the reserve clause became extinct and was replaced by a system that included free agency and arbitration. "The shame about the situation that's developed is that players move around all the time," Bob says. "When we played we usually stayed with one team, so fans associated players with particular teams. There was more of a feeling of closeness between the fans and players. Not any more."

Friend's viewpoints about the modern game come toward the end of an interview that began forty minutes earlier on a sunny April afternoon in 1999. A doormat that reads "Welcome, The Friends" lies at the entrance of a brick-faced home, where Lola and I are greeted by the six-foot former pitcher, neatly but comfortably attired in a white golf shirt and black pants.

We are led to a section of the living room with a mahogany table standing aside a wall supporting numerous framed photos and memorabilia of Friend's ballplaying days. One includes a shot of Bill Mazeroski rounding third after hitting his celebrated home run against the Yanks' Ralph Terry, giving the Pirates the victory in the finale of the 1960 World Series. "I was in the dugout when Maz hit it out," recalls Bob. "I had been pitching earlier. I thought I made two good pitches but [Bobby] Richardson singled to left, [Dale] Long singled to right, and I was out of there. The next thing you know, they had tied the score. I wasn't feeling good about it. I was thinking, 'What the heck do you have to do? I made two good pitches and I'm knocked out.' Then all of a sudden Maz hits the ball. I didn't think it was going out because the way [Yogi] Berra was drifting back it looked like he was going to catch it. But the ball went thirty feet over the fence."

For Friend, 1960 was the culmination of a baseball career that originated in Lafayette, Indiana, where he was born on November 24, 1930. Bob was a teenager playing for the Lafayette Red Sox, a semi-pro club, when a scout for the Dodgers named Stan Feezle spotted him. "Feezle had signed Gil Hodges and Carl Erskine out of Indiana," Friend notes. "He was a big fan of mine and was really behind me. I guess he and my dad encouraged me to pursue a professional career more than anyone. Unfortunately, my dad died of cancer before I turned pro."

Feezle worked for Dodger executive Branch Rickey, who, after being fired in 1950, went to the Pirates. He took Feezle with him. After several years of watching Friend's progress, Feezle convinced Rickey of the right-hander's potential. Friend signed for $17,000. Says Bob, "I went to the Pirate spring training camp at San Bernardino, California, in 1950, but they sent me to the Class B team in Waco, Texas, of the Big State League. Buddy Hankin was the player-manager. He was my catcher and was an outstanding motivator."

Friend had a good year in Waco, which included a no-hitter in his final outing. In July, he was shipped to the Triple A Indianapolis club of the American Association, where his pitching raised the eyebrows of skipper Al Lopez. Friend continued to impress at the Pirates' 1951 spring training camp and made the ballclub. "Billy Myer was my first big-league manager. He liked my arm and worked me into the rotation early."

Besides leading the league in ERA in 1955 and wins in 1958, Bob led N. L. pitchers in innings-pitched in 1956 and 1957 and in games-started from 1956 to 1958. "I'm proud of the fact that I was able to pitch every third and fourth day. Not too many guys could do that, or wanted to. I was eager to pitch, regardless of who was out there. I don't know how many times Warren Spahn and I hooked up. It seemed I would always face the best pitchers."

And best-hitting ballclubs. "I pitched against that tough Milwaukee team every series. Speaking of which, I was surprised to find out recently that I gave up 16 homers to Eddie Mathews and 11 to Hank Aaron over a period of 15 years. That's not too bad."

Although Friend often pitched effectively, he remained inconsistent during his first four years. Rickey contemplated a trade. "Then I pitched a game against Brooklyn at Ebbets Field that I would say was the turning point of my career. I was behind 3–1. They were going to take me out of the game but I kind of fought to stay in there. We ended up winning the game 6–3 and I had 10 strikeouts."

Friend describes other games in his career that are particularly memorable. "I struck out Stan Musial with the bases loaded and won 2–0 for my tenth win in 1956. I remember the game I won my 20th in 1958 after six tries. Dick Stuart hit a homer off Marv Grissom over the clock at Forbes Field and I won 5–4, then won my next two starts very quickly. Speaking of Stuart, I remember him liking to go for the long ball. And I mean *long*. If it wasn't *long*, he wasn't happy.

"In 1960, I had so many good games coming down the stretch. In a game in St. Louis, we were half a game behind and I pitched against Larry Jackson. I beat him 4–1 to put us back into first place. In September, our lead was down to three games and I beat the Dodgers 4–2 in Los Angeles. Nineteen-sixty was probably my best year because my 18 wins were important in helping to win the pennant."

The discussion turns to Game Seven of the 1960 Series. The Pirates were trailing by three runs in the eighth. "None of us had given up," insists Friend. "We had a mixture of veteran players and a team that made very few mistakes. And the team had so much resilience. We would always come back. We won about 40 games that year while trailing in the seventh. I don't know how many times we came back in Los Angeles. There was a game against Koufax that we were trailing 3–1 in the ninth and won 4–3. So we were confident all through the Series that we were going to beat the Yanks."

A bad-hop single off the bat of Bill Virdon caromed off Tony Kubek's throat, Roberto Clemente beat out a swinging roller when pitcher Jim

Coates failed to cover first base, and the Bucs took the lead on Hal Smith's timely three-run blast. The Yankees rallied to tie in the ninth, setting the stage for Maz's clout. "Smith's homer was very important, but Mazeroski's ended it. I believe it's still the only home run to end a World Series, so it's not surprising that it's the one remembered today, especially when you consider that the New York press thought we were going to get clobbered. It was a stunning blow.

"Mazeroski was the greatest second baseman I ever saw. He got rid of the ball on the double play faster than anyone. He should be in the Hall of Fame."

One of the players on the 1960 Pirates was Roberto Clemente, whom Friend labels a tremendous athlete. "When he joined us in 1955, you could see that he was going to be special. He was probably one of the top five ballplayers I've ever seen."

Clemente resented the 1960 MVP vote in which sportswriters snubbed him and gave the award to Pirate teammate Dick Groat. Friend understands how Clemente felt, but believes Groat was deserving of the honor. "He [Groat] won the batting title and was terrific in the field. He wasn't with us for two weeks in the season when he broke his wrist, but he had an outstanding season. But I don't remember Clemente complaining in the clubhouse that he should have been the MVP. Roberto would never do that. We heard about his disappointment through the press."

During his career, Clemente developed a reputation for being moody, and being somewhat of a hypochondriac. "He dressed right next to me and I always got along with him," Bob remarks. "All this stuff I hear about his being temperamental or always complaining, I never saw that. And as far as his being criticized for sitting out games, well, as hard as he played all the time, putting out one thousand percent, I can see why he probably had some injuries and would need a rest.

"The only negative thing I ever saw with Clemente is when he and [Danny] Murtaugh got into it in the clubhouse in 1960 or 1961, I'm not sure of the year. Roberto came twenty minutes late and didn't take batting practice before a doubleheader. I think he said he got caught in traffic. Murtaugh came in and told him not to dress. Murtaugh was looking for leadership from Clemente and was trying to maintain discipline, so he wanted to send Roberto and the ballclub the message that we had a chance to win this thing and we're not going to do it by having our top players not showing up. Of course, the press reported the incident. That was a downer for both Clemente and Murtaugh, but they patched everything up."

On New Year's Day of 1972, Clemente was killed in a plane crash while on a mission to transport much-needed supplies to Nicaraguan earthquake victims. Bob recalls hearing about the tragedy. "I was in Fort Lauderdale. Del Miller, the harness race driver, called me early in the morning. We were supposed to play golf that day. He told me that Roberto was dead. It was a huge shock, and then the news came out later that the plane should never have taken off, which made the tragedy even worse. Well, I was Allegheny County Comptroller at the time so I took a plane to Puerto Rico with some of the Pittsburgh politicians and Pirate officials. When we got there, I went with Joe Brown [Pirate general manager] to where the plane had crashed. We just kept looking out into the ocean, not believing what happened."

I ask Bob about his views on the modern game. "Long-term contracts cause problems. Some players can handle it and others can't. Some don't have the incentive to really bust every day when that long-term contract is in effect. Then you have some of these big contracts that are way out of whack. But you can't blame the players for that."

Despite his concerns, Friend is optimistic about the game's future. "Since the last agreement between the owners and players, things have settled down. And of course, last season's home run derby was just outstanding. That really brought baseball back. The interest is just tremendous. I just hope they are able to work out some kind of a system where the small market teams are going to be able to survive. For instance, this franchise here in Pittsburgh is 113 years old. There's a lot of history here. But right now, things are looking pretty good with the new ballpark."

Friend is referring to PNC Stadium, scheduled for opening in 2001. The day before our visit, Bob attended the groundbreaking ceremony. It followed the renaming of the Sixth Street Bridge to the Roberto Clemente Bridge. "They brought down the veil and it showed "21-Clemente Bridge." The bridge has a plaque showing Roberto. There must have been 20,000 people there.

"Then we walked over to the groundbreaking ceremony. All the politicians were there. I was invited with Dick Groat and some old Pirate players. The small diamond was there, and it goes 425 feet straight out to center field to the Allegheny River. It will be a small stadium, holding about 38,000 with a grass field. And the right field fence will be—guess what—21 feet high [Bob smiles], for Roberto's number. It should be a good slugger's park. I imagine the Allegheny will be holding a lot of soggy baseballs after they start playing."

Friend believes the trend towards cozier, smaller ballparks as opposed to the large symmetrical parks and domed stadiums of the 1970s is a change for the better. "When I played, we had Forbes Field and Crosley

Field with the terrace in the outfield. We had Ebbets Field, just a wonderful ballpark. Then you had the Polo Grounds, with the long center field and the facing. All parks had grass fields, and each had its own character."

After his playing career, Friend became involved in politics and served two terms as Pittsburgh's comptroller. "Tom Johnson, one of the Pirate owners, was the Republican Finance Chairman. He coaxed me into getting involved. Then I decided to get out of it and went into the insurance business with BABB, Inc., and I've been with them ever since. I'm kind of semi-retired now and play a lot of golf. I have a son, Bob, who's on the tour. I kind of follow him and have a lot of fun with that. He's doing well this year, making the cut eight out of 11 times. I expect he might win one this year."

Following the interview, Bob leads us to a hallway with additional memorabilia, including a photo of the 1960 world championship Pittsburgh Pirates. It was a team that broke the hearts of Yankee fans nearly four decades ago. The loss in the Series was the forewarning of a period of failure unprecedented in the history of the Bronx franchise. Although the Bombers appeared in the Fall Classic in the four years proceeding 1960, they won only once, and following their loss to the Cardinals in 1964, they would not come close to taking a pennant for the next 11 years.

Bob Friend at his home in Fox Chapel, Pennsylvania.

For this longtime Yankee rooter, the memory of Mazeroski's ghastly drive continues to haunt. How could the mighty Yankees lose to the horrid Pirates, a team whose nickname was derived from its stealing key players from opposing ballclubs in the late 19th century? The remembrance has, however, grown less tormenting with passing years and decades. What better proof than my amiable chat with Bob Friend, a key player on that hated 1960 Pittsburgh team.

Bobby Thomson

Most ballplayers would settle for Bobby Thomson's career stats. Throughout much of his 15 years in the majors, Thomson was the model of power consistency. The "Staten Island Scot" had eight 20-homer seasons, five coming consecutively. In five of eight years playing for the New York Giants, he led the club in home runs, and he topped the National League in triples in 1952. Thomson amassed four 100 RBI seasons, as many as collected by former Yankee slugger and Hall-of-Famer Mickey Mantle. He appeared in three All-Star Games.

Despite his long-term success, Thomson's achievements remain obscured by one brief but momentous swing, which for baseball fans evokes thoughts of Russ Hodges' emotional pronouncement, "The Giants win the pennant! The Giants win the pennant!"; of an ecstatic Eddie Stanky mugging Leo Durocher while the victorious manager awaits the completion of his conquering hero's victory run; of a forlorn Dodger, Jackie Robinson, standing with hands on hip in the infield, staring motionless in disbelief; of a distraught Ralph Branca, head down, sobbing in the clubhouse; of one of the most celebrated events in sports history—the shot heard round the world!

Fame brings exhilaration but may also lead to frustration and bitterness, especially if one's lifetime is defined by one extraordinary feat. So I ask the 75-year-old Bobby Thomson if he ever resented being remembered for the pennant-clinching homer of 1951. "I've always been glad to have that one shining moment in my life," he answers from his home in Watchung, New Jersey, on a pleasant May day in 1999. "Later on, very little time was spent thinking about what I had done in my baseball career. I had to go out and get a job and support my family. So it was kind of nice when cab drivers in New York would honk the horn and yell, 'Hey, Bobby!'

"If I hadn't hit the home run, Ralph Branca and I would have been forgotten about for the most part. I would have missed all the attention and invitations that I'm still getting. Let's face it, it's kind of fun. And it also puts me in the position where people come and ask me to pitch in for a lot of great charities. Being retired now, I feel good about helping out whenever I can."

Born in Glasgow, Scotland, in 1923, Thomson immigrated to America with his family three years later. His father put food on the table by working in carpentry and construction. He also became captivated by America's national pastime. "He used to be a Dodger fan," Bobby admits. "I'm not sure how that happened. Maybe it's because the Dodgers weren't having the best of luck at that time. He probably related to the underdog."

One day, older brother Jim brought home a baseball glove from his job at Sears & Roebuck, and Bobby was hooked. "It was something to get that glove," Thomson says. "Jim would take me out in the backyard and work with me. He'd throw the ball, and I guess the bat was kind of heavy because I wouldn't always hit the ball back to him. He'd get sore at me once in a while when I'd have him chasing the ball, but he was a guy who was always behind me. I guess you can say it was Jim who got me started in baseball."

Dad helped too. The senior Thomson would walk his youngest of six kids to wherever there was a ballgame. Bobby's skills as an infielder improved to the point where he was playing sandlot ball as a teenager. "Once someone kidded my father and said, 'Bobby will be with the Giants some day.' He said, 'Don't think he won't be.' To this day, I regret that he died while I was still in high school and never had a chance to see me play in the big leagues."

While playing for the Gulf Oilers of the Industrial League on Sunday afternoons, Bobby handled the shortstop position at Curtis High School on Staten Island, where Coach Harry O'Brien allowed the youngster two errors a ballgame. His first pro contract came in 1942 with the New York Giants. He was assigned to the Class D club in Bristol, Virginia, and played third base until wartime service in the Air Corps began the following year.

Honorably discharged in 1946, Bobby joined other big-league hopefuls at the Giants' camp in Jacksonville, Florida, in February. Thomson surprised himself by making the jump to Triple A ball in Jersey City. It was the same year Jackie Robinson was making his pro debut. "I played in Robinson's first game in organized ball. He played for the Montreal Royals. They won everything that year."

Called up by the Giants toward the end of the season, Thomson made his big league debut on September 9, played in 17 additional games, and finished the season with a .315 average, nine RBIs, and a pair of homers. His admirable performance did not earn an automatic roster spot the following season. During spring training at Phoenix, Arizona, Thomson competed for the third base job with fellow rookie Jack Rohrke and Sid Gordon, a regular in 1946. Giant manager Mel Ott rotated the trio in exhibition games. "At the end of spring training, we got on our own private train and barnstormed back east with the Indians, who were training in Tucson. Well, we were a week out of New York, and I guess Ott didn't like the looks of the second baseman. So he asked me to try. You know, second base is the worst place for an inexperienced guy to play but I guess he had seen me do things that made him think I'd be okay. I fouled up a double play on Opening Day, but I started to get the feel of it.

"Then it wasn't long before Ott asked me to go to the outfield. We had rookies out there who weren't playing too well. It was a very windy spring and balls weren't being caught that should have been caught. I was pretty fast. I had done well in some of the races we ran in spring training so I guess Ott thought I could cover ground. I loved it out there. I could run and go get 'em."

Thomson recalls Ott's personality. "Mel was easy to play for. He was the opposite of Durocher because he was laid back. He could get mad when he saw things that he didn't like. But when you mention his name, I remember him as being a real gentleman, somebody who you could invite over for dinner."

In mid-season of 1948, former Dodger manager Leo Durocher replaced Ott. "Back in those days, the Dodgers and Giants had a rivalry you wouldn't believe. Players just didn't like each other. Gil Hodges was the only Dodger I'd say hello to. It wasn't that we didn't respect the other guys. It was just the nature of the rivalry not to like them.

"So when Leo came over from those hated Dodgers and walked into our clubhouse for the first time, he looks at us and wipes his hand across his chest and says, 'Giants. Giants. That's what it's all about. Let's forget about all that stuff that's gone on before. We're all Giants and we'll play like a team.' And I don't recall there being any resentment toward him from the players. Even if there was, he had quite a personality so it wouldn't take long for him to win you over. We all wanted to win, and that's what he was all about."

In Durocher's first full season in 1949, the Giants finished fifth, eight games below the .500 mark, improved to a 86–68 record and third place in 1950, and were poised to challenge the Dodgers and Phillies for the flag in 1951. A miracle surge in the final two months erased a 13½-game deficit, necessitating a three-game playoff with the Dodgers. New York took Game One, thanks largely to Thomson's two-run homer off Branca. It is a feat forgotten by most fans, but not by Thomson. "To have the pennant on the line in a three-game playoff and to be able to come through in the first game was a nice feeling."

The club was trounced the following day, setting the stage for the dramatic finale. The Dodgers had a 4–1 in the ninth inning, but Al Dark and Don Mueller singled, and one out later, Whitey Lockman doubled in a run. Dodger manager Charlie Dressen removed fatigued starter Don Newcombe in favor of Branca, who would again pitch to Thomson.

Mueller had suffered a leg injury while sliding into third. It would play a significant role in the drama that followed. "I was waiting with my bat in hand, and Mueller's injury just took my mind completely off the game. It wasn't until they carried him off the field that it was back to baseball." A relaxed but focused Thomson strode the ninety feet from dugout to home plate. "I was psyching myself up, telling myself, 'Get up there, you S.O.B., and give yourself a chance to hit. Do a good job, you S.O.B. Wait and watch. Don't get overanxious, you S.O.B.' I had never done that before.

"I took the first pitch down the middle. The guys told me later that they wanted to kill me for taking that first one. But I wanted to wait and watch. You know, the good hitters do that. Williams was the best. He could sit back, wait for the ball, have a good look at it before cutting loose. Anyway, Branca tried to waste the second pitch high and inside, trying to set me up for a breaking pitch away. Remember, in the Polo Grounds you could hit it 500 feet to center and Duke Snider would do a pretty good job of running it down. But Branca didn't get it inside far enough. It was a ball, but I was very quick with my hands. You know, I had been hitting well the last three months of the year.

"I got around on it and hit it hard. I thought, 'Upper deck home run.' Then I looked at the darned thing and it must have had tremendous overspin. I just got on top of it a fraction. So now it's starting to sink and I'm thinking, "It's not a home run, it's just a base hit.' Then it disappeared in the lower deck."

As the celebration subsided in the Giant dugout, Thomson was approached with a $500 offer to appear on the *Perry Como Show*. Though he felt he could use the money, Thomson declined, saying he just wanted to get home to his family. When the offer was doubled, the newborn celebrity responded, "For $1,000, I guess the family can wait."

After the show, Thomson returned to the New Dorp section of Staten

Island where brother Jim greeted him. "I told him, 'Don't ask me what happened over there. The good Lord must have had something to do with it.' Then he said, 'Do you realize what you did? Something like that will never happen again.' When he said that, for the first time I looked at it in a completely different aspect. Before, I had thought that we beat the Dodgers, and that was it. Never did I think they'd still be talking about it."

Thomson's famed blast remains his most cherished of baseball memories. I ask him to recall others. "There was the time I made an over-the-shoulder catch for the final out, with us having a one-run lead and the ballgame in the balance. The reason I remember that game is because my sister and her husband drove down to watch.

Bobby Thomson at his home in Watching, New Jersey.

"Then there was the time when I was back to playing third base after Willie Mays came up. You always wonder how you'll manage in pressure situations. And you're always thinking you want to get that first man out. So Carl Furillo topped a ball down the third base line and I ran in and scooped it up with my bare hand. It was a do-or-die play and I made it. Later I thought, 'Hey, that was pretty good. I must have been pretty loose out there.'"

Thomson received a salary hike for the '52 season. "They offered me $2,000 more at first. Of course, I didn't sign for that." Early that year, the "Saintly Scot" of the Polo Grounds performed another miracle. Trailing by three in the bottom of the ninth, Bobby connected for a game-winning grand slam. But his heroic deeds weren't sufficiently numerous in subsequent seasons to satisfy management, leading to his trade to Milwaukee in 1954. "The Giants always expected more from me than they got, let's put it that way. And with Willie Mays coming back, they had the opportunity to get people they needed. So it [the trade] wasn't a surprise.

"If I had to be traded, I was glad it was to a team like Milwaukee.

And Gene Conley was on that team. He was a tough, sidearm pitcher. I remember he had hit me unintentionally on my thigh once, and that thing stayed with me for about a week. So I said to myself, 'Wow, at least I won't have to face him anymore.'"

The Conley incident diverts Bobby's attention to the way modern hitters react to brushbacks and beanballs. "When we got hit with a pitch, we didn't charge the mound like they do today. We got even. Durocher would say, 'Let's get two for one,' and we'd get a couple of their guys. I never thought I'd be rooting for the pitchers, but the batters these days give me a pain in the neck the way you're not supposed to throw inside. Pitchers have to throw inside. It's their job."

Thomson was sent back to the Giants in 1957, then to Chicago where he played for the Cubs for two seasons. He ended his career as an American Leaguer in Boston and Baltimore in 1960. "When I retired, I went to the Stephens Institute to take a battery of aptitude tests to find out what's between my ears. I only had a high school education, so they told me to try sales. I took a lot of interviews and ended up working for a paper company. Maybe in the long run my baseball career helped me in the business world. Sometimes, I'd introduce myself as Bob Thomson and I'd get back, 'Are you *the* Bobby Thomson?' But it wasn't necessarily the thing that helped move me along."

What rates as the most celebrated achievement in sports history? Gene Tunney's taking advantage of a long count to outpoint Jack Dempsey in their notorious heavyweight rematch of 1927? Jesse Owens' embarrassing a Führer in his homeland with a quadruple-gold-medal performance at the '36 Olympics? Tennis star Rod Laver's unprecedented second grand slam in 1969? The victory by the upstart AFL Jets over the heavily-favored NFL Colts in Super Bowl III of 1969, making good Joe Namath's pre-game prediction? Muhammed Ali's conquering rival Joe Frazier in a "Thrilla in Manilla" in 1975? Reggie Jackson's three-homers in Game Six of the '77 World Series? Mark McGwire's 70 round trippers in 1998 or Berry Bonds '73 in 2001?

Or was it Thomson's momentous Polo Grounds blast of 1951? It is no surprise that those who witnessed it are able to recall fifty years later precisely where they were and what they were doing at the time. No surprise, except for Thomson. "I've been a big fan of Bill Parcells [football coach] for some time, when he was with the Giants, then with the New England Patriots. Now that he's with the Jets, I've even become a Jets fan. He has a wonderful secretary, and she told me that Parcells still remembers my home run. He was ten years old, sitting in his back porch with his dog, listening to the ballgame. He even remembers what he was wearing. I couldn't believe it when she told me. Here I've been a big fan of his for years and didn't realize that he's been a fan of mine."

A month following the interview, Thomson visits Staten Island, New York, where his home town celebrates the U.S. Postal Service's new commemorative stamp honoring "The Shot Heard 'Round the World." Bobby appears at a ballfield named after him, takes a few swings, gives a speech, and shakes hands with students from P.S. 38, his old school. Two evenings later, Thomson appears at a cocktail reception in his honor, with receipts donated to a local charity. He autographs stamp books, shakes hands, listens to speeches given by dignitaries, and speaks briefly. "I can't say anything to justify all the nice things said about me," he remarks. "I'm just not used to all this attention."

Johnny Pesky

Having made one brief pit stop during a five-hour drive up 95 and 93 North on a May day in 1999, Lola and I arrive early in Swampscott, Massachusetts, for our two o'clock meeting with Johnny Pesky, former Red Sox infielder of the '40s and '50s. Located ten miles northeast of Boston, Swampscott is a picturesque and serene town nestled along Nahant Bay, an inlet off Massachusetts Bay. After some effort, we find a reasonably priced café and order predictably—chicken sandwich for Lola, veal parmigiana for myself. After lunch, we cross the street and relax on a plaza bench offering a panoramic view of the inlet prior to heading for Pesky's home.

Johnny and Ruth Pesky welcome us into the their handsomely-renovated 40-year-old ranch, then lead us through a living room containing a skylight ceiling and large stone fireplace, through sliding doors, and into an attractive and appealingly-comfortable den. Two conspicuous objects hanging on a wall adjacent the kitchen are a lithograph of Ted Williams and a photo of a young Pesky seated in the Red Sox dugout.

Pesky talks of having finally paid off the mortgage, that he "wouldn't have had it any other way," but wonders how his life would have changed had he played ball during a different era. "If I was about 25 years old today and could play for about five years, making about two or three million a year, that's all I'd need. Some players today ask me what my highest salary was and don't believe me when I tell them. Even the great ones weren't making the kind of money they make today."

Pesky's parents were born in what was Austria-Hungary before a world conflict altered the political map. "My dad had been a cook in the navy before World War I. He came to America with four other friends and brought my mother later. In fact, one in the group was the grandfather of Mickey Lolich [former Detroit Tiger hurler]. They went to New

York, to St. Louis, and finally to Portland, where they got jobs in logging camps."

Born John Michael Paveskovich, Johnny played high school, American Legion and semi-pro ball in Portland. Later, his younger brother Vinnie did the same, was eventually signed by the Yankee organization, and played for manager Lefty Gomez in the California State League. Despite failing to break into the majors (he abandoned his baseball quest, entered the University of Portland, and eventually obtained a masters in education), Vinnie's hardball experience in the Golden State made possible a friendship that would endure for decades. "Vinnie and Lefty really liked each other. After Lefty quit managing and joined the Wilson Corporation, he would give talks all over the country. Whenever he came to Oregon, Vinnie would pick him up and drive him all around. When I'd see him in Boston, Lefty would say, 'I saw your brother. He's still better looking than you are.' We were very fond of Lefty."

Pesky reflects with gratitude on his years in Portland. "I had a good childhood. We were lucky to have good opportunities. In the summertime, we would walk down the end of the block, meet with some kids, and go play baseball. In the winter, we'd be at the ice rink. There were no distractions like drugs or booze. And we all had families that made us understand that we had to be home at a certain hour. If we were told to be home at five o'clock, that meant five o'clock."

Labeling himself a frustrated teenage hockey player, Pesky was actually talented enough to try out for the pros in 1942 prior to joining the Red Sox. "I was working out with the players and was doing pretty good. But other guys who played the game told me that the NHL is tough and that I'd be better off as a ballplayer. So I chose baseball. The funny part of that story is that after the 1942 season ended, I worked in the winter as a hockey linesman in the Western Hockey League. I made five bucks a game."

Most of Pesky's baseball skills were developed while playing on talent-laden American Legion ballclubs in 1938 and 1939, which included several future major leaguers. He caught the attention of Boston scout Ernie Johnson. The former American League shortstop made a favorable impression on the prospect's mother. "Later I was offered more money by another organization. I can still remember what my mother said when I told her. 'No. Mr. Johnson will look out for you. Boston, Boston.' So I went to Boston and, of course, I'm glad that I did." Johnny's dad reacted coolly to the possibility of his son donning spikes, saying at one point, "If you be the best ballplayer, you'll be a bum," but got used to the idea. "He didn't really mind my going into pro ball," Pesky defends. "He just wanted me to be a decent person."

Pesky signed with the Red Sox in 1939 and the following year trained at Rocky Mount, North Carolina, where former Brooklyn Dodger Heinie Manush was coaching for the Red Sox. "When I first got to the training camp, I was holding the bat at the end. You know, when you're 19 or 20, you think you're so strong, even though I only weighed about 160 pounds. He [Manush] didn't say anything to me for about four or five days. Then, as we were getting ready to play, he saw me in a pepper game holding the bat at the end. He said, 'You know, Johnny, the way you're swinging that bat, they'll knock it right out of your hands. Try choking up a few inches and move closer to the plate.' So I took his advice and I hit .325 in my first year in pro ball. And I hit the same way throughout my career."

His outstanding season in Class A earned Pesky a tryout at the Triple A Louisville camp the following spring. Expecting to be shipped to the Double A club in Scranton, the 21-year-old was surprised to make the Louisville roster. "Playing in the American Association in those days was almost like playing in the majors. That year, 32 players went on to play in the majors—Preacher Roe, Harry Brecheen, Murry Dickson, Ray Sanders, Max Marshall, Harry Walker—they all played in the American Association that year. And all eight shortstops from that year went on to play in the majors."

Pesky's first shot at the big leagues came in the spring of 1942 when five shortstops were fighting for a spot on the Red Sox roster. "A kid named Merrill Combs, I thought, was the best of all of us, but he came up with frozen feet during the war." It came down to a battle between Eddie Pellagrini, a power hitter who socked 19 homers playing in the Coast League in 1941, and Pesky, who connected only twice that year but whose .325 average was appreciably superior to Pellagrini's. To assess their abilities, Boston manager Joe Cronin rotated them in exhibition games until a mid-spring injury became the turning point. "Eddie came up with a bad leg so I played against the Cardinals and Yankees two days in a row and did pretty well. As a matter of fact, I got a hit off of Lefty Gomez. He was close to the end of his career. I remember it like it was yesterday. I hit the ball over Joe Gordon's head for a single. I was standing at first, and Lefty said to me, 'If a little pea pod like you can get a base hit off me, I guess I *am* through.'"

In his first season in the majors, Pesky demonstrated what he had shown throughout his minor-league stint—he could swing the bat. The lefty hitter led the league with 205 safeties, becoming the 13th rookie to top the leaderboard in hits. His .331 average was runner-up to Ted Williams' league-leading .356. In 620 at bats, the five-foot, nine-inch rookie demonstrated a keen batting eye by fanning only 36 times in 620 at bats while drawing 42 walks, a sizable amount for a contact hitter lacking power. Pesky proved to be an alert baserunner and scored 105 runs, fifth best in the league. He was sure-handed and reliable in the field.

For Johnny, one game from that rookie year of 1942 is particularly memorable. "We were playing the Yankees in August in front of a full house on a Saturday afternoon. Spud Chandler was pitching. I used to hang up his jock strap as a youngster working in the Coast League. And here I am six or seven years later and I'm hitting against him. And he was a mean guy. He'd throw at your feet. Well, anyway, before the game Jack Mullaney, a writer for the old *Boston Post*, said to me, 'You know, Johnny. You haven't got a hit off Chandler this year. You're 0–14 against him.' Well, I knew he was right because you remember if a guy gets you out all the time. Ted [Williams] was sitting about ten feet away, so he comes over and says, 'Yeah, for crying out loud. You're trying to pull this guy and he's throwing you this hard sinker. How dumb can you be? My God, I'm a foot taller and 40 pounds heavier and I can't pull him.'

"So the game starts and my first time up—ground ball to second. And I'm thinking, 'Oooh, here we go again.' Second time up, same thing. Then in the bottom of the eighth, there are two outs with a man on and Dominic [DiMaggio] hits the ball down the right field line and [Tommy] Henrich gets the ball and throws it back to the infield.

"I'm the next hitter with two on and first base open. Before I go up, Ted pulls me by the sleeve and says, 'Now look, Johnny. For crying out loud, don't try to pull this guy. Just go up the middle. Man, you're dumb. I thought you knew a little about hitting.' So I said, 'Okay, I'll do exactly like you say.' So I turn to go up and he grabs me by the shirt again and says, 'You know damn well they're not gonna walk you to get to me.' That really gets me going.

"Well, I get in the batter's box and Chandler's looking at me with that scowl of his. He looked like a bulldog out there. So the first pitch is ball one, then strike one, then ball two, and here comes that hard sinker. Red Rolfe was playing third and is in on the grass cause I could run pretty good. I hit the ball by Rolfe and into left field. So now we're ahead 3–1 and Chandler is giving me holy hell. 'I'll stick one in your ear, you little bastard.' And I'm not paying attention to him. I'm just looking at Williams, the next batter. He's got a big grin and is giving me the thumbs-up sign.

"So Chandler gets set to throw and he steps off the rubber and looks over at me and gives me another blast. This time I answer, 'Hell with you. When you were in the Coast League, you were a lousy tipper.' Well, the first pitch to Ted he hits thirty rows in the bleachers. Everybody in our dugout got up to watch where the ball was going and when Ted comes in, he hears, 'Way to go Ted,' and 'You really got all of that one,' stuff like that. Well, I scored ahead of Ted and was sitting on the bench next to Bobby [Doerr]. I say, 'Christ, Bobby, I got the big hit in this inning and no one said anything to me.' So Ted says, 'Where's that horn-nosed little shortstop of ours?' And here he comes. Now, we're sitting side-to-side. He says, 'See, Johnny. Didn't I tell you how to hit this guy?' I say, 'Let me tell you something, Ted. He was so damn mad at me for getting that dinky little single he forgot you were the next batter.'"

Anticipating being drafted, Pesky and Williams attended flight school during the 1942 season. One week after returning to Portland at the end of the season, Johnny received orders to report to Amherst, Massachusetts, for war training school. Williams and Pesky were there for six months before being transferred to Chapel Hill, then to Indiana for flight training. "There were so many fliers that they came up with another program where station officers were needed for tower work at certain bases. A four-stripe captain, a Yankee fan, brought me into his office and told me I had just enough flight time to qualify. They sent me to Atlanta and that's where I got my commission. As a matter of fact, I think I got mine a week before Ted got his.

"But Ted was brilliant. He grasped things so quickly. When we were together in Indiana, Ted was going through the program like it was nothing and I was having more difficulty with it. After supper, I would work extra hours with my instructors. After about four or five months, Ted said to me, 'Johnny, why can't you get this stuff?' I said, 'Gee, Ted, I'm not you. I just need the extra work.'

"Ted was the same way as a player. After the war, we all got off to a great start, except for Bobby Doerr. Dom was hitting about .480, I was hitting .400, and Ted was probably hitting .600. But Bobby was hitting only about .260. One day, Dom, Bobby, and I were sitting in the dugout. Ted comes over and yells to Bobby from the field, 'Get up here!" Then he shows Bobby what he was doing wrong. 'For crying out loud, you've got your bat up, down, open, closed. You're using 14 different stances. Get a stance you can feel comfortable with and give it a try.' Well, Bobby is listening and hasn't opened his mouth yet. Finally, he tells Ted, 'But Ted, I am not you.' Williams throws his hands up in the air and says, 'You wanna be a lousy .280 hitter, be a .280 hitter.' But Bobby came out of it, and became a Hall of Famer."

In his first year back from the service, Pesky led the circuit in hits with 208, and was third in batting with a .335 mark. "If there was one game I recall more than any other that year, it was Opening Day. It was a dark, dreary day. The park was full. We were down 1–0 and I slid between Buddy Rosar's legs to tie it up around the sixth inning. Then we went to the bottom of the eighth and Dick Fowler was pitching. Now, I wasn't a pull hitter, I hit to all fields, but this time I hit it down the right field line, just inside the foul pole. Elmer Valo almost broke his arm trying to catch it. So we were ahead 2–1 in the last inning and the A's have the bases loaded with one out. The ball is hit to Bobby and it took a crazy hop and hit him on the shoulder. It caromed over to me about three feet away and I stepped on second and threw to first for the double play to end the game."

Most rewarding for Johnny in 1946 was his club's taking the pennant for the first time in 28 years. In the Series, the Sox lost to the Cardinals when in the deciding seventh game, Harry Walker's double scored Enos "Country" Slaughter from first. Baseball historians put much of the blame on cutoff-man Pesky, whose hesitation in throwing to the plate allowed Slaughter to tally. According to teammate Williams, the criticism is unwarranted. "Nobody yelled to him," Ted recalls in *My Turn at Bat*. "Not Doerr, or Higgins, or anybody. So you can't blame Pesky."

In 1947, Johnny hit .324, and his 207 safeties enabled him to lead the circuit for the third-consecutive season. "When you think about it, if I don't go in the Navy for three years, I would have had 1,000 hits in five years. That's never been done." He almost certainly would have cracked the 200-hit plateau one or two times as well. Nineteen forty-seven would be his final 200-hit season.

Nonetheless, Beantown fans witnessed many accomplishments from Pesky during his seven-year stint, which ended early in the 1952 season. In 1942, and from 1946 to 1951, Pesky hit over .300 six times, averaged 181 hits per season, and his combined batting average for the seven years was .315. He reached the 100-plateau in runs-scored in his first six seasons, and missed repeating the feat by seven in 1951. He drew 100 walks in 1949 and 1950, and was one short of the mark in 1948. Though his career statistics dropped dramatically in forthcoming seasons, Pesky's impressive first half and lifetime average of .307 warrant his being considered for the Hall of Fame. "When I first became eligible I didn't get many votes," Johnny acknowledges. "Writers called me and asked how I felt and I told them I didn't expect to get in. I'd love to be inducted but there are other guys that should be in as well. Dom DiMaggio. Bill Mazeroski. Why do they have to wait until guys have passed away to put them in?"

Despite being the mainstay of the Red Sox infield for seven years, Pesky was unloaded to the Tigers in a nine-player swap in June of 1952. "It was supposed to be a turnover year for the Red Sox. They had veterans

Johnny Pesky at his home in Swampscott, Massachusetts.

like DiMaggio, [Vern] Stephens, [Walt] Dropo, and me on the bench. They were playing kids like Gene Stephens in left, who was supposed to be the next Ted Williams. Ted was over in Korea. They had Faye Throneberry in right. Jimmy Piersall, who turned out to be one of the best center fielders, was playing short. Billy Consolo was at third, [Ted] Lepcio at second, Dick Gernert at first, and Sammy White catching. On June 12, (Don) Lenhardt hit a pinch-hit grand-slam homer to win the ballgame and put the Red Sox in first place. The next day, Lenhardt, Freddy Hatfield, Bill Wight, Walt Dropo, and myself all went to Detroit.

"Ruth and I were living at Lynn [two miles west of Swampscott] at the time and Cronin called the house and said, 'I've got bad news for you. I just traded you to Detroit.' Well, Walt Dropo was building a home in Marblehead [four miles northeast of Swampscott] and was living with us at the time. He was outside talking with his building contractor. So I went outside and told Walt, 'Cronin's on the phone. We're going to Detroit.' So he went in and talked with Cronin. We just thought the two of us were going but when we were in the car driving in to get our stuff, at the first traffic light we hear over the radio, 'Red Sox make a nine-player trade.'"

Two seasons with Detroit, half a year with the Senators, and Pesky's playing career was over. In the winter of 1954, Yankee general manager Lee MacPhail contacted Johnny and offered a coaching position on the Yankee farm club in Denver. He would be working with manager Ralph Houk, a former Yankee catcher. "That was one of the best things I ever did. I loved working with Ralph. We were very close."

Following the 1955 season, Tom Greenwade, the Yankee scout who had signed Mickey Mantle, phoned Pesky and offered a managing post at a co-op in Albuquerque. "No sooner did I put the phone down then John McHale of the Tigers called and asked me to manage a Class B team." Johnny accepted, and worked for several Detroit minor league teams from 1956 to 1960 before shifting to Seattle as skipper of Boston's Triple A club from 1961 to 1962. "The next year, [Pinky] Higgins left the dugout to become general manager and Mr. [Tom] Yawkey wanted me to take over. Thinking about it now, I wish I had gone back to Seattle for two more years. The Red Sox were not a good ballclub when I took over. But they were coming. And Yastrzemski—I had to bench him once for loafing. But we finally got things squared away."

Two second-division finishes by Boston resulted in Pesky being axed. He then worked as a coach for Pittsburgh, whose star player was Roberto Clemente. "He was a funny guy and had that delightful little accent. He never called me Pesky, he called me Pecky. None of the other players would think of calling me Pecky.

"I was there for three years and every spring Clemente would bring all the coaches a box of cigars and he'd bring perfume for the coaches' wives. I remember the time we went to Puerto Rico to play a series. Afterwards, we went to his place. There must have been 300 people there. What a spread he put out for us. The whole works. He was just a generous and fine man. And what a ballplayer. I can still see that gallop of his when he was running the bases."

After the interview, Ruth and Johnny lead us to the basement, where a collection of old photos are displayed on Johnny's Wall of Fame. One shows Johnny posing with his Navy outfit, which includes Ted Williams, Johnny Sain, and Bobby Doerr. Another is a team photo of the 1950 Red Sox ballclub, which set a still-standing team record .302 batting average. Johnny contributed with a .312 mark that year.

Before leaving, I ask Johnny to autograph a baseball. He is glad to do it. "I still get letters from fans today," he mentions. "I got one from a town in Texas and you could tell it was from a child from the way the envelope was written. Evidently, her teacher gave the students an assignment to write to a ballplayer. So I opened the letter and it said, 'My teacher will give me a good grade if you send your autograph on a piece of paper.' Then the next line read, 'Although I have never seen you play, my grandfather saw you play.' I loved that. I sent her an autographed photo."

Johnny escorts us to the minivan, thanks us for coming, and apologizes for prolonging the interview with numerous lengthy stories. I assure him they were a treat. While leaving Swampscott, Lola and I take one more admiring gaze at the breathtaking view of the inlet. It has been a most agreeable day.

Jim Kaat

Besides being a wonderful wife and competent camerawoman, Lola is a successful entrepreneur, having retailed in custom-made ladies wear for the past 15 years. Routinely, I drive her to midtown Manhattan on Mondays where she shops for supplies at various wholesale stores.

Returning home one Monday afternoon in mid-June of 1999, I check for telephone messages. The voice of Jim Kaat is discernible even before he mentions his name. The former lefty hurler and current Yankee broadcaster has received my letter requesting an interview and is phoning to arrange time and place. I return the call and suggest meeting at Yankee Stadium on Wednesday, since my 18-year-old daughter Jackie, Lola and I have tickets to the game that evening. Jim agrees to leave three passes at the press gate and meet us in the MSG press box at four o'clock.

We arrive at the stadium at three-thirty. Prior to entering, Jackie joins a sizable group of fans gathered near the players' entrance adjacent the press gate. There is a commotion as a tanned, handsome man wearing sunglasses stops to sign autographs. Jackie shoves a baseball between a forest of arms and into the hands of Rafael Palmeiro, star slugger of the Texas Rangers. Informed afterwards of the player's identity and team affiliation, she is noticeably disappointed.

Kaat has not yet arrived at the MSG booth, but his broadcasting sidekick, Ken Singleton, greets us warmly and invites us to wait. The view from the box offers an impressive panorama of an historic ballpark appreciably altered since visits during my youth. Gone is the picturesque upper deck facade that decorated the roof, with a portion now remaining in the unbefitting bleacher section. Monuments honoring former Yankee greats, more numerous today, are no longer delightfully-menacing obstacles to outfielders; they are instead hidden behind the left-center-field fence. The shortened distances to fences have made extinct Yankee Stadium's spacious

Death Valley, renowned for devouring even the lengthiest fly balls. Beyond the left-center to right-center fence are the bleachers, with Budweiser, The Wiz, Xerox, and Deer Park ads adorning the walls.

We watch as early birds Paul O'Neill and Tino Martinez take extra batting practice before Yank teammates join them 15 minutes later. Informed at four-thirty by a Yankee employee that traffic near the Third Avenue Bridge would further delay Kaat's arrival, Jackie and Lola decide to take a walk around the press level. They return with a report on food and beverage prices, markedly different from those in other sections of the park: hot dogs, 50 cents; soda, 75 cents; ice cream, one dollar (compared with $3.50, $3.50, and $3.00 at all other levels). It is decided that, following the interview, we would eat prior to taking our regular seats.

Jim arrives around five-fifteen, apologizes for the delay, and says he is glad we waited. The MSG booth being cramped, we are led to an unoccupied and more spacious press box. Jackie takes a seat, Lola prepares the camera, and the interview begins.

Kaat was born in 1938 in Zeeland, Michigan, population 4,000, and 125 miles north of Chicago. Explaining the sizable Cubs and White Sox following in a state that hosts Tiger games, Kaat says he grew up rooting for the Philadelphia Athletics. "My dad was an avid Connie Mack fan," Jim explains. "And for some reason, one of the first players he took a liking to was Lefty Grove. In fact, my dad once drove to Lonaconing, Maryland to visit the bowling alley that Grove owned, and he went to Grove's induction ceremony at the Hall of Fame in 1947. So I grew up following the A's and I could probably still name the starting lineup they had in the early fifties."

Modern professional athletes often excel in several sports in high school or college prior to deciding on one sport. Not Kaat. "From the time I was seven or eight years old I pretty much had my heart set on playing baseball." Kaat's imposing height of six-feet, six-inches belies a diminutive stature as an adolescent. "Funny thing, I was always the smallest kid in my class. People would ask, 'What are you gonna do when you grow up, little boy?' I would answer, 'I'm gonna play baseball.' And they'd say, 'Isn't that too bad. He's too small to play baseball.'"

Being pre–Little League, most of Kaat's youthful baseball experience consisted of six or eight neighborhood kids going to the local park until he was hired as batboy for a local team competing against various clubs around the county. "These guys were anywhere from 20 to 30 years old, and some had even played in the minors. When I was 16, the manager said I could pitch for the team. I thought I might be a little too young but my dad said to give it a shot. I pitched semi-pro ball, and that helped me a great deal."

Kaat explains the origin of a nickname that has endured for over fifty years. "When I went to spring training (with the Senators in 1957), I was the youngest player on the roster at 18 years old. Now, even today after being in the game for forty years, there are still some people who pronounce my name "cat," instead of "cot," the Dutch pronunciation. So everybody at the camp was calling me "cat." They would kid me about having a brother Tom or a brother Bob. Now, there were a couple of other pitchers before me who were known for being good fielding pitchers— Harry Brecheen had the nickname "Cat," and Harvey Haddix had the nickname "Kitten." The guys around the camp saw that I was a pretty good fielding pitcher, too. So they had the idea of naming me "Kitty," which also suited the way they pronounced my last name."

Kaat broke into the majors for the first time on an August day in 1959. He was scheduled to pitch a Double A game for Chattanooga when he was informed by manager Red Marion that the Senators were calling him up. "I was surprised because there were two or three other pitchers who were throwing better. I even told the trainer that my arm wasn't right. I couldn't throw from the top but had to come more from the side. I had sort of a catch in my back. But I went to Chicago on Saturday morning and started the second game of the doubleheader on Sunday afternoon. Probably the most memorable part of that start was that Louis Armstrong performed between games. I was a big Armstrong fan. They had him on a flatbed truck. When I was warming up, every three pitches I'd stop and watch Louis perform.

"As for the game—well, the White Sox had (Luis) Aparicio and (Nellie) Fox and Al Smith. They ended up winning the pennant that year. I only lasted a few innings."

After the season ended, Kaat returned to Michigan where medical tests and x-rays revealed a cyst lodged between two ribs. Surgery restored Kaat's pitching form. He returned to the Senators in 1960 and earned his first major league win. Jim smiles, "It came right here in Yankee Stadium against Whitey Ford. Moose Skowron, who I will see Monday at Yogi Berra's celebrity golf tournament, hit a home run off me early in the game. Jim Lemon came up in the seventh inning and hit a three-run homer. Then Pedro Ramos came in to relieve in the eighth and pitched the last two innings. I won 5–4."

It was his sole victory that season, but one of 283 in a superb 25-year career that included 898 appearances (among the top ten on the all-time list), three twenty-win seasons, five seasons with an ERA under 3.00, and a record 16 consecutive Gold Glove Awards. He was the key player on the pennant-winning Twins team of 1965; helped the Twins (1970) and Phils (1976) to division titles; and appeared in a career-high 62 games for the world champion Cardinals in 1982.

Hall of Fame credentials? "I could probably talk twenty minutes about why I shouldn't be in the Hall of Fame and about twenty why I should," Jim says. "But some day, I think the Veterans Committee will put me in.

"I recall Steve Carlton's induction. That same year, right-hand pitcher Vic Willis was also inducted. I was sitting next to his grandson on the bus going to the induction and he told me he was accepting the award on behalf of his late grandfather. At the time, I didn't have a grandson. I have one now who's going to be two years old in about a month. Anyway, I told him, 'Some day my grandson will be coming here and be doing the same thing for me.'"

Notching 300 wins usually ensures a pitcher's induction. Free agent Kaat had the opportunity to close in on the milestone as a starter with a different ballclub in 1982, but opted to remain as a reliever for St. Louis and skipper Whitey Herzog, whom Jim rates as the "best manager I ever played for as far as running a ballclub." Kaat explains his reasons for not leaving. "Whitey said he had a spot in the bullpen for me and that he was putting a good team together. So I stuck, and that's why I have a World Series ring. So I'm comfortable with the decision I made."

One of the most memorable moments for this author and longtime Yankee fan occurred in a 1967 game involving Kaat and the Twins. The sinkerball specialist clung to a 1–0 lead with two outs in the ninth when he faced aging, switch-hitting slugger Mickey Mantle. The count reached three balls, two strikes when Jim challenged Mick with a fastball near the knees. Mantle connected, launching the ball toward the furthest limits of Death Valley. Having no expectation of its clearing the unreachable bleacher wall, I kept hoping it would fall beyond the grasp of galloping left fielder Bobby Allison, but it continued to soar before settling into the fifth or sixth row of the bleachers. Mick's thunderous blast was proceeded by a rainstorm, and after an hour's wait the game was declared a tie to be replayed at a later date.

I remind Kaat of Mantle's heroics that night. He, too, vividly recalls the home run and reflects on its significance. "I came back a month later for the makeup game. They got a run in the first inning. Steve Barber, the lefthander, was the opposing pitcher and he beat me 1–0. So I pitched 18 innings, gave up two runs, got a tie and a loss, and we lost the pennant by one game that year. So when anybody asks me about my most disappointing loss, that was it.

"In that tie game, I had thoughts of pitching around Mantle, but the guy on deck was Elston Howard. Howard hit me better than Mickey did, and I didn't want to face him as the winning run. If you remember, right field was 344 feet away with a low fence, and Ellie used to go that way. I had struck Mickey out twice that day, so I felt confident that I could get him.

"I actually had pretty good success pitching against Mantle. He only hit seven home runs off me in my career and they were all solos. I remember Mantle getting a single once, and after the inning my teammate Harmon Killebrew came back to the bench and told me Mantle was complaining about how tough it is to hit my sinker in the air."

Most of Kaat's innings-pitched were accumulated in the sixties, a decade thought by some to be the greatest in baseball history. Kaat disagrees. "Even though I appreciate the way baseball was played in the sixties, in retrospect I still believe the golden era of baseball was right after World War II until the time they expanded. But the sixties was a great decade, with all the great stars that played at that time. Even though there had been expansion, it wasn't to the extent that we have today. Divisional play hadn't come along yet, so you were still playing the tough teams a great deal. Once it split, we ended up playing teams in the western division a lot more often than we did Baltimore, New York, Cleveland, and some of the traditional teams. So I was happy to have played when I did, but if I had my druthers I would have liked to have played between 1947 and 1960."

The conversation shifts to the modern game. Kaat, an outspoken critic of pitchers' reluctance to challenge batters with fastball strikes, explains the possible reasons for their caution. "There's a lot of information from scouts on how to pitch to batters, and pitchers are expected to use it. The strike zone is smaller. The ball is wound tighter. And hitters are much stronger. You used to be able to throw the ball on the outside corner and make the hitter fly out to right field. Now, you have guys like Derek Jeter who can hit it out of the ballpark that way. So it's a hitter's game and many pitchers are hesitant. But when you do see pitchers challenge batters and are successful, it tells you it's the right way for them to go."

Kaat assesses modern umpires who, a month following the interview, create a controversy by submitting their resignations as a means of protesting baseball's decision to bring umpires under the supervision of the commissioner's office rather than league officials. The umpires change their minds, only to discover that their resignations have been accepted. The backfired strategy puts union leader Richie Phillips in the hot seat. "It's tough for umpires," Kaat concedes. "They're closely scrutinized because of our television coverage. They're no longer the invisible men in blue. People know who the umpires are, which ones are good ball-strike umpires, which ones favor the pitchers, and so on. But they have a lot of power and they're hesitant to change. I think that in the spirit of what's good for baseball, there's got to be a meeting of the minds where administrators and umpires get together and agree that there's got to be change.

"After (Bob) Gibson had the tremendous year in '68, they had no problem saying we need more hitting in the game so we're going to lower the mound. They did it overnight. Now we have too much hitting, but they seem hesitant to get the umpires together and say, 'Look, we better go back to using the traditional strike zone.' I looked at the rulebook the other day, and it's supposed to be called a strike right here (Jim holds his left hand and arm horizontally at his chest). There hasn't been one called there in ten years. So I think you need to get all the umpires from both leagues together in one body, instruct them to enlarge the strike zone, and then get behind them. There's nothing wrong with a lot of action in games, but I don't think people like to see 24–12 games."

Jim is on a roll. "The biggest problem in baseball today is finding competent middle relief pitchers. Starters seldom go more than six or seven innings, so you have to deal with a lot of middle relievers who otherwise would be in the minors. And with games taking three hours and longer, why don't we shorten the game to seven innings? Of course, the answer to that is you can't mess with the history of baseball. It's too drastic a change. Well, look at the changes that have been made over the last few decades. Right here at the stadium, balls that are home runs now were fly ball outs during Mantle's era. You have astroturf, expansion, a smaller strike zone, a wild card, a designated hitter. It's changed drastically already. So seven-inning games would be a change I'd be in favor of."

I inquire about Jim's future plans. "I live in Florida in the off-season. I'm sort of a golf junkie. I'm going on 61 now and have one more year in my contract to broadcast games for the Yankees. So in a couple of years, I see myself relaxing in Florida and playing golf. I'd still like to be around the game. I've talked to some organizations about being a spring training coach. I've had some sessions with Dr. [Gene] Budig, President of the American League, who has said he'd like to involve me in baseball administration. So I think I'll take a look at what's out there that can keep me connected with the game in a sort of part-time basis."

After the interview, Jim invites us to watch the game from the press box. Lola and Jackie decide to try to meet some of the Yankees still

Jim Kaat in the MSG press booth at Yankee Stadium.

lingering on the field, but by the time they arrive all pinstripers are safely secluded in the clubhouse. To my delight, they do not return empty-handed, having taken advantage of the economical food prices in the press level to purchase hot dogs and soda.

What remains of the sunlight by game time shows partly cloudy skies, with temperatures in the 70s. The game is the second of a three-game set, the Yanks having taken the opener. Orlando "El Duque" Hernandez starts for the Bombers, trying to improve on a 7–5 record, while the Rangers counter with Rick Helling, with a 6–6 mark.

Prior to the opening pitch, the girls leave the booth for a more spacious, comfortable, and unoccupied one located to our immediate left. They are barred from entering by a Johnny-on-the-spot condescending employee who warns that the section is "reserved for guests of The Boss." Out of character, Lola capitulates without argument.

Hernandez retires leadoff batter Mark McLemore on a groundout, prompting applause from most of the 30,000 in attendance, including the three non-media members watching from the press box. We are politely reminded by Yankee broadcasting analyst Suzyn Waldman, seated to our immediate right, that vocal support for either team in the press level is taboo. El Duque dismisses the next two batters and, with Jackie's coaxing but some reluctance on my part, we head for our field level box seats located between third base and the left field foul pole.

A group of fans seated nearby soon become conspicuous for two reasons. At the conclusion of each half-inning, they react to the baseball being thrown toward the pitcher's mound with glee or gloom, depending on whether the ball remains on the dirt mound or rolls onto the infield grass. Winners are paid, and bets taken for the next half-inning. What also becomes noticeable and mildly irritating to some is their propensity for using the service of beer vendors during play, and to stand while being served, oblivious of shouts from nearby spectators to be seated. They are, nevertheless, an amiable bunch. Befriended by one, Jackie learns that they are job trainees from different regions of the country visiting New York for a weeklong seminar.

By the third inning, the Yankees are trailing 2–0 on a Lee Stevens monster home run into the most distant section of the right-field bleachers. Hopes come alive in the bottom half following a leadoff double by Scott Brosius, but are abruptly deflated when Helling whiffs Jeter, O'Neill, and Bernie Williams. Concern mounts when Jeter suffers an injury the next frame, jamming his wrist in a diving attempt at a ground ball, but the popular All-Star shortstop remains in the game.

Included among the job trainee group is a spirited Cleveland partisan making little effort to conceal loyalty for a team sporting the best record in baseball, and to forewarn Yankee rooters of the Tribe's inevitable sweep of the Bombers should they meet in a championship-series clash. I remind him of the outcome of the previous year's confrontation, that should the Tribe get by the Yanks in 1999 they would still need to win the World Series—something they had not achieved in their battle with the Braves in 1995 and with the Marlins in 1997, and that should they win the Series it would leave the franchise 21 shy of the Yankees' 24 world championships of the century. My strategy in checking his boisterous boasting backfires, as the knowledgeable Cleveland fan persists with between-innings discourses on the club's noteworthy history, with particular emphasis on Hall-of-Famers Tris Speaker, Bob Feller, Lou Boudreau, Larry Doby, and Bob Lemon. I want to remind him of early-century Cleveland hurler Addie Joss, but decide it would only exacerbate his vociferousness.

The Yanks trail by two with two gone in the fifth when Jeter reaches on an error, then swipes second. Bleacher fans' shouts of "Let's go Yanks!" subside when O'Neill lines out to right field. Out come the grounds crew, who song-and-dance their way around the infield to the tune of "YMCA."

Martinez's extra batting practice does not go for naught as he produces a one-out single in the bottom of the sixth. Chili Davis peppers a ball that is destined for the glove of left fielder Rusty Greer, as an exasperated Jackie moans, "We're running out of time." Lola echoes the sentiment when Helling's pick-off move catches Tino napping at first to end the inning.

After the Rangers notch another tally, and as our Cleveland rooter remains seated, Yankee fans stand for the seventh-inning stretch, with sounds of "Take Me Out to the Ball Game," then "Cotton Eyed Joe" pervading the park. The scoreboard informs the crowd of the first-period results in Game One of the NBA Finals—New York 27, San Antonio 21—prompting a roar and perceptible increased optimism prior to the Yankees' licks. Alas, Posada flies to Greer, ditto Shane Spencer, and Luis Sojo pops up. Yankee fortunes are looking bleak.

The Rangers are retired in the eighth, the frame ending with Jeter's circus catch of a liner. Brosius opens the Yankee half with a walk, and Jeter reaches on McLemore's muff of a grounder. O'Neill scorches a missile to deep left, but Greer intercepts its flight. With runners at the corners, Williams whiffs and is serenaded with a chorus of boos by those undoubtedly recalling his salary holdout prior to eventually signing a multi-million-dollar deal with the Yanks for the '99 season. Tino grounds out to end the inning. The ballpark begins to empty.

By the bottom of the ninth, the remaining crowd's exasperation is intensified by the scoreboard's half-time report indicating the Knicks badly trailing the Spurs, then by the Yankees going down in order. Our heroes have been convincingly defeated, unable to even once pierce the enemy's normally suspect defense.

There are, however, many satisfying moments during the remainder of the 1999 season. Precisely one month later, David Cone pitches the 16th perfect game in baseball history, the third by a Yankee, with David Wells having thrown a perfecto in 1998. There is a three-game sweep of the Indians at the Stadium in July, which includes a 21–1 rout. There is a shellacking of those same Rangers in the ALDS, the trouncing of the rival Red Sox in the ALCS, and the sweet sweep of the Braves in the Series, proceeded by another ticker tape parade, courtesy Mayor Rudy Guiliani.

For this longtime baseball and Yankee fan, one of the most satisfying aspects attached to the '99 season is the visit with an old-timer in the press box of the most historic ballpark in history. With the recent abandonment of Tiger Stadium, and Fenway's doom looming, one wonders whether Yankee Stadium will soon be made obsolete as well. Speculation has been abundant in recent years, with owner Steinbrenner often citing such Bronx problems as limited parking, traffic turmoil, and an unsafe environment as inhibitors to attendance. (Those detriments did not prevent the team's drawing three million to the ballpark in 1999.)

Yet, Steinbrenner has also repeatedly avowed his abiding respect for baseball tradition; it may be that reverence that has thus far saved the stadium from the bulldozer. It is, nevertheless, a compelling temptation for owners to seek more promising sites, and to build more fashionable green cathedrals offering lucrative luxury boxes. Hopefully, Steinbrenner will continue to resist the bait. Yankee Old-Timers' Day just wouldn't be the same anywhere but in the House That Ruth Built.

Frank Malzone

It has been written that in tragedy every moment is eternity. Frank Malzone understands, and remembers. "Nineteen fifty-six was a hard year for me personally," the former third baseman acknowledges midway into our conversation at his home in Needham, Massachusetts, in November of 1999. His light-hearted demeanor changes, exposing a lingering melancholy despite the more than forty years separating his confrontation with calamity. "I lost my first child, Suzanne. She was sick for a couple of days, maybe about a week. She had diarrhea and we didn't know what to do. Finally, the doctor told us to take her to the hospital. We brought her up that night, and in the middle of the night we get a phone call telling us to come to the hospital, that she had passed away. It took me a long time to get over it. It took Amy even longer.

"But we've had five children since then, and the fourth was a girl, Anne Susan. They're all doing fine today. And we have six grandchildren—three girls and three boys."

Frank was anticipating playing his first full season in the majors when the kick in the gut eradicated his exhilaration. "When I went to spring training, I was out of it," he says. "I did make the ballclub but by the trading deadline they sent me to the Triple A San Francisco club in the Pacific Coast League. But in the spring of 1957, I was back on the right track. The loss of my daughter was part of my past. And we were fortunate to find someone who could help Amy get over it."

Frank remained with the Red Sox for the entire season, finishing with a .292 average and winning the Gold Glove for third basemen in the first year of the award's existence, when only one was given for each major league position. When the custom of awarding one per league began the following season, Malzone again won, and claimed the prize in 1959 as well. Today, he is recognized as among the most consistent fielding third basemen of the fifties and early sixties, and holds the extraordinary though uncelebrated distinction of being the only player in major league history to finish a career of ten seasons or more with all fielding appearances coming as a third baseman. (At the end of 1999, still-active Astro Ken Caminiti remained eligible for the honor after playing in a dozen seasons.)

Ironically, this durable defender of Boston's hot-corner was born and reared in that perennially-despised locale for staunch Red Sox fans—the Bronx, New York—home of Yankee Stadium, whose construction has ofttimes been credited to a fellow named Ruth. The most famous former Fenway player in history is still blamed by belligerent Bostonians for a hex so potent it has thwarted each of their team's attempts at a world championship since the year of the Babe's trade to New York in 1919.

"I grew up in Clason Point near the Throgs Neck and Castle Hill sections," Frank informs. "The whole neighborhood was oriented toward baseball and sports in general. If it wasn't baseball it was football, if it wasn't football it was soccer. There was always something going on. So I just grew up liking sports. My brother, sister and I used to play ball at a field about a block away from our house. We had to take care of it ourselves, cut the infield out and so on. So we played a lot of baseball."

Malzone attended Samuel Gompers High School, and despite playing high school and semi-pro baseball was an aspiring electrician in his senior year. He recounts an incident that became the turning point in his professional life. "One day a bird dog for the Red Sox by the name of Cy Phillips approached me. He owned a sporting goods store in the area. I can remember going in there to buy a pair of spikes for the summer when he asked me if I'd like to play pro ball."

It was not the first such offer, as the New York Giants had previously approached Malzone. "I played in a game sponsored by a newspaper that gathered all the high school stars in the area. We played the game in the Polo Grounds. I got a couple of triples and after the game they asked me if I was interested in playing pro ball. But they wanted me to wait a year. Basically, they were trying to see if I would get bigger and stronger."

After graduation, Malzone interviewed for a job as an apprentice electrician. Then came Phillips' offer. Frank beams, "I jumped at it. It wasn't much. One hundred fifty dollars a month, and no bonus. Just enough to survive, but it was a chance to play professionally and I grabbed it."

Frank's father did little to discourage him. "Dad used to like to watch me play. He was kind of outspoken about my abilities. When I think about it today I laugh. He used to say to other players, 'Well, if you were all as good as my son you wouldn't have any problems. You'd win all the games.' But everybody knew him and liked him because he was a fun guy."

Malzone's first pro season was at Milford, Delaware, where his impressive .307 average earned a promotion from the Class C Eastern Shore League to the Class C Can-Am League. "I played in Oneonta, New York. That's where I met my wife, Amy. She used to like to go to the games. I happened to talk to her one day at the ballpark in 1949. Two years later, we were married.

"I had a great year in Oneonta. Hit .329. And I had 27 triples, which is hard to believe, but that's what I did. It set a Can-Am record."

Only one year after his marriage to Amy, Frank was drafted into the Army at a time when the country was still entangled in the Korean War. He chuckles, "I had tough duty. I spent two years in Hawaii." He elaborates on the events leading to the attractive assignment. "It was strange. I got inducted in New York and went to Camp Kilmer in New Jersey. The sergeant who was interviewing me asked, 'How would you like to go to Hawaii for your basic training?' I knew that from Hawaii they were sending them over to Korea. I said, 'No, I'd rather not. I'd just as soon stay in the States.' He said, 'Well, you're going anyway.' I said to myself, "What did he ask me for?"

Following basic training at Schofield Barracks, the setting for the Pearl Harbor film classic *From Here to Eternity*, Malzone was preparing to pack for Korea when he received a last-second reprieve. "My orders were already on the boat when the lieutenant came over and said that Colonel Hazlitt wanted to see me. He had heard that I was a pro ballplayer. So the colonel called me in. He said he couldn't keep me at Schofield and that he wanted to send me to Fort Shafter, which is on the other side of the island. So I said it was all right with me. They had to find a job for me so they put me with the MPs. I didn't know what I was doing there. I spent about a month with them. Eventually, I got in special services and had two real nice years there. I brought my wife over and we lived on the base. So the two years were enjoyable as well as a learning experience for a 21, 22-year-old. I was very fortunate. Some of the guys I trained with in Schofield got killed over in Korea."

Malzone played shortstop for the Army team. He acknowledges it was his preferred position. "I felt if you have talent, it's easier to play. Everything is right in front of you. You knew what the pitcher was going to throw because you could see the catcher's signs. At third base, you couldn't see them so you didn't know if the pitcher was going to throw a fastball or a slow curve. So at shortstop you could cheat, in a way, without the batter knowing it."

Following his Army stint, Malzone played winter ball in San Juan for a club managed by future major league skipper Ralph Houk. "I enjoyed playing for Ralph. He knew baseball, respected the players, and took a lot of pride in his work. Later on when he was working for the Red Sox, I worked for him as an advance scout."

Recalling his scouting duty for Houk prompts Malzone to recount a related story. "During spring training, I used to get in uniform and work with some of the players. I can remember the first year Wade Boggs joined our ballclub. We were told by the minor league people that Wade could hit but couldn't play third. So Ralph got a hold of me and said, 'Look, your job is to make a third baseman out of this guy.' I kidded him, 'Whaddya say?' He said, 'You're gonna stay with him all spring.'

"And that's just what I did. Worked with him all spring long. My locker was right next to his and we'd talk about playing third every day. I give Wade a lot of credit. He wanted to learn. Of course, he had a good attitude because he wanted to be in the big leagues and Ralph wanted him to play third. So I worked with him. For instance, I slowed him down in his preparation. He had a habit of taking three steps. I told him, 'Wade, there's no reason to do that. If you want movement, just dance in one position so you can go either way.' And practically everything I gave him he liked and tried. It was a long spring but he became a solid third baseman."

Malzone ends the anecdote with a smile, but a trace of annoyance. "Of course, we know what happens when they don't need you anymore. It's, 'See you later. Goodbye.' So you never hear Wade say anything about anyone who helped him."

Malzone played minor league ball at Louisville in 1954 and 1955 before getting his first taste of big-league competition toward the end of the 1955 season. "I got called up by the Red Sox and got in maybe six or seven games. I remember my first base hit came off a guy named [Bill] Wight. He was a lefthander with a great move. I remember the first base coach telling me to be careful. So I'm like, 'Yeah, sure, don't worry.' So I took two steps off first and—boom! Before you know it, I get picked off on my first major league hit! I learned in a hurry."

Frank also recalls his first two games played at historic Fenway Park, getting six hits in ten at bats in a doubleheader. "I figured this is easy," he laughs. "But today they'd make more of it than they did then. They make a superstar out of you even before you're in the big leagues. I was just trying to impress the managers and coaches. That's all I cared about."

Following the devastating year of 1956, Frank was mentally prepared for a comeback the following spring in Sarasota. "Everything was working out all right. Then all of a sudden we were playing games and for the first ten I didn't even get an at bat. So I said to myself, 'Here we go again. I'm gonna be sent back or sold or traded.' I told Amy that we might have to be making some kind of a decision soon.

"We left Sarasota and went to San Francisco to play the Giants in some exhibition games. The day of the first game the city had a slight earthquake. Of course, none of us knew what was going on. We weren't used to tremors and that stuff. Well, anyway, that night I got to the ballpark and I was standing out on the field and Pete Daley, the catcher who I knew very well, came over to me and said, 'Hey, you're playing tonight." I said, 'C'mon, don't fool around like that.' But when I went in to look at the lineup, sure enough, I was in there."

The rookie managed only one single, but nevertheless played in every spring and regular-season game thereafter. "I still don't have any idea what caused them to change their mind and give me a chance. Probably because none of the other third basemen did enough to show they deserved the spot. Then finally someone said, 'Let's give Malzone an opportunity.' I told one of my teammates, 'Maybe the earthquake woke them up.'"

Malzone does not recall the transition from minor to major league ball being particularly difficult, with the exception of having to face quality pitching more frequently. "For instance, you go into Cleveland and you get [Mike] Garcia, [Bob] Lemon, Herb Score and Early Wynn. That club always had great pitching. Later it was [Luis] Tiant and [Sam] McDowell. In Detroit, you had Frank Lary, Jim Bunning, [Don] Mossi. You go into Chicago and they had Billy Pierce. Every club had two or three guys that you knew when you stepped to the plate you've gotta work the pitcher. Then when you establish yourself, you sort of know how the pitchers pitch and what you have to do to stay in the big leagues."

Playing alongside Frank for the first six of his eleven seasons with the Red Sox was slugging superstar Ted Williams. Malzone talks about time spent with The Splendid Splinter during the Hall of Famer's twilight years in the big leagues. "In my first spring training, he was the first one to greet me in the clubhouse and welcome me to the ballclub. Of course, later on he would have something to say to me, just like he would with everyone else. He'd criticize my hitting and say, 'You dumb Dago. You hit the first pitch too much,' or something like that. I'd tell him, 'Well, maybe I am dumb, but I gotta do what I gotta do to be a player. I don't have the ability you have.'

"But I enjoyed being around him, not only for his baseball wisdom but because he was well-educated in the way of life. Did a lot of reading. Every time he talked about something, he seemed to know the subject more than the person he was talking to. And what a hitter he was. It was unbelievable watching him. I was looking at a guy who was 38, 39 years old and could still win batting titles. And he couldn't run. Not like Mantle anyway."

Malzone's roommate in his first full season was right fielder Jackie Jensen. Not in the same caliber as Williams, the San Francisco native was nonetheless an upper-echelon player of the fifties and would have been the top star on several other ballclubs. The righty swinger took advantage of the proximity of Fenway's famed left-field wall to string together six consecutive seasons with 20 or more home runs. He was a three-time RBI leader (Williams took no RBI crowns in the decade) and had two additional 100 RBI seasons. Jensen led the league in triples in 1956 and even topped the leaderboard in stolen bases one season. "Jackie was a good person," Frank emphasizes. "I liked him. He had a lot of pride in what he was doing. If there's anything about Jackie, he was, well, I wouldn't say jealous of Williams, but Ted would annoy him at times. Jackie would say, 'Why should Ted get these things? Why can't we all get some attention?' I think he just read the whole situation wrong."

Some considered Jensen to be an oddball, particularly in regards to his fear of flying. "I can remember when we first started short flights, he wouldn't get on the plane. He'd get there on time for the game, but he'd always take the train. Then when the West Coast games were in effect, it was hard for him to do it. That's one of the reasons he retired. They made him a nice offer to come back but he said, 'Naw, that's the end of it.'"

In 1958, Senators shortstop Pete Runnels was traded to Boston in exchange for outfielder Albie Pearson and part-time first baseman Norm Zauchin. Runnels would become a two-time batting champ with the Red Sox after nearly winning one in his initial season with the team. "Pete and Williams were fighting for the title going into the final day of the season," Frank recalls about his fellow infielder, roommate and "good friend" of five years. "Ted had been out of action for about two weeks of the season and didn't have as many at bats as Pete did, but he still had enough to qualify. Pete batted second in the order and Ted batted third. So Pete gets a base hit his first time up, then Ted gets a base hit. Next time up, Pete hits a double, then Ted comes up and gets a double. So Pete and I are sitting in the dugout, and I look at Pete and say, 'What's the matter?' Pete says, 'He's not gonna let me win this thing.' And needless to say, Ted got another base hit and Pete went hitless the rest of the game and Ted won the batting title."

Runnels was traded to the Astros in the fall of 1962 and Billy Gardner became Malzone's final Red Sox roommate. "Billy was another I was close with on that ballclub. And Pete Daley. I got to know him in the minors. And Ike Delock. As a matter of fact, we still talk with Ike and his wife from time to time. They used to live here in Needham for years, and then they sold their house and moved to Naples, Florida, about ten years ago. Glenna and Amy get on the phone once a month, and I kid Amy, 'How long are you gonna talk?' But they're great friends. And it's good to talk to Ike and some of the other guys and talk about the old players living in Florida."

Malzone speaks with pride of his former team and its abundant talent, which for a time included Williams, Jensen, and Jimmy Piersall in the outfield, Don Buddin, Runnels and Mickey Vernon in the infield, and Sammy White as the catcher. He offers his reasons as to why the club never won a pennant. "It's simple, really. We were competing against the New York Yankees. I'm guessing, but I would say that in my ten full years playing in the majors, the Yankees won the pennant seven times. Later on, I would go to those Old-Timers' Days at Yankee Stadium, and here comes all the players. They'd just keep running them out there. They would bring out Yogi, Moose [Skowron], Hank Bauer, Mantle, Whitey Ford, Tony Kubek, [Bobby] Richardson, Clete Boyer. I'd say to myself, 'No wonder we never won anything.'

"I think the Yankees always had a sound and consistent pitching staff and that's what separated them from the rest. They always had four or five pitchers who could stop you. We had good pitchers but none really who were one step above the rest. They had great stuff, but their control might not be as sharp. Then again, maybe playing at Fenway had something to do with that. As a confidence factor. You know, when you pitch in a big ballpark you say to yourself, 'Maybe I can give in a little to the hitter. Maybe he'll hit a nice fly ball to somebody.' Fenway doesn't work that way. You hit a nice fly ball and it winds up going against the wall. So our pitchers felt they had to pitch more carefully."

When Williams retired following the 1960 season, his replacement in left field was a lefty-swinging rookie named Carl Yastrzemski. Malzone and Yaz were compatible teammates, and Frank remembers giving the green but gifted ballplayer some early advice. "Yaz stepped into tough shoes and sometimes he tried to be like Williams. I told him, 'C'mon, who you kidding? Just be yourself.'"

Frank reflects on Yastrzemski's transition from spray to power hitter. "At first, Yaz wasn't a pull-hitter, more of a Wade Boggs type, everything up the middle or to the left side. But as we know, his career accelerated after the 1967 season when he established himself and he realized he could pull the ball, hit home runs, and still maintain a high average. When I think about it, I think Wade Boggs could have done the same thing if he tried."

Malzone played for several managers, including Johnny Pesky and Billy Herman. Pesky replaced Pinky Higgins in 1963 and lasted less than two seasons. "Pesky was a good manager but, unfortunately, wasn't well liked by the general manager. At that time, everybody blamed Yastrzemski for Pesky's being fired (there was friction between them), but it wasn't his fault. Yaz wasn't that strong at that time."

Pesky's replacement late in the 1964 season was future Hall-of-Famer Billy Herman. Malzone is candid about his disapproval of the nine-time National League All-Star second baseman and one-time Pirate skipper. "He was a good baseball man but he wasn't a good person. You know, the kind of person you wanted to play for. He showed his emotions too much. And he wasn't straight up with the players. I had been with the club for ten years, and he started platooning me. Never even talked to me about it. His feeling was, 'Well, you're a pro, you should understand.' Yeah, sure, I understand, but I'd still like a little courtesy. And I thought he was a friend of mine because he was a coach before that."

The conversation turns to Frank's career highlights. "At the time, I didn't think much about my winning the Gold Glove Award my first three years in the big leagues, but looking back now I'd have to say it's probably one of my most outstanding achievements. Also, my (six) All-Star selections come to mind right away." He recalls his first appearance. "I wasn't voted in by the fans. They voted for George Kell and I was chosen as backup. The game was in St. Louis and the thing I remember most about it is that Ted Williams and myself were the only players from the Red Sox who were selected. I rode on the plane with Ted and I didn't know what to expect in the game. He told me that it's a fun day, but the American League wants to win. We did win, with Casey Stengel as manager. I picked up Kell; he played the first four innings and I played the rest. I did get a base hit. It came off Larry Jackson of the Cardinals.

"In another All-Star Game, I hit a home run off of Don Drysdale. It was played in the old Coliseum, which was made for my stroke. Left field was a short poke away. I had never faced Drysdale. I got to know him well and, God rest his soul, he was a good man. But anyway, I knew of his reputation. I remember saying to myself, 'I'm not gonna let this guy get ahead of me.' So on the first pitch he threw this big curve ball, but he left it up. I didn't hit it real good but good enough to get it over that screen in left. I'm just glad they took him out of the game and I didn't have to face him again that day."

Frank Malzone at his home in Needham, Massachusetts.

His most memorable ballgames? Frank begins by confessing his disappointment over never being on a pennant-winner, so that his major contributions consequently went for naught. "But there was one game in Washington when I had ten chances at third, which tied a record at the time. I can remember another one here in Fenway when I hit a home run in the 11th inning off of Ryne Duren to win the game."

I ask Malzone how he generally fared against the bespectacled Yankee fireballer who had a reputation for erratic control, and would begin each relief appearance by throwing his first warm-up toss ten feet over the head of the catcher, a warning to forthcoming hitters to stay awake at the plate. "Actually, I always hit him well. I'd say to him, 'I can't help it, Ryne. You don't have a curve ball. I can hit a fastball.' He'd have those big glasses and throw that wild warm-up, but none of that stuff bothered me. In fact, I never really had any fear of getting hit. In my whole career, I think I got hit about four or five times."

Asked to choose the toughest pitcher he faced, Malzone names right-hander Jim Bunning, a Tiger for nine seasons prior to hurling in the National League for another eight. "His delivery was tough on right-hand hitters; he'd come from the side a little bit. The ball ran good and he had a good curve ball. And he was a strikeout pitcher. When you faced him, you knew you had to work hard. I got base hits off him, but I couldn't go up there confident that I was gonna hurt him.

"But I did kind of aggravate Bunning a little. I was tough for him to strike out, even though I was a right-hand hitter. He'd get two strikes on me, and I'd bloop one to right field. He'd give me this look at first base and I'd smile back at him. We understood each other."

Like other former players, Malzone believes modern pitching is less formidable than in past eras. "Pitchers don't come inside because the umpires protect the hitters. That's why all of today's hitters have that style of striding toward the plate. If you did that consistently in the days that I played, the pitcher would let you know about it. Boom! And the hitters respected them for it."

Frank offers examples. "Early Wynn and Dick Donovan were tough because they'd like to brush you back once in a while. Donovan's ball ran into you and he would take that one shot and push you off the plate. That was his style and you knew it when you went up there."

Malzone is annoyed at the cockiness shown by modern players. "They show each other up too much. With that home run stare or dance. Pitchers in our day wouldn't tolerate that sort of stuff. Their attitude was, 'You want to show me up? Let me show you something next time you come up.' We had respect for each other. That was part of baseball then."

After 11 seasons in Boston, Malzone became the property of the California Angels, where he served as a pinch-hitter and occasional replacement for third baseman Paul Schaal. Retiring at the end of the 1966 season, he contacted the Red Sox and inquired about any available positions. "I really wanted to come back as a coach, but they hired me as a scout."

Frank recalls a conference with Boston executives and personnel near the close of the 1967 season when four clubs, including the Red Sox, were battling for the flag. "They had called and asked me to watch the Minnesota Twins for a while. I got back to Fenway ten days later and they called me up to a big meeting. So I walked in, and there was Dick Williams [manager] and one of his coaches, Bobby Doerr. And there was Haywood Sullivan [scouting director], Dick O'Connell [general manager], and Mr. [Tom] Yawkey [owner]. We were all sitting around and I was thinking, 'What am I doing here? No one warned me ahead of time about this meeting.' But I sat there and listened until they asked me what I thought of the Minnesota ballclub.

"I didn't have any notes, but I went through the lineup and told them what I thought off the top of my head. Then when it came time for me to sum up, I told them, 'I just want to say one thing before I close. Don't let Killebrew beat us here at Fenway. He kills us here. If you have to walk him every time up, do it.' Well, we walked him quite a bit and ended up beating them in the three games, and we won the pennant. Later on, Mr.

Yawkey told me that he really appreciated what I had said at that meeting. And the next year, I became the advance scout."

In one of the games of that crucial season-ending series against the Twins, a soon-to-be Triple Crown winner received a valuable tip. "[Jim] Merritt, a lefthander, had a habit of tipping his glove before he threw a certain pitch. So when he came in to relieve and was warming up, I told Yaz. He said, 'Are you sure?' I said, 'Yeah, just look at him. You can see for yourself.' So he hit a home run off Merritt and we won the game."

Frank relinquished the advance scout position in 1994, but continued to scout and evaluate opposing players. By the new millennium, he will have been a Boston scout for 37 years. "I'm thinking of semi-retiring," asserts the 69-year-old who has undergone two angioplasties. "I want to keep working but I don't want to kill myself. We've got to come to a mutual agreement about certain things."

Following the interview, Frank leads Lola and me to a downstairs den adorned with enough memorabilia to satisfy the most ardent admirer of Boston baseball in the fifties, to which Malzone was a significant contributor. His career stats aren't comparable to those of contemporaries Williams, Jensen, and Runnels, but he was the mainstay at third base longer than any Red Sox predecessor. And if he was overshadowed by fellow third sackers and future Hall-of-Famers Kell, Killebrew, and Brooks Robinson during his career, the name Frank Malzone is nevertheless as recognizable today to fans who followed baseball in the fifties and sixties as any player of that era.

Dale Berra

Compared with other rendezvous with old-timers, travel time is brief to the Yogi Berra Museum and Learning Center for an interview with Dale Berra, the 44-year-old son of the legendary Hall of Famer. A twenty-minute drive north on the Garden State Parkway takes us to Montclair, New Jersey, then another half-mile takes us to the campus entrance of Montclair State University where we ascend a hill to a parking lot opposite the museum. Prior to entering, Lola and I withstand the frigid temperature of this mid–week day in the first month of the new millennium to observe through an iron fence Yogi Berra Stadium, situated adjacent the museum. As I would later learn, the stadium is home to the New Jersey Jackals, part of the independent fourteen-team Northern League.

A receptionist greets us, and while waiting for Dale we browse through brochures that explain the museum's history and goals. Founded in 1997, with the groundbreaking ceremony taking place in mid-year of 1998, the museum is dedicated to celebrating and chronicling the famed Yankee's life in and outside of baseball, while "reflecting his lifelong commitment to the education of young people."

To the latter end, the museum offers a variety of enlightening programs, conferences and exhibits designed to enhance public interest in the sport and its role in American life. To date, "Hispanic Heritage Month," "Black History Month," "The Business of Baseball," "History of the Baseball Glove," "Math and Science Week," and "Read Across America" have been presented. More traditional baseball events have been offered, such as "The Perfect Night," featuring talks by Yankee battery combos for perfect games (Don Larsen–Yogi Berra, David Wells–Jorge Posada, David Cone–Joe Girardi); "The Life and Times of Hank Greenberg," celebrating the career of the first great Jewish star; and "The Pride of the Yankees," with actress Teresa Wright discussing her role as Lou Gehrig's wife in a movie regarded as one of the best of the baseball flicks. The museum's greatest attraction is its exhibits honoring Berra's career as well as other significant players and events in baseball history.

Enter Dale Berra, whose uncombed but neat black hair, boyish visage and trim six-foot stature immediately corroborate his status as young old-timer. He invites me to take additional reading material including a copy of a commemorative Yogi Berra comic book, for which a two dollar donation is suggested. Dale leads us to a private area at the rear of the museum where the interview begins.

Born in Ridgewood, New Jersey, in 1956, Dale moved with his family to Montclair in 1958 where he lived for the remainder of his youth. Unlike other sons of pro ballplayers, whose dads played a major role in their development, Dale asserts that Yogi actually spent little time teaching him baseball skills. "I learned by playing with my two older brothers, Larry and Tim," Dale says. "If I'd ask Dad to play catch with me, he'd say, 'That's what you have brothers for.' We'd play on the sandlots or in the park. Or we'd play whiffle ball in the backyard. Even just throwing a ball against the side of the house. Every day. In fact, I don't have a recollection of ever not playing ball."

Larry would go on to play minor league ball, while Tim became an All-American football player at the University of Massachusetts prior to one season with the Baltimore Colts. "So they were both good athletes, five, six years older than me. Whenever they'd have pickup games and needed a man they'd ask me instead of looking for someone their age. That's how I knew I was so good. Playing with them gave me confidence."

Despite televised games being numerous during the sixties, Dale watched few. "Dad would always advocate playing for experience instead of watching. And that's just what we did." Although his older brothers had the opportunity, Dale never saw his dad play. His earliest recollection of being at the ballpark was when he was eight years old. "Dad was manager of the Yankees in 1964. I remember sitting in the trainer's room and locker room watching the players come in. Watching Bobby Richardson shave, Mel Stottlemyre being called up, Mickey [Mantle] sitting in the whirlpool, Joe Pepitone drying his hair, Frank Crosetti giving me a ball to play with, sitting with batboys in the back room where they washed uniforms and counted baseballs. Little bits and pieces."

When the Yanks fell to the Cards in the 1964 Series, Berra was fired. He was immediately hired as a coach for Mets manager Casey Stengel. "Now, I can remember everything you could possibly remember about the Mets. Going to spring training and putting on a uniform, playing catch with Ron Swoboda and Ed Kranepool and Tom Seaver, batboying for them. And I thought Casey was great. He loved Dad so much it was incredible. Mom would always tell stories about how whenever she picked Dad up at the airport after a road trip Casey would go out of his way to tell her how great he was. As far as he was concerned, Dad was the greatest player he ever managed."

Dale continued developing his baseball skills while working as a batboy. Although Yogi chased him away from the infield, concerned about hard-hit or bad-hop grounders doing damage to Dale's teeth or psyche, Dale shagged fly balls in the outfield. "On days there were games, I'd go to the park with my dad early, around three o'clock for night games. They would have guys who needed extra batting practice, maybe because they were coming off the disabled list. The pitching coach would throw to that one hitter for 15 minutes. I'd be the only one in the outfield, catching flies and throwing them in. I loved to do that."

Yogi eventually permitted his taking infield grounders, and Dale worked alongside Met shortstop Bud Harrelson during batting practice. At about the same time, he made the high school varsity club in his freshman year. "I played varsity ball throughout high school and in the summertime I'd work out at Shea. In my junior year, I played summer ball in county leagues. They were made up of older guys—thirty, forty years old. A lot of them were ex-minor leaguers, some ex-major league pitchers. It was a strong league and I was only 16. So scouts had seen me play both in high school and these county leagues."

By Dale's senior year in 1975, scouts informed Yogi that his son would be a high draft pick. Some requested he dissuade Dale from playing football that fall. "I remember Dad told me, 'Forget about it. Play all the sports. They're worried about you getting hurt. If you worry about getting hurt, you'll get hurt.' So I played football, hockey and baseball that year."

A Pirate first-round draft pick and 17th overall in 1975, Berra hustled from his graduation ceremony to Niagara Falls, part of the New York-Penn Rookie League. The next year, he played Class A ball in Charleston, South Carolina, made the big jump to Columbus, Ohio's Triple A ballclub in 1977, and broke into the big leagues late that season. "Rennie Stennett had broken his ankle and they called me up that night. I was in the lineup the next day. We were playing the Padres and Bob Shirley was the pitcher. I flied out to left field, then I walked and then they pinch-hit for me late in the game."

Returning to Columbus in 1978, Berra was leading the league in home runs and RBIs by July when the contending Pirates again brought him up. Playing part-time at third base, Berra socked six home runs in

56 games. "A couple of them won games. Toward the end of the season, we were one game out with three to play against the (first-place) Phillies. We won a doubleheader and were tied for the lead but we lost the pennant on the last day. I played in that game. It was very exciting."

During 1979 spring training, Dale battled and won a spot as utility man, but when the Bucs traded for third baseman and two-time batting champ Bill Madlock he became expendable. Berra headed west to play for the Portland, Oregon, Triple A club. "I spent July and August there. Then Tim Foli got hurt and they called me up around August 26th. They wanted me eligible for the World Series. So I boarded a plane in Portland and landed in Los Angeles where the Pirates were playing.

"As soon as I got off the plane, there was a message for me to call Pirate general manager Pete Peterson. He said he was sorry but he couldn't call me up until the end of the Triple A season. The problem was that I had still been on the Pirates' 40-man roster while I was playing minor league ball. The rule was that you couldn't call up a player who was on the roster during the last ten days of the minor league season. They were afraid the big league teams would take all the best minor league players during the most important part of the minor league season. Peterson said that if he had known about the rule he would have called me up the day before the rule went into effect, even without Foli being hurt, because he wanted me eligible for the Series. So if he had called me up two or three days earlier, I would have been in post-season play."

The minor league season ended on the final day of August, and Peterson immediately brought back Berra. Dale recalls playing 25 of the final 30 games, with the Pirates winning 20 to capture the flag. Although ineligible for post-season action, Berra was invited to be a bench-supporter during the NLCS and World Series. After overwhelming the Reds in three-straight and winning the world championship in seven against Baltimore, Pittsburgh players voted Berra a full Series share and a ring. "Even today, Chuck Tanner [Pirate manager] always goes out of his way to say that I played the most important games of the season at shortstop and that we wouldn't have beaten the Phillies out by one game without me. I think he's blowing smoke a little bit but it's nice of him to say that."

Dale remained with the Pirates throughout the 1980 and 1981 season, but the utility infielder's averaging only 240 at bats per season thwarted his hitting effectiveness and consistency. Given his first opportunity as regular in 1982, the righty-swinging Buc took advantage and today rates the season his most satisfying. Berra's .263 average, 10 homers and 61 RBIs in 529 at bats were not reminiscent of his dad's productiveness, but they were better than most shortstop stats that year and, along with his capable glove work, proved he belonged in the big leagues.

And as Dale points out, his numbers were accumulated while hitting in the eighth-place position in the lineup, normally regarded as disadvantageous for batters. "The eighth hitter in Chuck Tanner's lineup was an important guy. Phil Garner, an excellent hitter, batted eighth for years before me. We could have batted fifth or sixth anywhere else, but Chuck always wanted a good eighth hitter. This way, they would want to walk you to get to the pitcher. He thought that if he had a weak hitter batting eighth they'd pitch to him, get him out, and then you'd have the pitcher leading off the next inning.

"So I batted eighth and wound up leading the majors in intentional walks for three years in a row. I lost a lot of RBI opportunities because they'd walk me a lot of times with men on base. If I had been in a higher position in the order, I would have driven in 75 to 80 runs a year."

Tanner managed throughout Berra's eight seasons with the Pirates. Following the 1984 season, Dale was traded to the Yankees where he played briefly for his dad, then Billy Martin in 1985, and Lou Piniella in 1986. Dale talks about his favorite skipper. "Tanner was the best I ever played for. He instilled confidence and made me happy to be a major leaguer. Even if you were the worst player, Chuck would back you up. You could strike out three times with the bases loaded or make an error to lose a game, and he'd be the first to pat you on the back and say, 'Hey, there aren't many guys in this world who can make an error to lose a major league game. You're good enough to be in a position to do that.' Or during the game if you made an error, instead of snarling at you, he'd say, 'Don't worry about it. You're gonna win this game for us.'

"I was going poorly in the first part of 1982—I think I was hitting around .160 the first month. Chuck said, 'I don't care what you're hitting. You're my shortstop. So go out and play and don't worry about anything. You're playing every day.' Kind of like the Willie Mays thing when he first came up and was struggling and Leo Durocher told him, 'You're my center fielder.' Obviously, it wasn't the same scale. But for me it was."

Berra's strong season in 1982 might have been a prelude to better things, yet his production fell in forthcoming seasons. Part of the reason had to do with the corrupt atmosphere pervading the Pirate clubhouse from 1979 to 1985. By May of 1985, following testimony given to a Pittsburgh grand jury by numerous active major leaguers, including Berra, who were promised immunity for their help, seven drug dealers were indicted and successfully prosecuted.

Dale voluntarily reflects on an unpleasant part of his past, one that players with similar experiences are often reluctant to discuss. "I think I'd be remiss in not talking about my drug problem when I was a player. There is no question in my mind that I should have gotten better every year. Instead, my stats kept going down. No question the reason is because I got involved with drugs. Doesn't take a brain surgeon to figure it out. I have no doubt that I would have been ten times the player I was if I hadn't gotten involved. It was the biggest mistake of my life. It's a regret I have to live with, but fortunately I'm such a complete person today now that I'm void of that stuff. I'm a good father and try to be a good person every day. I'm proud of what I do. So the drug thing is in the past."

Although the Pirates were affected most by the drug trafficking of the eighties, they were not alone. One source reports that 40 percent of all major leaguers were using cocaine by 1980. According to Berra, the rate was closer to 50 percent. He assures that drug use and availability are not as common in the sports world today.

"Not even close," he says. "Today, the players are smarter. No question. I'm not sure if the big money has anything to do with it because we were making about the same amount in my day. I was making $600,000 a year, and I wasn't an All-Star. Just a regular player. Today, that would be worth two or three million.

"Of course, salaries today are crazy but I think players take their responsibilities seriously. The young guys like the Jeters, Piazzas, McGwires, Bonds—they're all terrific players. And I can tell from the way they play that they're not involved with drugs. They understand that they're role models. When I was playing, I never thought about it. Nobody ever came to me and told me that I was a role model and should watch my behavior. I wish they had."

Still, there are some modern athletes who display apathy, even resentment toward their role model status. Dale believes their indifference makes little difference. "His activities are public knowledge. Why would you want to do anything that reflected badly on yourself? Why would I want anyone—kid or adult—to know I was drinking or taking drugs or assaulting someone? The only way to avoid the bad publicity is not to do it. You don't read or hear anything bad about Jeter. Nothing."

Dale discusses his 1985 trade to the Yankees and how manager Yogi had nothing to do with it. "He's the kind of guy who would only give a suggestion in response to someone asking for advice. He wouldn't think of going to the general manager and asking for a trade. Of course, once the trade happened he was very happy about it.

"I knew the trade was in the works a couple of weeks before. I had great anticipation and was delighted when it happened. It was a terrific opportunity, going to play for Dad, even though I knew I wasn't going to be playing every day."

Dale became a pinstriper along with former Buc Jay Buhner, while Steve Kemp, Tim Foli, and $400,000 headed to Pittsburgh. Since the deal involved a significant amount of money, it required approval by Commissioner Peter Ueberroth, who hesitated in giving it. "It took him about a week. I remember I would call the Yankee PR man, Joe Safety, every day. He had been on the Pirates before going to New York so I knew him personally. I'd call and say, 'What happened, anything new?' He'd say, 'Nothing so far.' Finally, he called and told me that the deal had been approved."

The Yankees started slowly in 1985 and, in keeping with his reputation as an impetuous owner, George Steinbrenner fired Yogi after only 15 games. Berra reacted by vowing not to set foot in Yankee Stadium during Steinbrenner's reign, even on such cherished occasions as Old-Timers' Day. It was a well-kept promise until, in response to a conciliatory gesture on the part of the Boss—traveling to the Yogi Berra Museum and offering an apology—Yogi finally returned, throwing out the first ball in the Yank opener of 1999.

Dale discusses the reasons for his father maintaining a grudge that for fourteen years kept him away from a ballpark he had called home as a player, coach and manager for 30 years. "Dad was never upset about the dismissal. He knew taking the job from Steinbrenner, you were going to get fired. He knew he was hired to get fired. I remember him telling me the day it happened, 'Go ahead and have fun. I'm playing golf tomorrow.' The crux of the problem had always been behind locked doors. Today, we know that it had been the way he was fired—the fact that George didn't go down to the manager's office and fire him face-to-face. As a personal gesture. Don't have Clyde King do it. Dad likes King a lot, but he wanted George to call or tell him himself.

"Until last year when the problem between them was settled, I don't think George understood how Dad felt. When he came to apologize, I don't think he knew what he was apologizing for. He thought Dad was upset about being fired. Dad said, 'I don't care if you fire me. You should have told me yourself. This would never have happened.'"

Did the fact that the dismissal came at a time when his son was a Yankee further embitter Berra? "Not in the least. Wasn't a factor at all. Had I not been there and the same circumstances occurred, he would have reacted the same way. And George still wouldn't have known why because for those 14 years when Dad was gone, Dad never told anyone. Everyone assumed Dad was mad because George fired him, including the writers. No one really understood the real issue until now."

Dale recalls a scene from *Bridge on the River Kwai*, in which culprit Alec Guinness, while observing a Japanese train going over the bridge, whispers, "My God, what have I done?" He likens Guinness' emerging remorse to Steinbrenner's. "When George came here, he walked around and looked at some of the pictures and exhibits. He read some of Dad's quotes—how he always wanted to be a Yankee since the days when he was growing up, that he was never more proud than when he was wearing Yankee pinstripes. After reading them and walking around for 15 minutes, seeing all the stats and all the pictures and all the World Series rings, George literally shook his head, looked down at the floor, and said, 'My God, what did I do?' I think he realized the impact of his actions for the first time—severing the ties of the greatest living Yankee, with Joe's [DiMaggio] passing. All Dad is, besides being a father and husband, is a Yankee. That's all he ever wanted. And for him to be away for all that time, well, George felt he was responsible."

On-again, off-again Billy Martin, whose volatile personality had precipitated two previous Steinbrenner dismissals, replaced Berra in 1985. The third time was no charm for the Kid, though he managed to maintain the post for the duration of the 1985 season. Dale assesses the skills of the controversial skipper, disagreeing with critics who allege that Martin showed bias in handling players. "Billy was a great strategist. I think he gained that reputation when he managed Detroit (1971–1973). He was still good with the Yankees, but by then they had the DH so there wasn't as much strategy.

"Billy would do whatever was necessary for the good of the club. He wasn't afraid of the repercussions of benching Reggie Jackson. He had favorites, but all managers have favorites. They're trying to win, and they're not thinking of a favorite who they like personally. They're thinking of using the right player to win a ballgame. A manager justifies playing favorites by saying, 'That's the guy I think should be in there to help us win.' If a manager uses favoritism and foregoes the better choice, knowing full well that the other player should be on the field, then obviously he can't manage in the big leagues. Billy wasn't like that."

Dale talks about a couple of highlights in an 11-year career that ended in 1987 when he played sparsely for Houston manager Hal Lanier. "I hit two grand slam homers. One came off the Mets' Mark Bomback. It was in Pittsburgh, and the thing that was special about it was that the game was televised in New York so I knew all my friends and family saw it. The other one I hit was in St. Louis, which is where my dad was born and raised. I had a lot of relatives still living there too. Of course, just the thrill of hitting a grand slam is special. Dad always instilled in us the importance of

RBIs. He had been a big RBI man. So to get four at one time was great."

In discussing the modern game, Dale is awed not only by the amount of home runs, but the number hit to the opposite field. "We had big, strong guys when I played. You couldn't be stronger than Willie Stargell. Or Mike Schmidt. Or Greg Luzinski. Or Andre Dawson. Or Dave Parker. I mean, Parker was six-five, 250. And when he hit a ball over the left-field fence at Shea Stadium, we all used to say, 'Damn, how many guys can do that?' Now you see shortstops who aren't that big hitting them out the other way, and you say, 'That's impossible!' Couldn't have been done in my day."

Berra supports the live-ball theory in explaining the increase in home runs, unconvinced that modern pitchers' wariness to throw inside is a factor. "When they say they don't come inside, they don't clarify that. They mean that pitchers don't throw enough inside strikes. But pitchers still hit people. Guys get hit all the time. They still knock you down or throw at you."

Dale Berra at the Yogi Berra Museum and Learning Center in Montclair, New Jersey.

As the conversation closes, Dale talks about Yogi's public reaction to a museum dedicated to honoring his life. "When it opened, Dad said, 'Most people get these things when they're dead. I'm glad I'm here to see it.'" I inquire about Friends of Yogi, Inc., a non-profit organization responsible for building and operating the museum. "It was the idea of [President] Rose Cali. She's the wife of an entrepreneur and developer in Montclair. For the last 30 years she has been devoted to helping charities. She's done everything imaginable for developing programs here at Montclair State—funding libraries, helping with Reading Is Fundamental. Everything she does is related to some kind of charity work."

A longtime friend of the Berras, Cali suggested paying tribute to Yogi's achievements while simultaneously enhancing the education of young people and adults. It remains the chief goal of the museum. "In the theater, we give lectures. Larry Doby came to speak during Black

History Month. Ted Williams and Stan Musial came. It's endless the kinds of educational programs we have. Now they want to expand by putting in a computerized virtual reality room for kids. So even though it's all to honor Dad, at the same time it's an educational center that's getting bigger and better all the time."

Besides assisting with museum activities, Dale and brothers Larry and Tim operate business agency LTD, the sole client being their celebrated father. "We handle everything. Every middle man and outside agent is pretty much out of the picture. We arrange all of Dad's affairs, which are many because he's so sought after."

No longer directly involved with pro ball, Dale occasionally watches Jackals home games. "The independent leagues are becoming very popular. Most are made up of major leaguers who've been released and are trying to make their way back—and a lot of them get picked up again. Some are guys who could have signed but didn't, or guys who were injured before. I know the coaching staff, and once in a while I'll go down on the field and fool around with the players. But that's my only connection with the team."

After the interview, Dale takes Lola and me on a tour of exhibits honoring one whose exceptional performance on the diamond has been overshadowed in part by an endearing personality and propensity for jocular remarks that have reached legendary proportions in his own lifetime. "I think the greatest thing about Dad is his humility," Dale says. "It's the biggest asset in his life. Who he is—the fame and popularity—means nothing to him. Everybody who ever meets him is just amazed by the fact that he's such a regular guy. A normal guy. He emits something that makes him lovable. I don't know what it is. He doesn't try to do it, but somehow it comes out of him."

Larry Bowa

Around midnight on Tuesday, October 17, more than 56,000 fidgety fans at Yankee Stadium watch Mariner slugger Edgar Martinez swing at a low slider delivered by Yank closer Mariano Rivera. The ball dribbles towards shortstop Derek Jeter, who charges, fields, and fires to first sacker Tino Martinez. Thus do the New York Yankees successfully defend the American League pennant for the third straight time and earn the right to defend their world championship for the same number of consecutive seasons.

"Start spreading the news, New York, New York," announces broadcaster Bob Costas following the final out. With the Mets having already won the National League pennant, it was his way of saying that the Big Apple is assured of its first Subway Series since 1956 when "Dem Bums" of Brooklyn fell in seven to the mighty Bombers, a team that won eight pennants and six World Series in the decade. As the first junior-circuit conquerors of the new millennium celebrate with hugs, hollering and high-fives, commentators compare them with their pinstripe counterparts of the fifties. (One week, later, following the five-game conquest of their scrappy crosstown rivals, their fourth Series victory in five seasons, the current Yanks are hailed by many as the equal of any sports dynasty in history.)

Although experiencing their most gratifying season in five years, numb Seattle players gawk at stadium festivities with understandable dejection. Free agent Alex Rodriguez, speculated to have played his last game as a Mariner, gazes at baseball buddy Jeter, perhaps wishing it was he with three (soon to be four) World Series rings. Pitcher Mike Garcia, twice victorious over the Yanks in the ALCS, watches Latino rival Orlando Hernandez being congratulated by an interviewer for his seventh post-season victory without a loss (a streak snapped by the Mets, the team's sole consolation of the Series). Downhearted skipper Lou Piniella is gracious in defeat, reminding a clubhouse reporter of his Yankee roots as one-time player and manager, leaving no doubt with which team his loyalty lies in the Series.

Among the morose Mariners in the visitor's dugout is third base, infield and baserunning coach Larry Bowa, a former big league shortstop who understands the ecstasy connected with winning a world championship, having been a key member of the victorious 1980 Phillies. After watching the Yanks clinch, I am reminded of comments made by Bowa in January, when in the lobby of the Marriott Hotel in Conshohocken, Pennsylvania, I ask for his assessment of Seattle's chances for getting into post-season play for the first time in five years. "We put together a pretty good team," the still-youthful-looking 55-year-old asserts. "On paper, we're very good. If we can go out there and perform, then hopefully we can play in the World Series."

Larry is quick to qualify his prediction. "I don't like to put the horse before the cart. Last year when I worked with Anaheim [as a coach] and we made a lot of acquisitions, like Mo Vaughn, I thought we'd win the division. It didn't happen. We had all kinds of injuries." (Not long after my interview with Bowa, Seattle's slugging center field superstar Ken Griffey Jr. exercised his free agent rights and headed to hometown Cincinnati to play alongside his father and coach, Ken Sr. At the time, many "experts" maintained the acquisition assured a pennant for the Reds and doom for the Mariners. Instead, Cincinnati failed to repeat as a post-season participant while Seattle clinched a wild-card spot, defeated the much-heralded Central Division champion White Sox in the Division Series, and stretched the Yanks to six games in the ALCS.)

"I'm looking forward to working with A-Rod [Rodriguez]," Larry continues. "He's one of three shortstops they're always talking about these days—along with Jeter and Garciaparra. It's rare that you have hitters like them in the middle of the lineup, doing all the things offensively, who still have that defensive awareness. They're in a different class."

Larry knows firsthand about talented shortstops. During a career spanning the seventies and first half of the eighties, Bowa was considered among the elite at his position. A five-time All-Star and six-time leader in fielding percentage, he would have won many more than the one Gold Glove Award he captured in 1978 had Dave Concepcion and Ozzie Smith not been contemporary shortstops. Never a power hitter and a .300 batter only once, Bowa made up for his mediocre stick with alertness and speed on the basepaths, averaging nearly 20 stolen bases a season during his 16-year career. Yet, success did not come easily for the aspiring ballplayer who struggled throughout his life as a pre-professional, minor leaguer, and big leaguer.

Born in Sacramento, a hotbed for future hardball heroes, Larry recalls going to parks during the summer and playing, playing, playing. "They had five or six diamonds, but you still had to get there at nine o'clock in the morning to secure one for the day. Mom and Dad would pack me a lunch and come back at five o'clock to take me home."

Bowa remembers going to games played at the Sacramento Triple A ballpark as a member of the Knothole Gang. "At that time, Triple A was great baseball. A lot of those guys could have played in the big leagues today. At that time, there was just no room." He also regularly watched *The Game of the Week* on television. With the Yankees appearing more frequently than other teams, the youngster became a fan of one particular pinstriped player. "In the middle of the infield they had Phil Rizzuto. He was a small-type player and I used to like to watch him play. He and Luis Aparicio. I was very small, so from watching how good they were, in spite of their size, I had aspirations about playing in the majors myself."

Larry attributes his interest and development in baseball mostly to his father, who was a one-time minor league player and manager. "I guess I've been around baseball since the time I started walking. There was always a ball and bat in the house. My dad taught me everything." Larry's father ingrained in his son the heartache and struggles of life in the bushes. "He didn't want me to become a baseball bum—playing in the minors all your life, not having anything else to fall back on. He'd tell me, 'It's a tough grind'—riding the buses, away from your family, the terrible parks and conditions. He'd remind me that only a small percentage make it to the big leagues."

Bowa's father was nevertheless supportive of his son's interest in the game, without putting pressure on him. Larry illustrates with an anecdote. "When I was in high school, I got cut by the baseball coach in my freshman year. I was so embarrassed. Then I was cut again in my sophomore year. I didn't even tell my dad. I'd hang around the field during practice and dad would pick me up every night at the Seven-Eleven. Then one day, he ran into somebody at the store who told him. So we were eating dinner that night and he says, 'How's practice?' I said, 'Great. Everything's going good.' Then there was this big pause and I looked up because I knew something was wrong. He looked at me and said, 'You didn't make the team.' I remember sitting there and saying, 'Naw, I didn't, Dad. I really feel disappointed and embarrassed.' He said, 'Why are you embarrassed? As long as you gave 100 percent, you shouldn't be. Don't worry about it. That's just one coach's opinion. You can still play American Legion and summer baseball.' Which is what I did."

Labeled too small, Larry was again cut by his high school coach in his final two years, but with encouragement from his father he tried out for the team at Sacramento Junior College. Not only did Larry make the squad, he earned All-Conference honors both years. One day during his sophomore season, Larry caught the attention of a Phillies scout. "Eddie Bockman, who wound up signing a lot of major leaguers, came to watch me play a doubleheader. Afterwards, the Phillies called him and asked how good I was. He said, 'I don't know. The first game he got kicked out in the second inning; the second game he got kicked out in the first.' [Larry laughs.] I guess in those days, my temper preceded me all the time."

Although Bockman maintained an interest in the Sacramento shortstop, Bowa was passed over in the first-ever draft in 1965. Soon afterwards, Bockman surprised Bowa with a visit to his home. "He said he liked the way I throw and run but that he couldn't guarantee a lot of money. I told him I don't care if I didn't get any money, I just want to play. I remember he told me there was a contract in his car and for me to go get it. There was something like a $2,000 bonus, about $1,200 after taxes. Not much, but I signed. To this day, Eddie is a great friend. We still exchange Christmas cards."

Larry recalls his first game as a professional, playing for the Class A Spartanburg club in South Carolina. "I struck out four times in a row. After the game, I was sitting at my locker and Bob Wellman, my manager, came over and saw I had my head down. He asked me what was wrong. I said, 'There's no way I can play professional baseball. I'm completely overmatched.' He said, 'Trust me. This guy is something special. He's going to be a pretty good pitcher.' I said to myself, 'I hope so. If they're all like that I have no chance.' Anyway, the pitcher's name was Nolan Ryan."

Bowa had a good year at Spartanburg and was promoted to Reading of the Double A league in 1966. Following an outstanding year, Bowa was sent to the Instructional League where manager Bob Skinner immediately presented him with the choice of making the Phillies as a parttimer or spending one year in Triple A ball for the chance to become the Phillies' regular shortstop. "I remember what I said like it was yesterday. I told him, 'I'm not going to be a utility player. I don't want to sit on the bench. If I can't play every day, I don't want to play in the big leagues.'"

Aware of the talented infielder's main shortcoming, Skinner convinced the right-hand batter that his best chance for improvement came with learning how to switch-hit. "It wasn't easy. You do something one way for 18, 19 years and suddenly you have to change. I did all right (in the Instructional League), but then in Triple A at Eugene, Oregon, it was very difficult. I started out terribly. But I stuck with it and by the end of the year I ended up hitting somewhere between .290 and .300.

"My work ethic throughout my career was always outstanding. Again, that was from my dad. He'd say to me, 'Never shortchange yourself, your teammates, or anybody you play for. Whether I'm here on Earth or not, I want you to be able to sit down after every game and say, 'I gave 100 percent.' If you can do that, everything will fall into place.'"

Bowa's perseverance in Instructional and Triple A ball paid off. At the Phils' spring camp in 1970, manager Frank Lucchesi, Larry's former skipper at Reading and Eugene, assured the 24-year-old that he was the ballclub's regular shortstop. Bowa was enthusiastic throughout the spring, and ecstasy reached a climax on Opening Day. "Even today, that stands out in my mind more than any other game. After the critics said I wouldn't make it because of my size, my mom and dad staying with me consistently, overcoming all the negatives. Just standing on those lines, looking out on the field while they played the National Anthem is something I'll never forget as long as I live."

Unfortunately, the rookie faltered at the plate for the first three months, and held a pathetic .170 average in June. Critics were soon calling for a replacement. "A couple of writers said the only place I was going to hit was in Williamsport, which is where they play the Little League World Series. But they were telling the truth. I was terrible."

The fans in Philly, notorious for their impatience with struggling players, made their dissatisfaction known with catcalls after each batting flop. In retrospect, Bowa does not condemn them for it. "I know the fans are tough here. Maybe it's because they're mostly blue-collar. But I think it's fair. They pay good money to watch a product. If you don't perform the way you're supposed to they'll get on you. But if they see effort, they'll cut you a break. What they don't like is nonchalant play—walking to first when you hit a ball, not running out fly balls. When you work hard for your money and pay that kind of money to watch a game, you're entitled to 100 percent effort.

"You're from New York so you know this to be true there too. The Philly fans can be the toughest in the world, but they're also the greatest. I really believe that if I hadn't played in Philadelphia, I wouldn't have stayed in the big leagues. These people pushed me, made me want to work, made me want to succeed. And after that first year, I never had a problem with the fans that showed up."

Bowa credits Lucchesi for helping him survive that stormy, stress-filled rookie year. "I was working every single day with Billy Demars [hitting coach]. We hit extra, we hit extra. Finally, Frank called me into his office in June. I said to myself, 'He's gonna send me down.' But he said, 'Let me say just one thing. As long as I'm manager here, you will be my shortstop. I don't care if you make out until October.' Now, this is a rookie manager telling me he doesn't care what I hit."

Larry continued working with Demars, and by season's end had raised his average eighty points. "The one good thing about that year was that the team was rebuilding at the time. They knew we'd be coming in last, they knew we were going with kids, they knew they had a rookie manager. So that eased the pressure somewhat."

The Phillies played home games at Shibe Park for 33 years until its closing after the '71 season, so Bowa's rookie year was also the final one for the historic ballpark. "I loved playing there. The park had a personality to it. It was like Wrigley Field. You felt the fans were right there. You could hear them talking when you were sitting on-deck. It was unique. They had the iron fence in right field and the bleachers in left. It was well taken care of. And it was a very big park, which didn't hurt me because I used to bunt and slap the ball a lot. I was glad I played at Shibe because a lot of great players came through there. To be able to say, 'Hey, I played on this diamond,' was something special."

Bowa explains one drawback to playing at Shibe. "The only thing I didn't like was that it was in a bad area. We used to drive to the ballpark and guys would offer to watch your car for five dollars. You look at them and say, 'What are you talking about?' They say, 'If you don't get someone to watch it, there's a chance it won't be here when you come back.' So I had to give the guy five dollars a night."

A .250 average fell below his rookie expectations, but Larry's impressive turnaround in the second half made him optimistic when he returned to spring training in Clearwater in 1971. "That was the year the Vet [Veterans Stadium] opened. There was this big buildup. Everyone was talking about it." He recalls the Vet's inauguration. "On the day it opened, it felt strange. It looked like something from outer space when you first walked in. But it also felt good walking out on the field for the first time. And even though we were coming off a bad year, this place was packed.

"I think it was Jim Bunning that started for us and Bill Stoneman was the starter for the Expos. We beat them, and the game was special for me because I got the first hit at the Vet. Bunning retired the Expos in order and after Denny Doyle made out, I hit a breaking ball between second and first. They gave me the ball. I still have it today."

Throughout his career, Bowa rarely displayed power at the plate as he managed only 15 career home runs, although one was a grand slam in a game in which he had four hits in as many at bats. "The fans gave me a standing ovation (after the slam). When I got to the dugout, everyone was making like they were fainting. It was fun."

Bowa's occasional fence-clearing heroics did little to change his hitting philosophy. Aware of his limitations, he remained committed to hitting to the opposite field and making contact, explaining his outstanding career rate of one strikeout per 15 at bats. He compensated for his power shortcomings, taking advantage of the artificial surface by stroking the ball between outfielders for extra-base hits; in 1972, he led the majors with 13 triples.

In his current role as batting coach, Larry often explains to overeager middle-sized hitters the advantages of foregoing home runs for hits. "I see them with a big, long swing. They might hit 10 or 12 home runs but they'll hit .220. I tell them there's nothing wrong with being a singles hitter. Shorten up, put the ball in play, and you'll hit .280.

"But there are a lot of factors that make a player today want to try for homers. The parks are smaller, the ball is livelier, and the pitching isn't as good. And arbitration has ruined baseball because they only look at home runs and RBIs. They don't look at how many runners you moved over, how many plays you made in the field, how many double plays you turned over, how many times you gave yourself up with a man on second and no outs to try to get the runner to third. But when you look at the teams that play in October, they're the teams that do all that stuff. The team I'm with now—the Mariners—they've led the league in home runs the last four years but they've never been able to advance to the World Series. That tells you that slugging can take you so far but pitching and defense get you to the Series."

It took ten years before Larry's team got to the Series. Finishing ahead of runner-up Montreal by one game in 1980, Philly followed their division title with a hard-fought Championship Series victory over the Astros, winning the decisive finale in the tenth inning. They then bested the Royals for Philly's first-ever world championship.

Larry explains the circumstances leading to that eventful 1980 season. "We had gotten into the playoffs in '76, '77, '78, but we just couldn't get over the hump. We missed the playoffs in 1979, and then before the 1980 season it was more or less an ultimatum by the front office that they were going to give us one more chance—keep the team together, not get rid of any players, for one more year.

"Well, we were very mediocre the first half. We'd win a few, lose a few. Then at the end of July we just went crazy. We were on fire. You could feel the whole city coming together. You could feel it in the playoffs that you were going to win. You had the games in Houston—practically every game going extra innings—and then we beat Kansas City four games to two in the Series. It was incredible. And because we knew that if we didn't do it that year they were breaking up the team, it made it more special."

Special for the Philly players, and for the citizens of a championship-starved city. "They gave us a big parade. Millions of people lined the streets. It was unbelievable. Even now, when I go to restaurants around here, people always remember you. They tell you where they were when the final out was made. Or they tell you how important it was for their dad to have the Phillies finally win a Series. So you realize that you affected other people's lives and it makes you feel good."

Three players on that 1980 Philly ballclub were arguably the key contributors to the team's success. Two are current Hall-of-Famers—fireballer Steve Carlton, who led the league in wins (24), games-started (38), innings-pitched (304) and strikeouts (286) in capturing his third of four Cy Young Awards; third baseman Mike Schmidt, who topped the circuit in slugging (.624), home runs (48), and RBIs (121) in taking his first of three MVPs, two being consecutive (1980 and 1981).

The third is should-be Hall-of-Famer Pete Rose, whose value to the team cannot be evaluated by looking at season statistics, although he did lead the league in doubles with 42. Larry discusses the immediate impact Charley Hustle made when he joined the Phils as a free agent in 1979. "We always knew we were good but we also felt we were missing something. There's no question that Pete put us over the edge.

"And Pete was a very positive influence in the clubhouse. I'll give you an example. One day, we were all sitting around playing cards. Back in those days, you went to the park early to hang out with your teammates. There was camaraderie. It's not like today when you get to the park at four-thirty. Anyway, Schmitty always had a tendency to say, 'I hate facing guys I never faced before.' Well, that day Pete heard him say it. He looked at Mike like he was crazy and said, 'What did you say?' Schmitty repeated it and Pete says, 'Don't you think the guy on the other side is scared stiff to face you? He looks at your numbers—35, 40, 45 home runs. He's not scared?'"

Considering Rose's reputation as an in-your-face player, I ask Larry if there was initial resentment toward him from Philly teammates. "Not at all. You never liked playing against him, but always loved and admired the way he played. He brought that same intensity over here.

"Pete comes off different than the way he is. He comes off as arrogant but he isn't. And he belongs in the Hall of Fame. What he did in baseball was amazing. I didn't think the Gehrig record would ever be broken, and it was. But what this guy did—breaking the hit record—that *will* never be broken. First of all, they're not gonna have enough money to pay a guy to get 200 hits for 20 years in a row. That's an incredible number. So to have the all-time hit leader not in the Hall of Fame is something I just don't understand."

Bowa addresses the specific issues involved with Rose's ban from baseball. "Everyone's entitled to a mistake, and that's assuming Pete bet on baseball. Just knowing Pete, I've gotta say he didn't. When we played together during spring training, I know Pete used to go to the dog track every night. He'd go to Vegas. He'd bet on horses. But I can honestly tell you that I've never heard him talking about betting on baseball. And as far as keeping him out of the Hall of Fame, I'm sure you could rattle a whole lot of skeletons over there if you wanted to."

The antithesis of the fiery Rose was mild-mannered, unemotional Schmidt, who was the toast of the town in 1980. Fellow infielder Bowa remembers a time when the subdued personality of the slugger who displayed as much proclivity for whiffing as for wowing at the plate antagonized Philly fans. "His first year, he struck out 160 times. The fans started to get on him because he looked nonchalant. But that was just his way of relaxing. My way of relaxing was to show my emotions. Mike didn't do that. And maybe he came across as nonchalant because he was so gifted. He made everything look easy. But by playing with him for so many years, I knew he wanted to win as badly as I did, or Greg (Luzinski) did, or Pete did."

The efficient infield duo remained good friends throughout their ten years together with the Phils, despite a frosty first encounter in 1971. "Schmidt was a high draft pick, I think a number one. I remember reading about him, how great he was. On the day they signed him, he was supposed to work out with us before going to Reading. So he was taking ground balls at short and I went up to him and said, 'You know, I don't even know you. I'm sure you're an outstanding player. But I worked too hard for this. I'm gonna play shortstop here.' He looked at me like I was crazy but didn't say anything. So he started out as a shortstop in Reading, but when they saw me continuing to play well here they moved him to third base. So I still tell him today, 'If it wasn't for me, you wouldn't be in the Hall of Fame. You'd have so much ground to cover at short you'd have been too tired to hit all those home runs.' He laughs. But he was a great player and I was lucky to play with him and Pete."

The Phils made it to the post-season in 1981, but Bowa and his teammates lost to Montreal in an agonizing five-game division playoff in which Carlton was a two-game loser. There was more heartache for Bowa four months later when he was shipped to the last-place Cubs in an off-season trade for veteran shortstop Ivan DeJesus. Bowa's consistent play in Chicago was an important factor in the team's improved play the next three years which culminated in a division title in 1984, a season Larry rates as his most disappointing. "It was the first time in quite a while that the Cubs made it to the post-season. We won the first two games against San Diego, then they swept the next three."

Following another season with the Cubs and Mets, Bowa's playing days ended. "I guess the most satisfying thing about my career is knowing I played on a lot of winning teams. Both here in Philadelphia and in Chicago. That means a lot. The individual things don't mean much. I'd rather hit .240 and get in the playoffs than hit .300 and be watching TV. You've got to analyze what you do for the team. Do you bring intensity, looseness in the clubhouse? Did you have fun doing your job? I know I did. There were times I was miserable because things weren't going good, but every day I woke up I could hardly wait to get to the park. I still feel that way as a coach."

When asked for his most significant individual accomplishment in baseball, Larry picks the year that he played all 81 home games without committing an error. "I don't recall what year it was. It might have been the year I only made six errors all season (1979). But that was hard to do. Some people say, 'Well, you played on astroturf.' But there were drawbacks to that. You had to play deeper, which made the throws longer. The ball got to you quicker. So I don't think it takes away from the achievement."

Larry discusses factors about the modern game that are most disturbing. "Players are concerned about numbers. Can I hit .320? Can I score 100 runs? Can I steal 50 bases? I talk to some guys and say, 'Don't you want to get to the World Series? Don't you want a ring?' They look at me like I'm crazy. Like, 'Well, if it happens, it happens.' For me, I would have felt cheated if I never got to participate. I've played in All-Star Games and playoff games. Not to have gotten to that final level, there would have been something missing. I'm not saying everyone can get there. Ernie Banks, as great a player as he was, never got there. But that's what you've gotta strive for more than anything else."

Larry is also critical of the attitude shown by many of today's players and offers examples without mentioning names. "Players like to read about how good they are but won't talk to reporters after a bad game. You've gotta take the good with the bad. You've gotta let them know what

Author (left) with Larry Bowa in the lobby of the Marriott Hotel in Conshohocken, Pennsylvania.

happened on that muffled grounder. Be a man about it. It's a kid's game but you have to be a man to play it."

Having played a decade alongside a teammate who would accumulate 548 career home runs, Bowa nonetheless recognizes that home runs are more commonplace today, part of the reason being the increased size and strength of hitters. "They have better equipment and training. In my day, weight training was taboo. We were taught that more muscles tie you up when you swing. Now we see guys benefiting from it—guys like McGwire and (Sammy) Sosa. They rejuvenated the game. No question about it."

Still, Bowa is convinced that homer-happy hitters benefit from factors outside the weight room. "There's no question the ball is wound much tighter today. The bats are very hard-finished. And the parks are small. American League in particular. Boston's left field. Minnesota is small. Oakland is a joke since they enclosed it. Baltimore's Camden Yards is a joke. Up until last year, Seattle's Kingdome was a joke. They're like little league parks. The legit parks today are Kansas City, Anaheim and, now, Seattle."

Like other old-timers, Larry believes the batter's greatest advantage has been ineffective pitching, and blames expansion, a narrower strike zone, and an increase in batter-friendly counts as key factors. He contends that the knockdown rule has been most influential, with pitchers fearful of being thrown out of games even in cases of inadvertent wildness. "Pitchers pitch center away. So if I'm a hitter, I eliminate inside."

Because pitchers rarely come inside, hitters are unprepared for the few occasions that they do. Six months after the interview, Roger Clemens infuriated Mets fans by beaning their popular slugger Mike Piazza during a regular season inter-league game. Clemens rekindled their wrath during Game Two of the World Series by indignantly flinging the barrel of batter Piazza's shattered stick in the direction of the first base line, narrowly missing baserunning Piazza. The tormented hurler's action was more an unintentional reaction to pressure caused in part by a media that for days preceding Clemens' first start against the Mets since the Piazza beaning had spent an inordinate amount of talk and ink speculating about repercussions and retaliation. Following the unfortunate incident, Fox commentators Joe Buck and Tim McCarver were zealously critical of the right-hander throughout the game, while reporters in the post-game press conference virtually ignored the Rocket's masterful eight shutout innings and 12 strikeouts, harping instead on the bat-hurling incident. A public outcry led to Clemens being fined by baseball's dubious enforcer, Frank Robinson, renowned for having had a scrap or two during his playing days.

Old-timers can recall pitchers who threw at batters for no other reason than occasionally wanting to. "Pitchers aren't as mean today," Larry asserts as the interview nears an end. "Gibson, Drysdale and those guys used to pound you inside. When you faced them, as hard as they threw and knowing their personality and demeanor, you didn't dive into pitches like they do now, believe me. There's no fear factor today. And if a guy gets hit, even if he just gets nicked in the shirt, the pitcher gets a warning from the umpire. Or the batter runs to the mound. It's ridiculous. There would have been fights every day when I played if hitters acted that way. As mean as Gibson, Carlton, Seaver were, if you let them know it bothered you, you were gonna get hit more."

In 1987, Bowa returned to his native California as manager of San Diego, a team that had won only 74 games the previous year. The Padres continued to struggle under their new skipper, finishing last with 65 victories in 1987, then winning 16 of its first 46 in 1988 before Bowa was dismissed. Larry talks about the firing. "Ownership was going through a transition. Ray Kroc died and Joan Kroc [his daughter] took over. We had a different president twice. And as soon as they started changing ownership I knew I had no chance. But the positive about the experience was that after a slow start (in 1987)—I think we were something like 12–32—we had the best record in the National League in the second half. So we made great strides. The next year, we got out of the gate slow again, but that was because my two best hitters—[Tony] Gwynn and [John] Kruk—were on the D.L. (disabled list).

"But I have satisfying memories from managing. Some of the kids I worked with went on to have good careers. I worked with both Alomars (Sandy and Roberto), Joey Cora, Benito Santiago, Kruk. They're pretty good players. I'm not saying they wouldn't have made it without me, but to feel that I was a part of their growing process gives me a lot of satisfaction."

Would Bowa do anything differently had he the chance to do it over? "Hindsight being 20–20, I wouldn't have taken the managing job. The year before, I managed in Vegas and we won the championship. Soon after that, they asked me if I wanted to manage in San Diego. When you're just coming out of baseball as a player, and someone asks you to manage a big league team, you don't say no. But looking back, I could have used the experience of managing another year in the minors. Learning to handle the media, the players, the everyday occurrences. I think I was too soon removed as a player. I still had that player's mentality. When I practiced as a player, I used to take 100 ground balls. So when I managed, I wanted my infielders to do the same. But that's not how it goes."

Believing his negative results in San Diego to be the chief cause for an absence of managerial offers since then, Bowa closes the interview by admitting he hopes to someday get another chance. In October, one week after Seattle's elimination by the Yankees, the Philadelphia resident's hopes are realized when his former ballclub and cellar-dweller of the 2000 season requests his services as skipper. "There's a lot of good athletes here," Larry states at the press conference in Philadelphia announcing his signing. "I'm looking forward to the challenge."

If experience in facing challenges is a managerial asset, Bowa is the right man for the job.

Gil McDougald

Gil McDougald's first season with the Yankees was Joe DiMaggio's last. He is understandably hesitant when asked to assess the abilities of The Yankee Clipper. "I saw Joe's brother Dom play when I was a kid in San Francisco," the 72-year-old McDougald says from his home in Spring Lake, New Jersey, on January 31, 2000. "He played for the Seals. And I thought Dom was, I mean, just a great outfielder. But Joe, I only saw him in his worst year, when he had the sore hose. We had to go way out to get relay throws. So I'm not the one who would ever try to answer questions about his playing skills."

Gil corroborates what others have said regarding Joltin' Joe's reclusive nature. "He just didn't enjoy conversation unless it was a person he was really very fond of. He was a very into-himself individual. Hard to talk to. Later on, guys would ask me about Joe, the kind of person he was, and I'd say, 'I couldn't really tell you.' I played a year with him, and the most it would be was, 'Hi,' and that's it.

"And I think I was in the majority. Probably 95 percent of the guys in the clubhouse, that would be the conversation. It wasn't that he was, you know, a snob. He just wasn't like the other players who really enjoyed each other. And I can understand it because I can see how tough it is being harassed every time you walk into a place. In that one year, I don't think I ever saw him one time in the hotel or dining room—morning, noon, or night. He just tried to avoid people. That's the best way to describe it."

Gil's first encounter with Joltin' Joe came not as a Yankee rookie but as a teenager living in San Francisco. "A good friend of my dad's, Reno Barchiachini, who was also a good friend of Joe's and was his best man in his marriage to Marilyn Monroe, introduced me to him one night at a place called Dominick's Bar. Again, you gotta know Joe to understand that the conversation is very light."

McDougald was born on May 19, 1928, in San Francisco and attended Commerce High School in the downtown section of the city. "Today, it's a city building. I didn't really play too much baseball there. They had me pitching, but I had a rotten arm and all I did was throw curve balls." Teenager Gil gained valuable infield experience playing semi-pro ball, practicing with such future big-leaguers as Eddie Joost, Jerry Coleman, Frank Silvera and Bobby Brown. "We'd work out together. It gave you a better knowledge of what you can do and can't do. And if you saw someone doing something that you couldn't, you say, 'Oops, I better work on that.'

"In 1951, the Yanks had training in Phoenix, Arizona instead of St. Pete. And we fielded an all–San Francisco nine. I don't think that would ever happen any other place, any other time. But it was easy to understand for those growing up in San Francisco. It was a hotbed for baseball. Many players got paid better playing in the Coast League than the majors. You went one week to one club, one week to another club, and then you went home for a couple of weeks. It was really beautiful, a great situation. And they used to say that everybody was a .300 hitter and every pitcher was a 20-game winner. That's how good it was. And all those towns today are major-league clubs—San Diego, San Francisco, L.A., Seattle."

Notwithstanding the baseball ambiance of his hometown, Gil accepted a basketball scholarship from the University of San Francisco upon graduation from Commerce High. "I always felt basketball was a much more enjoyable game. Baseball, you know, is very slow moving, even though it's more a thinking game and you have to be more prepared and able to anticipate. But in basketball, it was go-go, quick, a lot of action and reflexes involved. In baseball, you could play third base for the whole game, and there isn't even a ball close to you."

Despite McDougald's preference for basketball, he disliked playing in college. After seven weeks, he abandoned his scholarship for enrollment at the City College of San Francisco. "Unfortunately, I ran into the wrong coach at USF for the style I wanted to play. Pete Newell coaches all the centers for the NBA. He's an old-timer and real student of the game. At the time, the game was starting to turn into racehorse basketball, which I would have preferred since I was a guard. But that wasn't the case at USF. If you knew Pete Sewell, the scores would always be 14–12 or 12–10, after playing the entire 40 minutes."

Deciding to concentrate on baseball, McDougald signed a minor league contract with the Yankees in 1948 and played his first year with the Class C club in Twin Falls, Idaho. He was promoted to Class B the following year and played for Victoria, British Columbia, part of the Western International League that included teams from Yakima, Wenatchee, Salem and Spokane. "After that year, I thought I was ready for the majors."

The Yankees were unconvinced, but believed he was good enough for Triple A. "I says, 'Naw. You're gonna send me to a league that's all fastball pitchers. I'll hit .350 and I haven't seen anyone who changes speed.' Well, that's not the way it is up in the big leagues. The Texas League was known for having guys who are sore-armed pitchers from the majors. And they needed to use a lot of off-speed pitches. So I asked them to send me there. I played at Beaumont and was the Most Valuable Player."

The Beaumont manager was former big league great Rogers Hornsby, whose reputation for intense dedication to baseball was matched by an unlikable personality, prompting criticism from teammates, owners, sportswriters and, most recently, his biographer for an alleged supercilious and overbearing attitude. Do not include Gil among Hornsby's critics. "I thought he was great. He wasn't like a lot of these guys who would try to get you to change something if you were in a slump. Right away they tell you that you're holding the bat wrong or you gotta do this or that. And they make a head case out of you. Hornsby was never like that."

McDougald talks about his first spring training. "In 1951, they had a pre-squad—a rookie camp before the regular training started in Phoenix. Well, when you live in San Francisco you're ready to play because everybody's working out; you're playing every weekend in semi-pro leagues. So I was in shape and ready to go when a lot of guys from back east weren't. They took spring training as a place to get in shape."

Another rookie at the Yanks' Phoenix camp was a sinewy, naïve Oklahoman by the name of Mickey Mantle, who was being publicized as the Yanks' next superstar. "I don't think they'll ever be a guy who'll come along and have a spring training like him. He got about $20 million worth of press in a month." Even more startling than the circus atmosphere surrounding Mantle were his displays of seemingly inhuman strength. "You know, he hit balls ... they talk about that Washington homer he hit [tape-measure blast off Chuck Stobbs on April 17, 1953, at Griffith Stadium]. What a joke. At Southern Cal that spring, he hit a ball—I've only heard a couple of guys from the club mention it since then—but no contest. The one in Washington was wind-blown as far as I'm concerned. Gus Triandos was with us and he hit a pop that looked like it was for the infield and while he's jogging to first thinking it's an out, the wind blows it into the seats. The Southern Cal campus had a fence that was 300 feet in right field, and they had a field house that was like 800 feet further out in open land. Well, I'm telling you, when I say 600 feet I'm being conservative."

McDougald recalls the switch-hitter's propensity for long home runs and strikeouts from the left side. "Right-handed, he hit on top of the ball and it died. Left-handed, he'd get that loft with that uppercut swing. But he was a much better hitter right-handed. And the righty pitchers who threw hard would crucify Mantle. Like [Walt] Masterson. I remember when we played the Senators one time and Masterson was pitching, Mantle said, 'I'm good for four today.' And sure enough, four Ks."

McDougald's infield competitors in the spring of 1951 were third basemen Billy Johnson and Bobby Brown, second basemen Jerry Coleman and Billy Martin, and shortstops Phil Rizzuto and Jim Brideweser. "Brownie was one of my good friends. And Brideweser, from Southern Cal, I tell you, he was one helluva ballplayer. He hit something like .545 that spring. And he was the second-fastest guy on the club getting down to first, next to Mantle. I was third. And Jim was so smooth. Did everything easy. But Casey didn't like Brideweser. It makes me laugh. But, you know, like every manager, they got their own ideas."

One other player competed for an infield spot, albeit briefly. "Mickey came to spring training as a shortstop. And when I seen him there, I said, 'Oh my God!' I laughed and told Crow [Frank Crosetti], 'This kid's gonna have to drive in a lot of runs to play there.' (Gil laughs.) If you saw him throw balls, he was clearing out the whole section behind first base, you know. What a scatter-arm!"

McDougald was used sparingly that spring and it appeared he would have difficulty making the team until he received support from an old ally. "We were barnstorming down the coast. When we got to L. A., Hornsby was there. He was on his way to manage the Seattle club, which was one step up from Double A to Triple A. He stopped by, and all the photographers wanted to take a picture of Casey with Rogers. So I'm standing there with them and Rogers says, 'You playing tonight?' I say, 'Ask the manager.' Well, Rogers was pretty blunt and the way he felt about something, you couldn't convince him otherwise. So he looks at Casey and says, 'What's wrong with you?' You know, they were pretty good friends. He says, 'He's the best ballplayer of all your players. Period.' Well, Casey put me in the lineup at third, and from that point I played every game that spring."

Once the season began McDougald again found himself on the bench, with Stengel opting to play Johnson and Brown at third, using Gil as a late-innings defensive replacement. On May 14, one day shy of the deadline for ballclubs to cut down their rosters, McDougald was summoned to the manager's office at Municipal Stadium prior to the start of the Yanks–Indians game. "There were about 70,000 at the ballpark. You know, big crowd. So he calls me in and says, 'I'm sending you back to Kansas City.' I says, 'You're not sending me anywhere. I'm going back home. Forget it. I'm not interested in playing anywhere but in the big leagues. I gave myself three years. If I can't make it by then, forget it.'"

The Indians were scheduled to start a right-hander, but shortly before game time skipper Al Lopez decided to use lefty Lou Brissie. After hearing the news, Stengel made a last-minute switch and inserted McDougald, who responded by playing flawlessly at third while driving in all the runs in the Yanks' 4–0 win. "After the game, all the writers want to know how I felt after playing my first start. I tell them 'Look, I don't feel like talking. You go in and talk to Casey Stengel.' I couldn't wait to get the hell outta there after what was said before. I really didn't want to play for him based on that feeling.

"The next morning, I get up, go to the park and head for the clubhouse. You know, it was get my gear and see ya later. So Pete Sheehy [clubhouse manager], who was a beautiful guy, says, 'What the hell ya doin'?' I say, 'What do ya mean, what am I doin'? I'm getting my stuff and going home.' He says, 'You're not going anywhere. They just got rid of Billy Johnson. You're still with the club.' I go, 'C'mon Pete. Don't play games.' But they sold Johnson to the Cardinals and after that I played any time I was physically ready for the next ten years."

If McDougald was given a reprieve, fellow rookie Mantle was not. By June, the slumping slugger was shipped to Kansas City, which was still a Yankee farm club in 1951. "It was a big disappointment for him following the great spring he had, and all the write-ups. But when the season began, all of a sudden the pitchers started pitching Mickey in and up when he batted left-handed, and he had problems. He had to learn to take the high ones instead of swinging at them.

"But his ballplaying experience growing up wasn't half as good as mine. He wasn't playing against the same quality competition, so he wasn't quite as ready. But it was nothing to be embarrassed about. The Yanks had 26 farm clubs, so there were at least 26 guys you had to beat out before you reach the majors, where they got guys who beat everybody out."

Following his ten years with the Bombers from 1951 to 1960, McDougald finished with a respectable career batting average of .276, and twice reached the .300 mark—hitting .306 in his rookie season of 1951 and a career-high .311 in 1956. Although proficient in gathering doubles and triples—he led the league in three baggers in 1957 and was runner-up in 1959—McDougald never reached the 20-homer mark in a season, his best being 14 in 1951 and 1958; he accumulated only 112 lifetime round trippers. His unimpressive homer totals are indicative of the ballpark's disadvantageous dimensions for righty batters more than McDougald's shortcomings as a power hitter. "After I quit, Jim Thompson invited me back to the stadium after they made all those changes. Jim was the superintendent of the grounds. It made me laugh. It looked like a little league field after playing ten years with Death Valley out there.

"When I think of guys like Bauer and Skowron and Howard and DiMag, so many of them would get robbed. Then you look at the left-handers who plop the ball 300 feet and they've got homers, and you go, '*grrr*.' My limit of hitting a ball might have been maybe 430 feet. In Death Valley, that's just an easy grab for an outfielder. And in Yankee Stadium, when the wind was blowing out, that was the worst, because it hits those stands and you get a back-draft. So the ball just dies out there. A lot of times, guys would hit the ball to left-center and I would see Gene Woodling go out with his back to home plate and catch 'em like a tulip, like they're coming back to him. Crazy, you know. It was not an enjoyable park to play in, at least for myself."

Gil did feel comfortable taking grounders at the hot corner. "The park did have a good infield. They had a good groundskeeper, who eventually went out to Cleveland. It was never a fast diamond because [Dan] Topping [Yank owner] always wanted the grass to look good for TV and all that nonsense. So you couldn't drive the ball through. It was like sod. That affected a lot of hitters. Most of us couldn't wait to get to another ballpark."

At the time of the interview, the Yankees had won three of the previous four World Series. A member of eight pennant-winning and five world-championship Yankee teams, Gil laughs when asked whether the modern pinstripers are the best ever. "You gotta be kidding. I had my buddy call me after they won the first Series and he's tellin' me, 'Gil, this is the greatest club.' I'm not mentioning his name. And I say, 'Who are you talking about, the Celtics?' Where are we at, you know? Come on. For gosh sakes, what constitutes a good ballclub? Were we better cause we had six Hall-of-Famers? Does that make *us* better? Or is it because we won eight out of ten when I was there? And if these hitters today faced the type of pitchers we faced, it would be a different story. They would knock you down, and all you'd better do is get up quietly and dust yourself off."

Besides his Yankee teams, McDougald feels other clubs of the fifties deserve attention, including the Milwaukee Braves. "They probably had as good a hitting ballclub as any team in the National League. They were the equal of the Dodgers in the fifties, the Giants in '51, Cincinnati in the seventies with Bench and Perez. So to talk about the greatest in anything, it's tough.

"If you had one guy that stood out over everybody—like Michael Jordan—it wouldn't bother me saying he's the best basketball player, period. During my time, Hank Luisetti was the best. Ask anyone from that era and they'll tell you. Luisetti was the one who started the one-handed push shot. Later, Oscar Robertson was the best. He'd just walk you right in under the basket and put it in. He was such a great team player. And they make a big deal about the double-triples these days. Robertson would do it every game—scoring assists, rebounds."

Given the Yankees' success throughout the fifties, I ask Gil if their losing the pennant to Cleveland in 1954 was a shock to him and his teammates. "Even with our success, every year we knew we had to be ready. At that time, there were eight clubs and every pitching staff had at least two good starters. Detroit, you think of [Hal] Newhouser and [Virgil] Trucks and [Dizzy] Trout. You look at Cleveland's pitching staff and they have three Hall-of-Famers [Bob Feller, Bob Lemon, Early Wynn]. Plus, Garcia, who was the toughest guy to hit. And they had the two best relievers in [Ray] Narleski and [Don] Mossi. We used to tell our pitchers to keep the game close. We didn't want Mossi or Narleski to get in there.

"So losing to Cleveland wasn't such a shock. Even though we split the season series with them, nobody else could beat them. They just ran through everybody. We won 103 games, the most we ever won when I was there, and we still lost."

Besides the 1954 Indians and the pennant-winning White Sox in '59, two other clubs played spoilsport during the fifties, preventing the New York franchise from sweeping the decade. Both the Dodgers (1955) and Braves (1957) downed the Bombers in the Series. Gil recalls an incident that he believes helped motivate Milwaukee in '57. "Howard Cosell used to have all those radio and TV shows. Well, before the Series he was interviewing Hank Aaron, Eddie Mathews, and manager Fred Haney. And his first question to Aaron is, 'Well, Henry, I understand the Yankee pitchers got your number.' Aaron looks at him and says, 'Whaddya mean?' Cosell says, 'Well, they're gonna knock you down. Whaddya gonna do about it?' And Aaron says, 'Get up and dust myself off.'

"Then Cosell says to Haney, 'Well, Fred, I guess you'll get Yankeeitis like all the rest of them. Right?' And you could see Haney light up, like he was ready to deck him. It made me so mad watching that interview, cause if anything could upset the apple cart it's doing something like this to get the guys so mad that they're gonna really put out."

McDougald connected for seven home runs in World Series play.

His first, a grand slam off Giant hurler Larry Jansen in Game Five of the 1951 Series, remains one of his most memorable moments. I ask Gil about his mindset prior to that historic plate appearance. "My mindset? It was made up for me real quick. Casey called me over, and I thought he was gonna take me out. I was ready to rap him with the bat, because he's done this so often. A guy could have had three homers in a game and his idea is, 'Not too many guys have ever hit four, so let's put somebody else in.' It would absolutely drive a hitter up a wall.

"So he calls me over and his words are, 'Hit one out, Mac.' Just like that (Gil slaps his hands). I look at him like he's crazy. You wouldn't believe it, but the guys who were there in the dugout heard him. Unreal. I remember going back up and smiling to myself and thinking, 'What kind of an idiot would call you over and tell you that at a time like this when you're trying to concentrate.' But it happened. I hit one out."

How did McDougald like playing for Stengel? "I had five of the most horrible years. If you want to say I disliked him, yes, I disliked him. With a passion. It was nothing personal. Strictly from a player's standpoint."

The enmity appeared to be reciprocated by Stengel, who took every opportunity to chastise his third baseman during clubhouse meetings. In 1955, an incident occurred that helped soothe their mutual discord. McDougald's story begins after the 1955 Series loss to the Dodgers when the Yankees traveled overseas to play their first exhibition games in Japan since the end of World War Two. "Except they weren't just exhibitions to some. Like my roomie, Hank [Bauer], who fought for forty-four months in Okie [Okinawa], which was a slaughterhouse. And only three of his company came back. I met those three guys. They were all from the Boston area. We used to meet them every time we went up there. After the game, they'd come up to our room and have a beer. Then Hank would go to sleep, and I'd listen to them tell stories about him. The type of man he was."

Gil is digressing, but I'm all ears. "It's funny, I was reading (Tom) Brokaw's book, *The Greatest Generation*. He was talking about how some of the guys who fought at Okie don't like to ever mention anything about it. And I'm thinking, it was the same with my roomie. In the nine years we roomed together, I never heard Hank talk one time about it. And it was the same with guys who fought at Guadalcanal or over in Europe in the Bulge, like Ralph Houk. Never heard them say a word about it. It was like, put it behind you. Forget it. But there was this tremendous animosity with Hank. For him, these exhibition games were like a third world war if they beat us. Seriously. Anyway getting back to Casey…"

Gil explains how the Yanks released Rizzuto following the Series and were in need of a shortstop in Japan. "The only others who had ever played short were Martin, and Jerry had played some in the minors. So Casey has a meeting and says he needs a shortstop. I say, 'Case, I'll play short. No big deal.' You know, you're thinking maybe you can give the other guys a break. They're only exhibition games."

McDougald's gesture eased their relationship somewhat and set the stage for a final reconciliation. "Casey had told us that the only bar that was off grounds was the hotel bar. Well, my wife had just left. She got homesick for the kids and told me she was going back. I wasn't too happy but I said okay. Well, one night it was real hot. It must have been one o'clock in the morning. I couldn't sleep. You know, I was sweating. So I decide to go down to have a beer. I look around. Nobody's there, right? At least I thought. And as soon as I get to the bar and order a beer, I hear this voice that I would know anywhere. He's got an entourage of Japanese reporters with him. I wish I could read Japanese because I would have loved to read the papers the next day to understand what the hell they were talking about. It must have been hilarious."

Gil orders another beer and is drinking quietly by himself when he feels a tap on his shoulder. "He says, 'Mac, who's the best pitching coach in baseball?' I say, 'Jim Turner is, you hired him.' He says, 'I didn't ask you that.' I say, 'Everybody knows Mel Harder's the best.' He says, 'That's the way to tell it!' That's the kind of guy he was. He could care less I was having a beer.

"Well, he stays with me to have a beer. I says, 'Look, Case, I gotta get this off my chest. I have the feeling you hate my guts. Rather than me have an ulcer and you get an ulcer from screaming and hollering at me, why the hell don't you just trade me? I'd love to get outta here. I'd take no pay if you sent me to Boston or someplace like that.'"

Stengel turns and stares into the eyes of McDougald. "He says, 'You're going nowhere. There's two reasons I get on you. Number one, you're a better ballplayer when you're mad. Number two, can you picture at meetings me getting on that guy that rooms next door to you?' So I know he's talking about Phil. Case knew that if he ever got on Phil, he'd die on him. And I think Phil was our meal ticket. He was the strength of our club up the middle. Sure hands. Hit it to him—double play! Easy. Flips the ball so nice and light. Makes you look good. So there were certain guys you couldn't get on. Yogi, Mickey. Basically for the same reason. They'd die on you.

"So I told him, 'Okay, I understand to a certain degree. But let me tell you something right now. I'm not changing. I'll get mad when I have to get mad. But my play on the field will not change one way or another.' And he says, 'Good enough.' And I loved the guy after that."

In 1956, McDougald experienced his most gratifying season; gratification derived principally from the challenge of playing a position for the first time since "fooling around" in pickup games during his youth. "In every ballpark the infield is cut out different. If you look at Cleveland, it's cut out really deep. Now, I used to be the first one to say this, I had a garbage arm. Well, when you have a garbage arm as a shortstop you have to catch the ball clean, get rid of it in a hurry. Like Phil, he had a garbage arm. And when you look at the young kids now, with the guns they got—Jeter, [Rey] Ordonez, Rodriguez—they all got great arms. I think if I had that kind of arm it really would have been fun playing, you know. So the challenge for me was knowing where to stand on the infield so you could throw the guy out. If you were too deep and caught the ball, the guy would beat it out."

In 1957, the Yanks acquired veteran southpaw hurler Bobby Shantz in an 11-player swap with Kansas City. Shantz had a couple of outstanding years with the A's when the franchise was still in Philadelphia. Most noteworthy was his 1952 season when he was among the top five in eight pitching categories, including a league-leading 24 wins, earning him the Most Valuable Player Award despite his club's fifth-place finish. By 1957, most considered Shantz a tired-arm, washed-up hanger-on and the Yanks took him in the deal almost as an afterthought. With the exception of slick-fielding Clete Boyer, who would become a Yank mainstay at third base for eight years, Shantz proved the most valuable pickup in the transaction, as his 11-5 record and league-leading 2.45 ERA were key contributions during the club's successful quest for the flag.

McDougald remembers how Shantz would take cortisone injections to relieve pain in his left shoulder prior to starting assignments. He also recalls one of Shantz's first games with the Yanks, and how he reacted with unusual appreciation following routine plays by fielders. "I was playing third and the guy hits a grounder to me and I get the big hop and throw him out. Bobby goes, 'Great play, Gil.' I look at him. Another routine grounder and I throw the guy out. And again Bobby says, 'Way to go, Gil.' I say, 'Where did you play?' I know Eddie Joost could have made any one of them plays. Then there was a play in the ninth. Maybe it was a little tougher play, you know. And I start the double play and we close them out. Bobby was so happy. At that time he was just trying to hang on. You know, they talk about Brecheen being a good fielder. There was nobody better than Bobby Shantz. *He* was a cat. Casey even put him in to play defense in center field sometimes."

Despite his obvious individual and team achievements, McDougald is remembered today mostly for an unfortunate plate appearance involving Tribe fireballer Herb Score in a game on May 7, 1957. Having led the league in strikeouts the two previous seasons, Score seemed yet another Cleveland pitcher destined for Cooperstown when McDougald made contact with one of his heaters. The ball struck Score in the face, and struck fear in the heart of the hitter. The lingering anguish is still visible on Gil's visage 43 years later. "It sort of brings you back to reality about baseball being just a game. You don't want to see somebody get hurt. Herbie threw the ball 100 miles per hour. And he was a little gangly. So to get that kind of speed on the ball, I guess you have to reach way back. And if you remember Herb, he used to rear all the way back with his left arm.

"So he throws a low-outside pitch, one I shouldn't have hit. I just flicked at it and the ball hit him in his right eye. If you're a lefty pitcher with a good follow-through, it should hit you in the left eye. I didn't even get out of the batter's box. I guess I was in shock. All I saw was the blood. And I never wanted to see the replay. To this day, I won't watch it. I have no idea what happened."

Gil discusses the immediate aftermath. "At first, they were afraid he was going to lose his eye. C. I. Thomas, who was the Cleveland team doctor, called me that night to tell me about Herbie's condition. Then we went on the road the next night and Thomas would call me every night to tell me that Herbie was fine. His mom, who was a devout Catholic, called me and told me it wasn't my fault, that you don't have control over what happens once you hit the ball. I mean, it was nice to hear people tell you that. But I already knew it. You don't have control over those things. But when you're the guy who does it, you're still upset."

Score missed the rest of the season and upon his return in 1958 quickly lost his effectiveness, winning fewer than half the number of games in his final five years that he did in his first two. Many today claim that an elbow injury in 1958 had more to do with Score's sudden decline than any trauma caused by the accident. Gil remains unconvinced. "Score was never, ever the same pitcher after that. It made him change his motion. He would recoil during the follow-through. He was afraid of getting hit with the ball. And he used to take medication that might have affected him as well."

The incident also had a deleterious affect on McDougald, as he had difficulty concentrating on the field. "I really didn't want to play anymore. But Casey would say, 'You're getting paid, you're gonna play.' He didn't want me to brood." A couple of déjà-vu experiences only compounded Gil's distress. "We went into Detroit and the papers were writing, 'The

Killer Arrives.' So that night, Frank Lary, their best pitcher— he and Jim Bunning—was pitching. I hit a bullet off his knee and they had to cart him off the field. So then they're really getting on me.

"Then we went into Baltimore where they had some really tough, get-on-you type fans. And I remember Skinny Brown was pitching. And if there was ever a time I thought I almost killed a guy from hitting, that's the time it happened, outside of Herb. Brown was a knuckleball pitcher but he tried to slip a fastball by me. I was late on it and hit a bullet. I seen his head go back and the ball graze his cap."

McDougald resolved that he would prevent future close calls by pulling every pitch. "So I went 0 for 50, something like that. I couldn't care less. Casey would get mad at me and say, 'You're giving up.' I'd tell him, 'Put somebody in if you think they can play better.' And, you know, you're only gonna hurt your teammates if you don't try, and every time I was on the field, I'd try. But at bat, the gut feeling was never the same again."

Gil McDougald at his home in Spring Lake, New Jersey.

Believing baseball was becoming burdensome, McDougald made up his mind to get out of the game as soon as possible. "That winter, I started a building maintenance company. And every winter I'd work on getting accounts so I could eventually walk away from baseball into something I could make a comparable amount of money. And by 1960, I was able to quit ball.

"In 1959, I told Casey and George Weiss that 1960 would be my last year. That I was quitting. And, you know, at that time they think everything's a salary ploy. So I told them, 'I don't care what you think, I'm just telling you that you'd better get yourself another shortstop.' And in 1960, well, I just couldn't wait to get out. The game just wasn't fun anymore since that Score thing. We lost to Pittsburgh and I couldn't care less afterwards. It was a joke Series anyway. We out-hit them, out-scored them. We did everything, and lost every one-run game. The best team doesn't always win in sports. But I didn't care. I was happy for Bill Mazeroski."

I ask Gil if he ever again faced Score following the notorious mishap. "I don't think I ever did. I don't think I could have put myself through it. If I did, I might have just taken three and gotten the hell outta there." A couple of years after Gil retired from the game, Score called it quits but, like McDougald, found equitable-pay employment, serving as the Cleveland Indians broadcaster for several decades. "The morning after his last game announcing, he gets in his car on his way to Florida, pulls out, and—wham—gets wiped out. He was in the hospital for two months.

"Well, I saw him recently. Now, I know I can't hear well even with the cochlear implant, which was a miracle for me. But I couldn't understand a word he said. It was terrible. I had my son with me and I asked after we got through, 'Tod, did you understand Herbie?' He shook his head. From a physical standpoint—you look at him, he's great, almost as young as he looked years ago. But ... (Gil pauses), maybe it had something to do with the affects of the accidents. I don't know."

Gil elaborates on why he needed a cochlear implant. "In 1955 or 1956, we were taking batting practice. I was over with Crosetti near second base behind the big batting screen. I bent to pick up the ball and Bob Cerv hit a bullet that struck me on the left side of my head. They took me to Lennox Hill to take x-rays. They said the x-rays showed nothing. (Gil laughs.) You know, nothing upstairs.

"Anyway, by 1970 my hearing was pretty bad and I went to the Mayo Clinic. The doctor said my hearing channel was fragmented. Probably caused by the ball Cerv hit. There was nothing they could do. By 1980, I couldn't hear a thing. I was deaf for 15 years. Couldn't hear zip. If I didn't have a couple of great girls in the office, I would have chucked the business long ago. Then I had my cochlear implant in 1995, which restored much of my hearing. Like I said, it was like a miracle for me."

In the three years following the successful surgery, McDougald spent much of his time traveling across the country, going to hospitals and universities and speaking on behalf of hearing institutes in an attempt to raise funds. Gil even testified at a hearing in the nation's capital, hoping to obtain government grants. "It was very rewarding. I ran into so many beautiful people. Doctors, patients. And they all felt the same way I do. The joy of hearing after being deaf for so long is, well, indescribable."

Gene Garber

Throughout his adult life, including 19 years spent as a big leaguer, Gene Garber has remained a farmer at heart. "There's always stuff to do, but I still love it." The 53-year-old former relief specialist is speaking on February 1, 2000, from one of his four farms, which total 400 acres spread across Elizabethtown, located midway between Harrisburg and Lancaster in southeastern Pennsylvania. "I've been doing it all my life. Working in the barn and milking cows before going to school in the morning. Milking cows when I went to college.

"Even after I became a major leaguer, I was milking cows in the winter. And there's nothing like the switch of a messy cow tail at three o'clock in the morning on a cold winter day to bring you back to reality—Oh, you're a big league player are you? *Swoosh!* (Gene swings his arm in a horizontal motion.) See how you like that!"

The Garber farms yield corn, soybeans, wheat, and barley, which produce profits supplemented by 108,000 egg-layers sheltered in a colossal chicken house. Gene is a vocal supporter of farmland preservation, and heads a local non-profit organization dedicated to preventing land in the Elizabethtown area from being used for residential, non-farming construction. "I grew up here and hope to die here. When I do, my kids will take over. I have two boys. The older one's been out of school for a couple of years and lives on one of the farms. The younger one's a senior at Messiah College and he says he wants to stay in farming too."

Garber was born in Lancaster, but spent his entire youth in Elizabethtown. Growing up with an older brother and younger brother and sister, Gene and his siblings went to a one-room schoolhouse during their first eight years of formal education, as had their parents. "My parents' schoolhouse is still standing about a mile from here. In fact, my mother was born a short distance from here. Maybe you saw it on the way over—a brownstone house with red trim."

It was during his first year of school that Gene became interested in baseball. "I was terrible. In fact, I was so bad that they made me stand behind a giant oak tree that we used for first base. I would watch from there. So they started calling me the spy. Then after some of the older kids moved on, I got to play. My mother made a bat for me out of a wooden plank four inches wide. I would play with some of the other kids in the schoolyard and churchyard. Then when I was ten, I started playing little league. I played shortstop and pitched every so often."

Throughout his youth, Gene did not stand out as an exceptionally gifted ballplayer. "I guess I was one of the better ones when I got older but I don't remember things that way. (Gene laughs.) I feel like I struggled when I was a kid, and I struggled my whole career. But I could hold my own."

Garber credits a namesake neighbor with helping to develop his skills. "Dick Garber. Very distant relation. About four or five years older than me. We'd watch him until he came in out of the field in the evenings. And pretty soon we'd be together. Even if it was for only ten minutes, he'd take the time to play catch or hit some balls with me and my brothers."

Playing all nine positions during his youth, Gene eventually became a pitcher only because he was not quite good enough anywhere else on the field. "If I had my druthers, I'd have much rather been a Larry Bowa-type, a shortstop. That's a position I really loved playing. In fact, I signed my first contract as a pitcher/shortstop. But they took one look at my hands and range and said, 'You're a pitcher.'"

Gene played four years of high school ball, but was not perceived as a prospective major league pitcher until his senior year when Abe Weidman took over as coach a few days before the start of the season. Weidman had been an accomplished player in the Florida State League where he played for future big league skipper Tom Lasorda. "As soon as Weidman saw me pitch, he said, 'Gene, you throw well enough to play professionally.' Obviously, when he said that he gave me hope that I had a chance. I mean, I only weighed 135, 140 pounds. So I certainly didn't ever expect it to happen, but Weidman gave me the incentive to really bear down all the time. He taught me to be serious and to be mean when I was pitching."

Garber was involved in the first major league draft of 1965, but when the Pirates grabbed him he was one of the last to be selected. In retrospect, he believes the draft did him more harm than good. "I know a couple of other teams were interested in me and it would have been nice to have a choice. And after pitching eight years for Pittsburgh, I would have loved to have a choice because I would not have picked that organization."

The Pirates offered Garber a $1,700 bonus with a promise to pay four years' college expenses. Gene planned on attending Elizabethtown College after his first season as a professional ballplayer in Class A ball at Batavia, New York. The Pirates approved of Garber's fall plans, but for another reason. It was around that time that the Vietnam War was escalating, and the organization wanted its prospect eligible for military draft deferment.

After signing with the Pirates, Garber pitched a game in Salem, Virginia, before heading north to Batavia, where the ballpark was a nightmare for pitchers—324 feet down the lines, 356 to the alleys, and 380 feet to straight-away center. Its diminutive dimensions led to a permanent transformation in Garber's pitching style and philosophy, so that, ironically, the bandbox ballpark indirectly accelerated his climb to the majors. "About the second inning of my first game there, I realize I gotta do something to get the ball down. That's when I changed from an overhand, here-it-comes-type pitcher to a sidearmer. I had always toyed with sidearm every so often, and I realized I could get the ball down better that way because it was sinking better. So from the second inning of that game until I retired, I was a sidearm pitcher."

Concerned that Garber's college deferment would not hold in 1966, the Pirates advised him to enlist in the Marine Reserve, a six-year option taken by other major league prospects. By doing so, Garber would be fulfilling his military duty without missing any significant amount of minor league training. "The Pirates had a full-time person at that time who did nothing else but scan the country looking for openings in the military reserve. Their quickest connection was the Marine Reserve."

Garber spurned the Pirates' advice and kept his deferment, although during the final semester of his senior year he enlisted in the Pennsylvania National Guard. "Part of the reason [that he kept the deferment] being that the Pirates' Double A team was at York, twenty miles from where I lived. That way I could play in the springtime while I'm finishing my semester, join the Pirates for the last two weeks of spring training, come north with them and join the Triple A club at Columbus, Ohio."

One prospect who took the Pirates' advice was pitcher Bob Moose, who had signed on the same day as Garber, and with the same scout. "He signed me in the morning, Bob in the afternoon." Moose's enlistment with the Marine Reserves indirectly led to Garber's first taste of major league ball. "Bob made the ballclub in 1969, but he had a two-week (military) commitment that season. So I covered for him."

On the Monday evening of June 15, Garber arrived in Pittsburgh. The following night, he watched from the Forbes Field dugout as the Pirates played Leo Durocher's first-place Cubs, who held a four-game lead. "Jim Bunning was pitching for us and Al Barlick was umpiring. Apparently the two of them had been feuding for years. They just didn't like each other for one reason or another.

"So in this game, Bunning would call Barlick every name in the book, then he'd throw a pitch right down the middle and Barlick would yell out, Ball! and look right out at him. Bunning would yell and scream and curse some more. The next pitch would come in and if the guy didn't swing, Ball Two! Barlick would look right out at him again, as if to say, 'What are you gonna do about that?' Finally, they had to come for Bunning in the third inning. Gave up about six runs. As he was walking to the dugout, that's when Barlick threw him out of the game. He figured he wanted Bunning knocked out of the game before he threw him out. So I'm watching this game—my first as a major league player—and I'm wondering what in the world I had gotten myself into here."

The following morning, the rookie read in the papers about the possibility of his pitching in the doubleheader that day, which was confirmed when he arrived at the ballpark. "During batting practice, I was shagging fly balls. Deacon Law, the pitching coach, came out and asked why I was shagging. I told him that's what pitchers do before ballgames. He says, 'Well, you're pitching the second game.' I told him nobody said anything to me about that.

"So we're standing out there in center field. And Forbes Field is massive; it's about 460 or something to center. And Deacon says, 'Let me go check.' He runs all the way in, and once you hit the dugout you still had a long ways to go underneath the stadium to get to the clubhouse. About 15 minutes later, he finally gets back and says, 'Well, you're pitching the second game. You can go back and lay in the trainer's room or go back to the hotel if you want.' I told him I'd just as soon stay around and shag. He said I couldn't do that, but I said I wanted to. It's the way I always prepared before pitching—shagged, took ground balls, and went through the normal procedure. But in the majors, they didn't like you to do that."

When the time came for taking the field for his first start, Gene was feeling the jitters. "I was a 21-year-old farm boy coming to the big leagues. It wasn't that I didn't think I could pitch there, but I only knew three or five guys on the ballclub. They were the ones I had played with in the minors. When I got there Monday night, I wasn't even called into the manager's office. So I'm pitching and I haven't even met the manager yet, who was Larry Shephard. Or the coaches. The first one I met was Deacon Law when he told me I was pitching. So I'm given the game ball under those circumstances."

Garber's major league debut got off to an auspicious start as he fanned Cubs leadoff hitter Don Kessinger. The right-hander then yielded his first major league hit to Glenn Beckert, but Billy Williams rapped into a double play and Garber had the first inning under his belt. He hurled a perfect second and third, and entered the fourth frame having faced nine batters and gotten nine outs. Kessinger led off with a fly to center that sailed beyond the reach of Matty Alou, who had been playing shallow. "Then he jogged after it. And Kessinger, who never ran too great, got an inside-the-park home run. That sort of infuriated me. I mean, this is my first big league home run I'm giving up."

After Garber got Beckert, Williams hit one "that might have killed some people out in right field. (Gene smiles.) Went about 400 feet." He retired Ron Santo, but Willie Smith, labeled by Garber "a converted pitcher," blasted a homer that matched in distance the one hit by Williams. "Hit it about 800 feet—400 up and 400 out.

"So after the third home run, Shephard comes out to the mound. Now remember, this is a manager I never met before. Well, he has his hands on his hips and he's looking up and around while he says his first words at me—he didn't say them *to* me, he said them *at* me—'A few f—ing rainmakers, heh kid?' Then he turns around and walks back. And that pretty much describes the way it was for me in all my years at Pittsburgh. My recollections of being there are not happy ones."

Garber made one other appearance that year, pitching an inning of relief at Shibe Park, or as Gene calls the former A's and Phillies ballpark, Connie Mack Stadium. "That was the fulfillment of a boyhood dream. When I was a kid, on Sundays we'd come home from church and gather eggs. We'd go out to the porch and have our lunch while we took turns every four or five minutes taking out a basket of eggs from the egg washer and putting another one in.

"While we were doing this, we'd be listening to the Phillies on radio. And I remember saying to my dad one day when I was about ten years old, 'Some day I'm gonna pitch for the Phillies in Connie Mack.' Well, he never forgot that and never let me forget it. And here, in my second big-league game, I was pitching in Connie Mack. Of course, I wasn't pitching for the Phillies. That came later, at Veterans Stadium."

Having attended a few games at Shibe as a youngster, Gene recalls some of the Philly players of the late fifties and early sixties that he saw in action, including Del Ennis, Willie Jones, Granny Hamner, and Robin Roberts. "And I remember Ryne Duren with those big glasses. I saw him pitch in the tail end of a doubleheader one night. Came in throwing gas at about twelve o'clock at night. I mean, he was throwing beebees. Struck out something like twelve in about three or four innings."

In 1970, Garber appeared in 14 games, all in relief, and was generally ineffective as he failed to notch a win or a save. Gene offers one explanation for his difficulties. "I had always been a starter in the minors. They felt that the best way to give a guy experience was to let him start. Which was fine because that gave me the pitching experience I needed. But starting doesn't give you relief experience. It's two totally different games. Probably more so then than it is now.

"When I was in the minors I had always started except for when I played for Johnny Pesky at Columbus. I was a short reliever. I enjoyed that, but still I was a young player and so, naturally, I felt I wanted to start."

Garber played in the minors throughout the 1971 season, and the following year appeared in four games for the Pirates without a win or save. He was traded in 1973 to Kansas City for lefty hurler Jim Rooker. Since Jack McKeon was a first-year manager, Garber went to Royals' spring training feeling he needed to quickly prove himself to a leader who was likely under the gun himself. "They had an awful lot of pitchers. I felt if I could make the club, I'd get my opportunities once the season started."

His fine spring performance not only landed him a spot on the roster but also provided the opportunity to share top bullpen duties with Doug Bird. Appearing in 48 games, 40 in relief, and hurling a career-high 153 innings, Garber split 18 decisions and notched 11 saves. His frequent activity changed his outlook, as he actually preferred the role of reliever. "I enjoyed it. I did everything. Pitched long relief, and that was the first year I did some short relief as well. After that point, I didn't want to go back to being a starter unless they gave me 12 or 15 straight starts. I felt if they allowed me to start every fourth or fifth day and stay in the rotation for twelve starts, I could have settled in as a starter.

"Had I been given the opportunity, I'm convinced I would have been a pretty good starting pitcher. But once I got a taste of short relieving, I loved relief pitching. Especially after I went to the Phillies."

Shifted to Philadelphia in midseason of 1974, Garber was used by manager Danny Ozark as the club's number one right-hand short reliever. During the next three years, Gene established his reputation as a pitching workhorse. He led the league in pitching appearances with 71 in 1975, led the Phillies in appearances in its division-winning season of 1976, and led the club in appearances and saves in the division-title repeat of 1977. "I really got to love that position (of short reliever). After that, I think I started one game, and that was in center field at Dodger Stadium."

Traded to Atlanta in June of 1978, Garber remained with the club until his return to Kansas City in August of 1987. In nine years with the Braves, he averaged 62 appearances, 92 innings and 15 saves per season. In three of those years, he was among the top five leaders in saves, including his career-high 30 in 1982, which was runner-up to Bruce Sutter's 36; he was a major reason why the Braves made it to the post-season for the first time in 13 years.

It was during his stint with the Braves that Garber pitched in a game for which he is most remembered by modern baseball aficionados, and one which Gene considers the highlight of his career. "That's only because everybody keeps reminding me about it. Just this past year, twenty years after the game, there were writers calling me wanting to know this or that."

Garber was a Brave for six weeks in 1978 when he faced the Reds in the sixth inning of a game in which his club already held an insurmountable lead. The lop-sided contest still held significance for the 31,000 spectators, as Pete Rose was attempting to extend his 44-game hitting streak, having failed in his first two tries against lefty starter Larry McWilliams. Garber got Rose on a double-play liner to third, but Pistol Pete had one more shot in the ninth. "The only strategy I had in my head was not to walk him. That's the only thing I was nervous about. Never, in my whole career, have I ever been scared to walk somebody. I've faced batters with two outs in the bottom of the ninth and the bases loaded, and it didn't bother me. Never thought about it. You don't ever plan on walking guys, but even if you do it's not the end of the world.

"But if that streak had ended by me walking him I'd be a goat for the rest of my life. I mean, this is Pete Rose. This isn't some rookie who's got a twenty or thirty-game hitting streak. By 1978, he's already a superstar. So I knew if I walked him, I'd never live it down. History would have borne me out; I'm just glad we'll never find out."

Garber threw five pitches; the last was foul-tipped into the glove of catcher Joe Nolan for the third strike. As described by the all-time hit leader in his autobiography, *Pete Rose: My Life*, Garber leaped into the air after ending Rose's quest. Gene admits feeling satisfied, but claims the elated reaction was related to a sense of relief as well. "I'll be honest, I wanted to end his streak. I was never fond of Pete as an opponent. I respected him, and would have loved to have him on my team. Sal Bando was another one. Couldn't stand him, but would have loved to have played with him. So there's no doubt about it, I really wanted to get Pete out. But my priorities were—first, to throw strikes; second, to end the streak."

You could not have convinced Pete, who grumbled after the game about how Garber had not thrown one strike. Gene smiles when reminded that Rose also complained about Garber's pitching the last at bat like it was the seventh game of the World Series. "It was the biggest compliment he could ever have given me. That's the way I wanted to play in the 900-some games I pitched. That's the way I had to play. Remember, I didn't have the size to compete. I had to give everything I had on every pitch. And going to Atlanta only reinforced that feeling. I pitched with a Hall of Fame pitcher—Phil Niekro. In my mind, one of the greatest pitchers of his era, which includes an awful lot of good pitchers. Did Niekro have super abilities? No, he was pretty average. You might say, 'Well, he threw a knuckleball.' Yeah, he threw a knuckleball. But the reason he was so good was because of his competitiveness. His philosophy was to make every pitch as though it's gonna be the last pitch you'll ever make. Nobody took the competitiveness to the mound that he did."

Gene believes Rose more than anyone should have expected no less than a 100 percent effort from any pitcher in any circumstance. "Pete didn't have super abilities. There were a lot of guys in baseball who had a lot more ability. But not too many people brought to the game Pete's competitiveness and confidence. And his work ethic! I mean, he worked hard. I think his background has a lot to do with that. I know with Niekro, his dad died of black lung disease. He was a miner. So Phil grew up with people who were miners. Hard-working people. With Pete, he was a street kid. Street-wise. Learned how to deal with all kinds of stuff. So competitiveness is ingrained in guys at a young age."

Gene recalls how reporters besieged Rose after the strikeout, even before the despondent batter had reached the dugout. "One thing that nobody wants to point out is that when I struck Pete out, he was the last out of the game. He left the batter's box, and he had cameras and reporters in his face. Now, you have to understand, Pete has supreme confidence in himself. He knows he's gonna go on to break DiMaggio's record. In his mind, there wasn't a sliver of a doubt. So now it ends, and before he has time to reflect—hey, the streak is over, what am I going to say, how do I react to this?—it was, (Gene slaps his hands) *bam!* Strike three! (Gene slaps his hands again.) *bam!* Here's the microphone, 'what do you think about this?'

"Well, they asked me to go to the interview room to answer questions. I said I'd be happy to, just give me a minute or two to get a Coke. So I went into the clubhouse, and the TV's on. While I'm sitting there figuring out what I'm gonna say, here's Pete live, just ripping me up one side and down the other. I'm thinking, 'I'm not going in that interview room.' So after about ten minutes of this, Pete finally said, 'That's enough. I don't want to get Garber any more ink.' And I remember looking right into the screen and saying, 'Pete, you just gave me all the ink I'd ever want.' If he'd have never said a word about me, it would have been forgotten. But they're still talking about me and the streak twenty years later."

I ask Garber the obvious question, whether Rose's ban from baseball should remain. "Pete was one of the greatest con men that ever lived. But his gambling problem turned out to be one of those times he wasn't able to con people. Should he be reinstated? Does he deserve to be in the Hall of Fame? Absolutely not. Pete and I played under the same rules. Every dugout we ever played in had posters slapped on the walls as to what you can't do, and if you do it what's gonna happen to you. In every runway and clubhouse. And it said that if you gamble on baseball, you're banned. So we all played under the same rules.

"If I did it and was kicked out of baseball, would they reinstate me? They wouldn't even think about doing it. Nobody would be talking about it. I wouldn't have had a chance. So why should Pete? And just because he's a true Hall of Fame performer, if the rules say you're banned from baseball how can you bestow baseball's greatest honor on that individual? I mean, he absolutely deserves to be in there, based on his merit as a ballplayer. Probably more than anyone who's ever played. But unless you want to put another one of those asterisks in the books to make him an exception to the rule, he's banned from both baseball and the Hall of Fame. That's it!"

The Rose match-up in 1978 was his most memorable performance, but Garber rates another as being his most significant. It came in the division-winning season of 1982. A 13-game winning streak in April helped the Braves build up a sizable lead, but the margin disappeared toward the close of the season. "In the last week in September, we finished up on the West Coast with the Dodgers and San Diego. We were one game behind the Dodgers with six to go. We split the first two in Los Angeles. In the final game of the series, it went extra innings and I pitched the 11th, 12th, 13th and 14th innings and we beat them in the 14th. Now, I had been with the Phillies through two championship seasons, but we clinched early both years. So that game I won in Los Angeles is probably the biggest of my career.

"We went on to play the Padres Friday night with Niekro pitching. Now again, when you talk about a Hall of Fame player, this is a forty-year-old that's pitching to play in post-season. And Niekro pitches a two- or three-hitter and hits a three-run homer to win 3–0. I mean, *these* are the Hall of Fame individuals. The guys who have that extra when the team has to have it and everyone in your city is pulling for you. So that's two good things about my being traded to Atlanta—having Niekro as a teammate, and not having to face him any more as an opponent."

Asking Gene to rate the hitters most troublesome for him, I am not surprised when he first mentions Bobby Murcer, having watched the Yank slugger drill three home runs off Garber in a 1973 game at Yankee Stadium. I recall reading the post-game comments attributed to Murcer and Garber that implied hard feelings. Gene reacts with a smile, then explains. "After the second home run, he circled the bases sort of slowly. Taking his time. So the next time up, I knocked him down. Got him out that time. But I didn't get him out the next time. Anyway, he had three home runs, five RBIs, and I lost 5–1. I only gave up one other hit and didn't walk a batter. So Murcer beat me by himself that game."

Having pitched two innings the previous day in Milwaukee, Gene was making one of the last starts of his career that night in New York, as he started eight with Kansas City in 1973 and not another for the remainder of his career. "Just before that Murcer game started, the guy who was supposed to pitch had a blister on his finger. Another starter was back home for a high school reunion. So the pitching coach, Galen Cisco, who's working with the Phillies these days, called all the pitchers together and said he needed someone for that night. So I said, 'Give me the ball. I'll give you nine innings. I'm not gonna guarantee what they're like.'

"Nobody remembers this—maybe except for Bruce Del Canton, who was my teammate in Pittsburgh and then at Kansas City; he and Bruce Benedict were my best friends in baseball—but I had a severe cold. I was taking a lot of Contac. So I'd be falling asleep on the mound. Then all of a sudden I'd be wide awake, and it was, 'Okay, let's go!' I'm not a drug guy, but I can understand what they mean by highs and lows because, literally, that's the way I was feeling the whole game."

Labeling Murcer a good hitter with good power and a "Yankee Stadium swing," Gene acknowledges the Yank's continual success against him while playing for the Yanks, and later for the Giants and Cubs. "He obviously picked up the ball very well against me." As did Frank Robinson and Johnny Bench. "There was a four or five year period that Bench was so dangerous. He had the greatest plate coverage I've ever seen. He could hit balls six inches inside off the plate or six inches outside, and take you outta the yard. A lot of hitters can hit those pitches, but they're not gonna take you yard.

"I only faced Robinson eight times in my career. The first five times, he hit three homers and two doubles. Frank stood so that his right elbow was right in the middle of the plate. And I was a sinkerball pitcher, so the ball would move down and in and I felt that I didn't have any pitching room. Well, after facing him those five times, I started talking to sinkerball pitchers and they said to make sure the ball dropped to the knees. So the next three times I faced him, I made sure the ball stayed down and I got him out all three times. It was only a matter of a four- or five-inch adjustment, which shows you how subtle major league baseball can be."

Gene Garber at his home in Elizabethtown, Pennsylvania.

The conversation turns to Garber's views about the modern game. Like most old-timers, he offers harsh criticism of umpires for not calling the inside strike. "Why won't they call them? Because they don't want pitchers throwing inside. Why? Because when they throw inside, hitters get hit, and when hitters get hit they get mad. Why do hitters get mad? Because they're never expecting any pitches to come inside. It's ridiculous.

"Even late in my career, the same thing was happening with me. Let's put it this way. If they had given me the inside pitches the way they give the outside pitches to Maddux and Glavine, I'd still be pitching today. Because I had that control where I was always in that one spot. Right there, all the time. But you never get that call an inch or two on the inside. Outside, yes.

"I made a whole career pitching lefthanders on the outside. I never came inside on lefties. I just wasn't gonna get beat by those kind of pitches. I'd get them out by getting strikes on the outside edge. But with righty batters I had to pitch inside and when I did, that same pitch that was an outside strike for lefty hitters was a ball for righties. Why? Because it was inside. It's the same situation today. The hitters know they have the inside pitch. Anything inside is a ball. So they're just sitting on that outside pitch waiting to whack it."

Garber suggests a couple of solutions. "Get rid of the DH. That's what started all this because now pitchers don't have to worry. They can knock down whoever goes up there and never have to face the opposing pitcher. Number two, just let the teams go at it. If one team knocks down a batter, let the other team retaliate. The way it is today, you have umpires giving warnings when pitchers hit batters with hanging breaking balls, for crying out loud. Or when a batter gets hit, all of a sudden you see the umpire flying out in front of home plate to make sure the batter doesn't charge the mound, which only serves to make the batter think, 'Hey, he must have been throwing at me.' It's gotten to the point where umpires won't allow anything."

At the time of his retirement following the 1988 season, Garber ranked fifth on the all-time major league list in pitching appearances (931), seventh in relief wins (94), and eighth in saves (218). "I guess the thing I'm most proud of about my career is my longevity. What made it significant, I think, is that it wasn't until I was 25 years old that I finally made it to the big leagues to stay. I had so many doubters along the road—you know, people telling me that I wasn't big enough or strong enough to throw in the big leagues. So to last as long as I did is satisfying."

Garber pitched in the big leagues during the sixties, seventies, and eighties. That he failed to play in four different decades is one of two regrets pertaining to his career, the other being his failure to participate in a World Series. "I was given my independence by the Royals on July 4th, 1988. By that time, the boys and [wife] Karen were living here at home in the summer. I could have tried to hook up with another club when I got my release, but I was forty years old and unless it could have been with a contender I wasn't interested. It would have been too big an adjustment for the boys. They would have had to go into a new school system. They had started to play Little League here so they were not anxious to go live somewhere else after school was out. And I couldn't blame them. So I told myself, 'I've had my day in the sun. It's time for me to be around my kids and see them play some ball.'

"Plus, knowing what I wanted to do after baseball made it easier for me to walk away. I felt like I could have played a couple more years. Physically, that wouldn't have been a problem. I was in good shape. I didn't have arm problems. But I knew I was going to be a farmer and owned some farms back here already. So family matters took precedent."

Gene gives baseball an "A" rating in assessing its place in American sports. "You don't have to be six-foot six, 300 pounds like you gotta be in football. And it's a game of strategy. Fans can get into the real intricacies of it and follow what's going on. Regardless of whether you have a lot of home runs or if it's a pitcher's duel, there's a lot to be fascinated with when you're at a ballgame, from the strategy standpoint.

"Baseball's still America's number one game. Always has been, probably always will be. A farm kid like me can still wind up having a pretty good career in the big leagues."

A fitting closing comment from a man who, aside from his love for God, family, and country, has held two things dear throughout his lifetime—farming and baseball.

Billy Sample

For the past three years, I have taught a baseball history course at the Piscataway campus of Rutgers University as part of its Continuing Education program. It is generally a small class, totaling six during the spring of 2000 when in mid-semester I announce that former big-league outfielder Billy Sample will be a guest at the final session on March 9 for the purpose of doing the interview for this book.

On the evening of his appearance, I introduce Billy to the group with an overview of his educational and professional background. His lengthy and impressive résumé includes a bachelor of science degree in psychology from James Madison University; a nine-year major league career spanning 1978 to 1986; Players Association Representative for the Texas Rangers from 1983 to 1986; member of the Players Association Licensing Committee from 1986 to 1987; a contributor and columnist for such prestigious newspapers and magazines as *New York Times, New York Daily News, Sports Illustrated, USA Today* and *USA Today Baseball Weekly*; sports broadcaster, commentator and host for various television and radio networks; actor and consultant for television and movie projects; script advisor for New York University's Creative Arts Program; and his current position as consultant to Major League Baseball in umpire evaluation.

Born in a suburb of Roanoke, Virginia, in 1955, Billy relates how most pregnant women in labor were taken to Burrell Memorial Hospital by an ambulance provided by a local funeral home. "This was still in the heart of segregation so they wouldn't pick my mom up. She had to find some other way to get to the hospital and deliver me. Funny how you remember stuff like that, way back then."

Shortly after Billy's birth, his mother and father moved to Brooklyn in quest of improved financial opportunities, while Billy lived with his grandparents in Salem, a town adjoining Roanoke. At age three, he joined his parents in Brooklyn before the Samples returned to Salem two years later. "I went to school there. We didn't desegregate until later on—1966 or 1967—and I can tell you that separate but equal is not the same. In my fourth grade class we had fifty, which seemed a little large. But I enjoyed school. In fact, I missed only six days of school in 12 years, and that's only because of illness—chicken pox or measles. I thought that was a big deal until I got here and found out some people didn't miss school at all."

Although smaller than Roanoke, Salem was a good athletic town. Along with amateur teams in several sports, it offered a minor league baseball team. Teenager Sample would frequently attend games and speculate about someday facing professional pitching. "I would interact with some of the players before or after a game—finding out what to ask for when I got drafted, learning some of the little nuances of the game."

Sample remembers it was a professional ballplayer who sold him his first car. "There was a guy named Doug Bair. Right-hand pitcher. Went on to pitch a little bit with Cincinnati and St. Louis. Not very big, but pretty good stuff, good velocity. In 1971, he sold me a 1960 Corvair for $60. Thirty dollars up front. It leaked oil, too. (Class laughs.) Well, years later we're at spring training. I was with Texas and he was with Cincinnati. We were at Pompano Beach, a great city to train in. Off the field as well, if you know what I mean. I went up to Bair and said, 'Do you remember that 1960 Corvair you used to own? I'm the guy who bought it from you.' He just started to talk forever after that."

Playing baseball and basketball in high school, Sample actually excelled in football. He was selected Second Team All-State Wide Receiver in his sophomore year, and remembers the Titans, the subject of the Denzel Washington flick, giving his school a thrashing in 1971. By age 15, he decided his best professional opportunity lay not with the pigskin but the horsehide. "If I had been six-one, six-two or as big as some of these guys (referring to the class), I probably would have played football. But I figured for my size and talent and skills, if I was going out of Salem I would have to do it with baseball."

After attending several tryout camps in his senior year, Billy was drafted in 1973 by Texas scout Joe Branzell, whom Billy labels "one of the few honest scouts I've ever met." Disgruntled with being picked 24th in 28 draft rounds, the 18-year-old commented to Branzell, "I didn't think they had that many rounds," then received the blunt reply, "Twenty-three teams passed over you 27 times." Says Billy, "It was as if he was saying, 'Don't blame us for drafting you that late.' I don't remember what they offered me. David Clyde was the first-round pick, so I'm sure he got all the money that wouldn't filter down to the 24th round."

Uncertain of ever making the big leagues, Sample rejected the Texas proposal, preferring matriculation at James Madison University in Virginia. "I didn't get a scholarship per se, but I didn't pay for anything either. And I played a pretty good freshman year." He then joined the Shenandoah Valley League, which consisted of college players, semi-pros, and former draft picks—some of the most skilled ballplayers on the eastern seaboard. "I didn't have a particularly good year. Probably because it was the first time I saw a hard slider. I saw it and said, 'What was that?' I used to hold my bat up high, like I was Cesar Cedeno and was just going to whale away at everything. Let me tell you, that slider brought that bat down somewhere around here (Billy pretends to hold a bat at a more conventional level.)

"Later on, when I played in the minors and some teammates were complaining about the conditions—and they can be tough—I told them, 'Guys, when I played in the Shenandoah League, I had to work during the day, play at night, drive an hour over the mountains to get back home, and wake up early the next morning to start all over again.' Shenandoah was good training. I played against some of the best, which allowed me to know that a rather unheralded player like myself could measure up to these guys."

Several Shenandoah players eventually became major leaguers, including Jim Pankovits, Dave Tobik, and Tom Brookens. "And there was Gene Richards. He had the National League record for most stolen bases by a rookie until Tim Raines broke it. Now, he's a hitting instructor for the Angels. He went to South Carolina State, same alma mater as Willie Aikens. Funny, South Carolina dropped its baseball program despite Richards and Aikens being the top picks in their draft."

Following a horrendous sophomore season on the field, Billy returned to the Shenandoah League in the summer of '75 and notched the Most Valuable Player Award. In 1976 the Rangers again drafted him, this time in the tenth round. "I knew I was going to sign no matter what round. Considering my size and age of 21, I pretty much had to. I wasn't going to get bigger and I couldn't get much older if I wanted to make it."

Sent to Sarasota for Rookie Ball, Sample and other hopefuls practiced at a training academy also used by Kansas City. "I think Ewing Kauffman [Royals owner, 1969–1981] started it. I believe Frank White is the only player of note who came out of there. Maybe U. L. Washington, but I'm not sure.

"We trained about 15 miles from town. And there was no transportation. No car, nothing. So you're young and virile, and no amount of saltpeter's gonna help you out there. You're all by yourself. Then the time would come when a guy would get a car. Everybody would pile into this one guy's car to drive with him into town for the only club and bar around. By the time you got out, your clothes were all wrinkled so you're not very presentable when you're trying to get a rap with somebody. It was hilarious."

Sample talks about playing for Sarasota manager Joe Klein, who later became farm director for both the Rangers and Tigers. "Joe's one of my best buddies in the game now. Anyway, at the time Kansas City had a much better team on paper than we had—bigger, older, stronger. Ken Phelps was on that team, and of course he made it to the majors. And they ran a lot. Jose Martinez was their manager, and he'd have these guys run and run and run. And then they'd run some more. He'd have them out there practicing all the time. Lightning could be striking all around and they'd be practicing. So Joe says to us, 'I don't think baseball is a track game, but we'll see.' Meaning that we'll see how well we do against the rest of the league, and against Kansas City in particular. Well, we beat them seven out of nine and won the league."

Although his .382 average was a league-high, the promising 21-year-old realized the odds were still against his ever making the Rangers' big league roster. "I can remember a meeting we had with Joe—I guess there were about 25 of us—and he said, 'Take a look to your left and your right, pick out another person, and that's all that's gonna make it to the majors.' And he was about right. From my group, I think Steve Comer made it. He was a 22-year-old out of the University of Minnesota. He made it because they needed to fill out a roster and I guess his coach had a working relationship or something. But Comer pitched quite a while in the majors. Changeup artist. Would throw you a changeup off a changeup. And then there was Brian Allard who had the proverbial cup of coffee. Steve Finch might have had a day or two. But that was it."

Sample finished rookie ball, went to Instructional League, and returned to James Madison to complete his degree. "I took twelve hours in one semester. Took some interesting courses, come to think of it. I remember arguing on behalf of the Equal Rights Amendment in a psychology class. It was kind of tough because my biggest opponents were females. So I didn't have a leg to stand on when I'm arguing for the ERA and the women are against me." (Class laughs.)

Billy's mention of women's rights prompts me to ask about his later involvement with the rights of ballplayers. Smiling, Sample recounts his acquiring the position of Player Representative for the Texas Rangers in

1983. "I got the job not from stepping forward, but from everybody stepping backward and I was left standing there. Okay, I'm being overly facetious. I took over the reins from Jon Matlack or Rick Honeycutt. I don't recall which one. One of them just came to my locker and dumped all the information as if to say, 'Your turn. I've had enough.'"

Reluctance to get involved with union activities may have been a result of the turmoil-filled season of 1981 when owners and players battled over a new labor contract. The major issues were ownership demands for restricted salaries and for compensation for loss of players in annual re-entry drafts. When the deadline for a deal expired in mid-June, players struck. An agreement was reached at the end of July, with both sides claiming victory—owners received draft compensation (each team received a veteran player from a pool of surplus players provided by all teams), and players thwarted the owners' attempt at a salary ceiling. "I don't blame him [Matlack or Honeycutt, for relinquishing the Player Rep position]. It's not that we, the Ranger players, had a more contentious relationship with management than other clubs, but there was certainly a lot of it with the long 50-day strike. So it was a tough job. It really was. You had to answer for a lot of things that weren't very popular."

Sample believes fans' perception of players as greedy during the '81 strike was partly a result of unfavorable press coverage, and put pressure on the union to settle. "People don't usually side with workers because when you see goods and services taken away, you have a tendency to blame the actual person or group that's taking it away. Even though we didn't make a lot of money back then, I guess we were seen as ingrates.

"I have a good friend, Paul Hagen, who writes for the *Philadelphia Daily News*. We have discussions regarding the relationship between the media and players, usually running into the early morning hours. My thinking is that sportswriters have to continue to have access to the people that are in charge. So it's a lot easier for them to side with management because the players could be gone later."

According to Sample, he was never "intrinsically anti-management," and even sympathizes with the owners' concerns. "I can understand why they want to have ceilings on salaries. I really do, because I think the pendulum has definitely swung from the time I played until now. Too many of a ballclub's decisions are based on whether or not the club can afford it. I think management deserves the right to make a living too. They're taking all the risks."

Still, Sample blames owners for causing many of their problems. He labels as "not a good PR move" their knee-jerk decision to halt pension contributions during the 1994 strike, a work stoppage resulting in cancellation of the World Series for the first time in 90 years. "Sometimes they do things that make me shake my head and think, 'Who thought this up?' But I shook my head when I was sitting in negotiations back then, too, when we were fighting for our existence. Now, they're just quibbling over dollars."

Sample contrasts today's financially secure union with the tentative conditions of the early eighties. "Back in my day when you went on strike you were on your own. In '81, I worked at a radio station." Recalling his connection with the union's licensing committee ("I just rubber-stamped stuff"), Billy explains how today's numerous deals with various enterprises have created a lucrative contingency fund. "In my time, work on the committee entailed only Topps revenue; that was basically our only licensee. Now, with the fund in the millions, the players can say, 'Okay, you force us to go on strike, but it's not a problem because we have these extra funds to keep us going.'

"My first contract—even though I was pro-rated when I came up in 1978—was only $21,000. Imagine $21,000 as a major leaguer during double-digit inflation. You figure you're netting maybe 14½. So you had to work in the off-season. My spouse had a $500-a-month job working in a shelter for battered women. That got us through one winter. Things have changed. Consider that the first $3 million contract was 1987—Kirby Puckett and Rickey Henderson. So it's escalated greatly and quickly."

Returning to the subject of his minor league career, Billy recalls hitting in a Double A league that included future major leaguer pitchers Al Holland, Rod Scurry, Nelson Norman, and Honeycutt. "And I remember hitting against Don Robinson for the first time. He threw me a two-strike curveball that broke really late for strike three. My knees shook while walking to the dugout. I was wondering if anybody could see them shaking. To this day I shudder. (Class laughs.) And granted the lights weren't as great in Shreveport, Louisiana, as they would be in the majors, but it was just one of those experiences you never forget."

An experience not limited to inexperienced minor leaguers. "When I was a broadcaster or umpire evaluator, I remember seeing Michael Jackson, now with the Phillies, throw Charlie Hayes a first-strike slider that buckled his knees. You could see it from where I was—'oooh-huh'—that's how he reacted. And you know at that point, he's done. Four pitches later, he's walking to the dugout. He just didn't have enough time to adjust to the pitch. He wouldn't have had enough time if he came back the next day."

Sample adjusted well to the sharp slants of Double A pitchers, resulting in a .340 average and promotion to Triple A ball in 1978. "Bob Welch was my first Triple A at bat. I was a good high-fastball hitter. I mean, if you had a fastball I had a swing for it. If you threw me something with a wrinkle in it, I was susceptible. But if you had some gas? Yeah, all right, let's go. And he struck me out with a 97-something fastball that took off. I threw my bat and helmet to the dugout and walked to the outfield and thought, 'Yeah, it's gonna be tough now. If they throw like this, it's gonna be real tough.' Of course, by the third at bat he got it down to something like 94 and I got my bat on it."

By September, Sample was third in the league in hitting and was informed by manager Rich Donnelly, future coach of the Rangers and Pirates, that he was being called up by Texas at the end of the Triple A season. Billy flew from Tucson to Milwaukee where the Brewers were hosting a night game at County Stadium. The Rangers were still in the hunt for the 1978 pennant, adding to Sample's surprise when he saw his name at the top of the lineup card posted on the locker room wall. "What bothered me was that they had me playing second base. I signed as a second baseman, and I still have to this day the Texas League record for most errors by a second baseman.

"Our shortstop at that time—Blair Stoffer, University of Texas— would never give me a clean feed. It would always go in his glove twice— sort of a double pump. Which didn't matter cause I wasn't gonna turn a double play anyway. So they moved me to left field because I was used to being there; that's where I'd wind up by the time Blair gave me the ball— I was getting killed." (Class laughs.)

Alarmed at the prospect of returning to his former position, Sample received encouraging words from Rangers outfielder Richie Zisk, borrowed an infielder's glove, and took batting and fielding practice in preparation for his major league debut. "I led off the game and hit the first pitch. I thought it was a screaming line drive. Later, they told me it was just a soft one that went off the glove of a diving Sixto Lextano for a base hit. I'm at first with this Cheshire Cat grin and Bump Wills comes in to pinch-run for me. So I'm done. They were just giving Bump one fewer at bat. He was a switch-hitter and was struggling from the right side. So it was my first major league at bat and it was downhill after that. (Billy smiles.) Actually, I had a few more hits that year during the race."

On the team bus in Seattle following the next-to-last game of the season, manager Billy Hunter motioned for Sample to sit in the front seat next to him. "I thought, 'This is nice. The manager's taking some interest in me. He doesn't have to do that.' So he started going over with me the team for the following year. He told me that John Grubb and I were going to alternate in left field. So I'm thinking, 'This is great. Beats the minor leagues.' Well, the next day they fired Hunter. *Aaaahhhh!* (Class laughs.) How about that for an auspicious start to your career?"

News of manager dismissals became routine for Sample, as he played for eight during his nine major league seasons: Hunter, Pat Corrales, Don Zimmer, Darryl Johnson, and Doug Rader with Texas; Yogi Berra ("I just say Yogi; sounds nice," he says) and Billy Martin with the Yankees; and Chuck Tanner with the Braves. "Don Zimmer was my favorite. Cause he's so sick! (Class laughs.) Naw, I'm just kidding. I probably cussed him the way I cussed the rest of them. But I thought Don told it to you about as straight as it could be told in a profession where there are too many egos than there are avenues for those egos to be satisfied. So I always appreciated that about Don."

Although he had a 12-year career as infielder during the fifties and early sixties before accumulating a winning percentage in a managing career that spanned 13 seasons and 1,744 games for four ballclubs, Zimmer is more recently known for being coach and premier bench buddy of Yankee manager Joe Torre. Demonstrative in the dugout, argumentative with arbiters, but revered by players, the rotund, pumpkin-cheeked throwback to old-time baseball is arguably the most endearing character still wearing a major league uniform. Encouraged by students to relate an interesting anecdote involving Zimmer, Sample cites the time the manager lost his job during the 1982 season. "If you go into or out of DFW Airport in Dallas today, you'll see Amon Carter Boulevard, named after the former Texas owner. Well, about the same time they told Zimmer he was fired, Amon died. They didn't want the firing of Zimmer to overshadow the tribute to Carter, so they asked Zim to stay on a couple more days before leaving. (Class laughs.) I think they fired him on a Thursday and asked him to stay until Monday.

"There's another story. The late Eddie Chiles [Texas owner, 1980–1987], who had a great heart, brought over a lot of his strategy and business acumen from his oil company. Mike Stone, his president, also came over with him to the club. They wanted to work more on performance criteria, for lack of a better term at the moment. The way that would manifest itself with us is that if you were a position player, the manager would have to call you in and ask how many hits you thought you would get over a certain period—a week, eight games, 30 at bats. And afterwards, they'd compare it with how many you actually got. If you're somebody like Al Oliver, who never lacked confidence—for good reason, a lifetime .300 hitter—he'd say, 'I think I'll get 15 with any luck, if my line drives fall.'

"So now it's my turn. I'm in and out of the lineup half the time, but

I might have been playing for a sustained period during this stretch. So Don looks at me sheepishly with his paper in his hand. He's trying to explain this format, which he hates. I mean, he's willing to do it but he's old school—this is old Brooklyn Dodger we're talking about. So he asks me, 'Okay, in your next 30 at bats how many hits do you think you'll get? Seven? Eight?' Well, I can tell he's struggling with this, and I'm probably one of the last he's asking. I grab the schedule off his desk and say, 'Well, let's see who we're facing. There's (Jack) Morris one day. What about a walk? Does that count for anything?' And I'm going on and on." (Class laughs.)

Although Arlington Stadium drew over a million spectators in all but one of his seven seasons with the Rangers, Billy asserts that promoting baseball in a traditionally football-conscious metropolis is difficult. "Nolan got there in the late eighties. I think he did so much for the marketing. He, Bobby Valentine [manager] and Tom Grieve [general manager]. But that was such a tough club to market. You're in Cowboy country. Baseball is just something else to do. You'd be standing in the outfield, hear a cheer, and say to yourself, 'This is an odd time for anybody to be rooting.' You didn't realize that they brought their TVs to the game and the Cowboys had scored a touchdown on *Monday Night Football*."

Billy questions some of the strategies formerly used by the Rangers to increase revenue. "I remember they tried to force people to buy concessions. They would confiscate your food at the turnstiles. I don't know how great a PR move that is. Whatever money you're going to get in concessions you're probably going to lose in public relations.

"There was one time when a lady had some food taken away, and by the time she got to her seat she realized this was not the way she had envisioned things. She went to file a formal complaint, and as she was walking by the turnstile where she had entered one of the ushers was eating her chicken. (Class laughs.) After you take a beating like that, public relations-wise, or not-so-wise, you say to yourself, 'Are they thinking? Are they trying? It's tough enough out here in this heat. We gotta deal with this, too?'"

Citing the almost unbearable conditions playing in a notoriously torrid town, Sample recalls a stretch of 43 consecutive days of over 100-degree temperatures. "Whew! Hello! You know, it's a lot easier for the ballplayers now because the infrastructure in the new park is such that you don't really have to practice outside for more than 20 minutes. You can do a lot of work inside. But the old stadium was a minor league stadium that they sort of built up. So once you walked outside you just baked. If you wanted to work on something extra—let's say bunting for a base hit—you had to make a conscious decision whether you were going to go out there at three-thirty, when it was about 104, or conserve that energy for seven thirty-five, when it was only 102."

The discussion shifts to Sample's current work in umpire evaluation. He refers to the owners' stern stance in accepting the resignations of umpires in 1999. "What we saw last year was the employer deciding that he or she had rights. They felt that the umpires were a little like Supreme Court Justices in that they didn't have to answer to anyone.

"I think by accepting the resignations, it added a sense of clarity to the umpire's union as to what management wanted from them. It's unfortunate that it had to happen that way, but it's kind of hard to blame management. The umpires are the ones who actually initiated the work stoppage. Even though I understand what they were thinking. They thought they were going to get locked out and wanted to bring the negotiations closer to where they had the greatest amount of leverage. In retrospect, what they did worked in management's favor because they could then accept some of the resignations. They didn't say, 'Let's get rid of all the guys we think are a grade lower,' but they probably picked and chose so they wouldn't get caught trying to target one particular area. Still, within that framework, they probably accepted resignations from some people that they were only too happy to see leave the game."

Billy analyzes the vote by umpires to form a new union following the resignation debacle of 1999. "There's always been a schism between the National and American Leagues, so the vote went along league lines— the American voting for a new union, the National being the most staunch supporters to keep the old one. Then the 22 that they [the owners] had hired voted with the American League, which makes sense if you know how management wants you to vote. They're the ones giving you a job after you've been in the minor leagues for ten years and you can make $70 thousand as opposed to $15 or $20 thousand."

If chances are slim for a minor league ballplayer making it to the majors, competition is greater and jobs far fewer for minor league umpires. Billy is sympathetic. "They really do have a tough go of it. You can be a good umpire and spend ten years in the minors making no money, in tough conditions, working two, three to a group. And it's hard to get in the profession anyway."

Demands for umpire reforms have been more vociferous and numerous during the nineties than perhaps any previous decade. Management addressed one issue at the onset of the new millennium with a directive that allowed for indiscriminate use of umpires, which supplanted the century-old policy of a separate set of umpires for each league. Sample foresees

Billy Sample at Rutgers University in Piscataway, New Jersey.

other reforms and is cautiously optimistic about baseball's commitment to improving umpire effectiveness. "I think baseball has the opportunity now to make it better in regards to the umpires being a part of the entertainment package. I think they are a part. I think we're all in this together. And hopefully, it will get better. They have the technology—simulators, in which you can call balls and strikes, safe or out, obstruction calls. So I hope baseball is not just giving lip service to us and will indeed try to improve every aspect to make it better, not only for umpires but for the whole game."

One change Sample does not support is constant use of instant replays to overrule close calls, claiming the "angles are too tough" to justify the innovation. He does, however, maintain that "getting it right is what it's all about," and advocates increased umpire conferences to ensure proper decisions. "Granted, they can't conference like they can in basketball because of the distances involved. But I do think we can move a little bit closer to the NBA where they have conferences in certain situations." Sample admits umpire conferences may initially create more problems than solutions. "You might have a situation where one manager runs out, then the other runs out. That's the kind of Pandora's Box that I'm not sure they want to see opened. But I do think it would be better for the game in the long run."

I ask Billy to assess minority-hiring practices by ballclubs in the 13 years since Al Campanis' notorious remarks on television's *Nightline*, when the Dodger general manager made disparaging comments, albeit unwittingly, regarding black players, climaxed by his alleging they lacked "the necessities" to be managers or front office executives. "I wasn't offended by the swimming part of his remarks. I swim like a rock anyway. (Class laughs.)

"But to be serious, I think, initially, there was something positive following his remarks. There was a movement—a good one, I was part of it—called Baseball Network. Willie Stargell, Frank Robinson, and Ray

Burris were the top leaders. We would put together a group of candidates for whatever job openings there were. I thought it was functional for improving the numerical ratio of minority hiring. After a while, that sort of waned a bit, and then maybe there was a mini-push here or there. It's one of those areas I hate to think you always have to stay on top of, but I think, unfortunately, you do.

"I do think it'll change a bit as non-whites have more management positions—from owners to general managers on down. I think owners would probably trigger more change than any other position. There was a time—I heard this from a reporter—when an owner who was selling his club wouldn't sell to a Jew. Today, you have more Jewish ownership in baseball. Unfortunately, I had a former agent that made sure I'd be working for the IRS too many years, so I don't have the kind of money to get into ownership."

Does Sample have any regrets about his ballplaying career? "I guess for most players, their careers ended sooner than they would have liked. Mine came at the onset of collusion where they were setting salaries and keeping free agents from being literally free. But I don't know, there are very few professions where you can be an adolescent into middle age."

What does he miss most? "The camaraderie. I think most former players will tell you that. Number two, I miss the competition. There are not many places where you can round third representing the winning run and have (Mike) Scioscia there blocking the plate and you've just gotta score. You just don't get that kind of adrenaline rush anywhere else. I'd like to find it somewhere else, but I haven't.

"I remember talking once with Ted Simmons. Ted was vice-president of a bank somewhere in Missouri where he lived. He was still playing at the time. And I said to him, 'Instead of trying to stay in baseball for another year, why don't you just get out and take control of this bank? You're smart and you can make a lot of money.' He said, 'Cause there's no three-two sliders in the outside world.' Kind of poignant, isn't it?"

Billy fields a few more questions before showing a genuinely entertaining video of fielding, base-stealing, and hitting highlights from his career. I thank him for generously giving his time, and after Lola takes a group photo we head home while Billy continues talking baseball and football with the students.

With his career extending deep into the eighties, Sample may be regarded as a young old-timer. He is, in fact, suggestive of the prototypical modern major leaguer, whose intelligence and eloquence is as perceptible as his athletic prowess. Yet, that may be where the similarity ends. From listening to his recollections of life in the bushes and big leagues, Sample must have maintained a degree of enthusiasm which some critics claim is lacking in many of today's ballplayers. (Indeed, Billy still displays a palpable love of the game, evident throughout his conversation at Rutgers.) Skeptics would insist his devotion remained constant because monetary rewards were not sufficiently ample to distract him from the game. From the few hours spent with him, it is difficult to imagine financial affluence having a negative effect on Sample's performance.

Nellie Briles

The baseball season is in its second week by the afternoon of April 12, 2000, when Lola and I enter the clubhouse of Pittsburgh's Three Rivers Stadium. Informing the receptionist of our appointment, we are greeted minutes later with a warm smile and handshake from the five-foot, ten-inch, silver-haired president of the Pirates Alumni Association—former righty hurler Nellie Briles. He escorts us into his office where the interview begins with a description of his town of birth—Dorris—located on the California side of the Oregon-California border. "Doesn't exist any more," says Nellie. "Might be a gas station there, but that's it. The lumber industry was prevalent there in those days, and my parents worked side-by-side in a lumber mill."

Born in 1943, Nellie actually lived in the adjacent town of Alturas until the age of eight, at which time the family moved to Chico, situated approximately 100 miles north of Sacramento. "That's really where I grew up—through the last part of elementary school, through junior high and then high school.

"In grammar school, they had playground programs after school, and whatever it was—baseball, soccer or basketball—that's what I played until it got dark and I went home. I just loved playing sports. Just loved being outside. I had two older brothers who were twins and were ten years older than me. They played sports, so maybe their love of sports rubbed off on me. I would say they and my father were the ones who most influenced me when I was young."

According to Briles, many of his friends received similar encouragement from parents to get involved in sports. Unlike some today, who harbor hopes of their children becoming millionaire major leaguers and whose "support" translates into intimidation and pressure for the youngsters, the parents of Chico had a different objective. "Being that most people from our area were wage-earners—hourly workers—perhaps sports was seen as a way of keeping kids busy, keeping them off the streets. My parents, for instance, always knew where I was."

Nellie's youth baseball background includes Little League, Pony League, Babe Ruth, and American Legion. "Once you play in an organized sport for the first time, where there are different teams, uniforms, winning and losing and structure, I think that helps develop and increase your interest." Coinciding with his participation was the advent of regularly televised ballgames, which, according to Nellie, "helped plant the dream" of becoming a big leaguer. "I'd watch the *Saturday Game-of-the-Week* and listen to Dizzy Dean. Didn't miss too many. And it made me think, 'Boy, wouldn't it be great if I could be a major league ballplayer?,' not knowing how tough it was gonna be and how fortunate you have to be to make it. But it was something in your subconscious more than any actual attempt at pursuing a goal."

That came later, about the time he was impressing as a 15-year-old pitcher in high school and American Legion ball. "There was one Legion team in Chico and we'd travel to towns all around northern California and play other Legion teams. I don't know if it's still a record or not, but I struck out 34 in one game. At the fair grounds in Chico. Went 14 innings. The level of competition wasn't real high, but we're talking 34 strikeouts."

Briles did not breeze through his entire teen years, as he was occasionally roughed up in semi-pro weekend games by players five to fifteen years his senior. "It was a tremendous experience," Nellie insists. "These guys knew how to steal bases with proficiency, so I had to learn to hold guys on. And I think that was the time my competitiveness really started to show for the first time. If I got knocked around I still wasn't afraid to get back on the mound and do better."

Notwithstanding those rough outings, word got around about Briles' pitching potential and he received several offers from scouts during his senior year. "At that time, most high school coaches were what you'd call bird dogs for major league teams—keeping an eye out for prospects. They were probably given some kind of a commission. That's probably how scouts first became interested in me. Still, I was from a small town in northern California, so scouts are skeptical—they wonder about the kind of competition a kid is facing. But they were interested enough to have a look."

Spurning all offers, Briles opted for a baseball scholarship at Santa Clara University and led his team to the national championship in his freshman year of 1962. After a summer of toiling in a Chico plywood mill and pitching semi-pro night baseball in Oregon, the right-hander rejected an offer from the Cardinals, completed his sophomore studies at Santa Clara, then played summer ball in the Western Canadian League. "Each team was more or less sponsored by a major league club. Calgary was sponsored by the Giants, the Dodgers had one in Edmonton, St. Louis sponsored one in Lethbridge. We traveled by car from one city to the next. I had a great time."

Toward the end of his third year at Santa Clara, a family tragedy became a turning point in Nellie's life. "My dad died of cancer at age 52. Naturally, he never got to see me play pro ball, which is one of the real disappointments that I have. Anyway, that summer the scouts knew if I got the right contract I was gonna sign, because I had a younger brother to take care of along with my mother, whose health was just so-so.

"I called my college athletic director and told him, 'You know my family situation. My father passed away. Scouts are offering me a contract and I'd like permission to register a few days late so I can hear what they have to say.' He said, 'If you're not here tomorrow, you don't have a scholarship.' Really hard-nosed me. Obviously, he was trying to force me to come back. But his strategy backfired. Before I spoke with him, I really hadn't made up my mind to sign; just wanted to listen to what the scouts had to say. But when he gave that response, I said, 'Well, if that's your attitude toward me, you just made my decision.'"

After calling Santa Clara coach Patty Cattrell, who sympathized with Briles and supported his decision, Nellie contacted Bill Sayles, former general manager of the Portland Beavers of the Pacific Coast League who had recently been hired as supervisor of scouts for St. Louis. "There were a lot of other teams that made offers, and it's not that Sayles made the best, but it was the best opportunity.

"I think it's important here not to forget a gentleman by the name of Eddie Bockman. He played third base for the Yankees and Pittsburgh and became a scout later, and still is today. At that time, he was a scout for Philadelphia and he had scouted me since high school. Took a great interest in me. As a matter of fact, after my father passed away, he would pick me up from home and take me to school because I didn't have a car. Once Philadelphia was out of the picture, Eddie acted in the best interests of my mother and me. We looked at the minor league rosters of teams that were interested—how many young pitchers they had already signed, who got bonuses, how many eggs were going to be in my basket if I signed with a particular club. St. Louis happened to look like a team that I might be able to make it through their system quickly if I performed. So it just seemed like the money and everything else was right."

The Cardinals paid for the remainder of Briles' college tuition, awarded him a $75,000 bonus, and gave him a first-year salary significantly higher than other minor league players. Within a two-day period, Nellie paid all outstanding bills and purchased a car for his mother, then headed for Instructional League in St. Petersburg, Florida. "The Instructional League was all about being introduced to pro ball. The intensity was expected of you. The level of competition was strong, about the same as Triple A today. You played games every day and worked on the finesse side of baseball. Polishing the diamond, if you will.

"Eddie Stanky was the farm director at that time. He was tough, very serious, very direct. The first words out of his mouth when I met him were, 'I'm farm director Eddie Stanky. I understand we just signed you as a bonus baby. We expect a lot out of you. You gotta lose 20 pounds.' I got to a low weight but didn't perform well cause I lost strength. By next spring, I got the weight back and was throwing well again."

In 1964, Briles was assigned to Tulsa of the Double A Texas League. The 20-year-old impressed with an 11–6 record and selection to the All-Star Team. Despite his outstanding performance, Nellie today recalls the not-so-glamorous aspect of life in the bushes. "You traveled throughout the state by bus so you had some long, long road trips. And in the heat. Whole lot of fun."

Toward the end of Briles' Tulsa stint, manager Grover Riessenger delivered the news that he was to join the Cardinals in New York. "From Chico to New York—that's a big step. We [the Cardinals] were staying in the Commodore Hotel—today it's the Hyatt. They still had elevator operators that used the manual lift to take you up and down. That didn't matter to me. I was in the big leagues.

"My first roommate was Joe Morgan—not the Reds player but the one who became the Red Sox manager. Like me, he was a minor league player who they brought up toward the end of the year; good pinch-hitter off the bench. He told me, 'Hey kid, I've been up a few times. Stay with me. I'll show you how to eat on a nickel.' (Nellie laughs) So we went to every corner drug store in New York. We were eating the greasy eggs, the whole bit. We laugh about that today."

Briles recalls his first day as a bona fide major leaguer. "When I was in college, I once worked out in Candlestick Park, but now I was in the big leagues. You know, you have your own major league uniform. So when I walked through the tunnel at Shea Stadium and onto that field, it was something special, a dream realized for my parents, brothers and, of course, me—from the time I was eight to 21 years old. All my dreams were realized at that moment. Like I said, it was really special."

It did not take long for the proverbial bubble to burst. Having arrived at the stadium at two o'clock, five hours before game time, Briles was alone on the field save for the trainer and clubhouse personnel when a member of the grounds crew approached him with a message to report to the office of manager Johnny Keane. "Of course, I was nervous. I went in there and Keane says in that gravelly voice of his, 'Hey, kid, I hear you had a good year.' I say, 'Yes, sir, I did.' He says, 'Good fastball, huh?' I say, 'Yeah.' He says, 'I hear you keep your fastball down. Moves pretty well.' I say, 'Yeah, your information is correct.' He says, 'Understand you have a good overhand curve ball. Not afraid to throw it when you're behind.' I say, 'That's right.' He says, 'Well, I just wanted to tell you that you're not gonna pitch.' (Nellie laughs.) I mean, he's gotten me all the way up to here (Nellie raises his right hand over his head) and then he just jerks the sheet from under me. So I say, 'Excuse me? What do you mean?' He says, 'Nellie, I'm going with the guys that got me here. We put this whole pennant race together in the last six weeks. Twenty runs up or twenty down, I'm going with guys that got me here. Just sit back, relax, and enjoy the ride.' He kept his word. I didn't pitch one game."

Despite his inactivity, Briles asserts the late-season experience was beneficial. "You saw the pressure. You saw the press. You saw how every pitch could mean everything. Saw this veteran ballclub scrapping and fighting every inch of the way. I was really introduced to the intensity of major league ball, the camaraderie, the kind of devotion to one another you had to have on a winning team."

Taking Riessenger's advice to keep his mouth shut and ears open, Briles was well received by Cardinal veterans, who found the rookie receptive to advice. "I was like a sponge. Sitting in the bullpen, listening to the veterans who are thinking along with the pitcher in the game, discussing strategy and hitters and basestealers and defensive positioning. Constant conversation. For 25 days. What an education."

The pennant race went down to the final day, with three teams still in contention. While the Phillies shellacked the Reds, the Cards battered the Mets at Sportsman's Park and St. Louis had its first flag in 18 years. When time came to select the team roster for the Series, Keane contemplated filling the final spot with a pitcher or an outfielder. "If it had been a pitcher I would have stayed with the club and been eligible for the Series. They decided to take Carl Warwick, who ended up getting some key hits in the Series. So the Cardinals went on to win the world championship and I went back to Chico."

Briles was appreciably more relaxed and confident at Cardinal spring training camp in 1965, for a number of reasons. "There was somewhat of a comfort zone. I had been with them for a month the year before so I wasn't among strangers. Johnny Keane was gone and Red Schoendienst was much more easygoing in his approach. And when I signed, the bonus rule was that if you received $8,000 the club had to put you on the major league roster after your second year or you might be lost in the draft. So I was gonna be on the club regardless. All these things made spring training much easier."

Briles did not see action for the first two weeks of regular season, then was used in the bullpen until getting his first big league start toward the end of the year when the Cardinals were out of the pennant picture. "We were flying to our next road game against the Dodgers. And keep in mind, when we flew in those days, we were still in the turbo props—four-engine propellers—so from St. Louis to Los Angeles was seven-and-a-half hours. Somewhere during that flight—I guess it was over the Grand Canyon—Red Schoendienst calls me to the front, sits me down, and says, 'Nellie, we've had a change of plans. We're out of the race, so we wanna give you your first start.' I had no clue this was coming. Totally unexpected. I said excitedly, 'Yeah? When, Red?' He said, 'Tomorrow night.' Now, we're talking Friday night in L.A. Fifty-six thousand. And being a California kid, it's pretty special. I don't even ask who I'm pitching against. Doesn't matter. I'm making my first major league start. Boy, you talk about adrenaline starting to shoot out of your fingers.

"Let me tell you something about that Cardinal ballclub. They had guys that would needle you. From Bill White to Kenny Boyer to Gibson to (Ray) Sadecki to McCarver to [Mike] Shannon. All those guys. Man, they'd needle each other all the time. Well, everybody had known that Red was gonna give me the news. So when he tells me, I get up and start walking down the aisle back to my seat. I could hear snickers and laughing and everything else. I turn around and say, 'What's everybody laughing at? I was just told I'm getting my first start.' They say, 'Yeah, we know. You know who you're pitching against?' I say, 'It don't matter.' They say, 'Yes, it does. It's (Sandy) Koufax.' Well, I'm getting my first start so, you know, I'm pretty cocky. I say, 'It still don't matter. I can beat him, too.' And they kept needling me the rest of the way."

Briles matched Koufax pitch for pitch through seven scoreless innings. In the eighth, Dodger Willie Davis reached on a bobbled grounder by normally sure-handed Julian Javier, then promptly stole second base. Nellie came inside with a fastball on Ron Fairly, who blooped a broken-bat RBI single to left. "I'll never forget when Koufax took the mound in the ninth, you could see a change in his demeanor—like, This game is mine. And he beat us 1–0.

"The next day, the Dodgers were coming off the field from batting practice and the Cardinals were getting on. Sandy, whom I had never met, went out of his way to come over to me. He said, 'Nellie, I just want you to know it was a great ballgame. It's too bad you had to lose, but I'm glad it was you who lost.' He kind of chuckled, but then he said, 'You're gonna be just fine,' which I thought was a nice thing to do. Well, right behind Koufax comes Drysdale. Later, he and I became very good friends. He tapped me on the shoulder and said, 'Kid! First big league tip from the opposition! If you're facing Koufax or Drysdale, you better not give up the first run!' And he just giggled and ran off the field."

Briles won only three of 12 decisions in 17 starts in 1966, and accumulated an overall record of 4–15. "But I had an ERA of 3.20. It was just one of those seasons when everything went wrong—there'd be a dropped ball or one bad pitch that would lose a game. But then I got my feet on the ground playing winter ball in Puerto Rico. I started every fourth day and went 13–1."

In 1967, Nellie continued to be used in the bullpen and as spot starter. As is often the case with aspiring major leaguers, Nellie's big break arose from a bad one for a veteran. "After the All-Star Game, we played Pittsburgh. Clemente hit a line drive off [Bob] Gibson and broke his shin. The next day, Schoendienst called me in and said, 'Nellie, you're taking Gibson's spot.' Well, talk about some shoes to fill. But at the time I saw it as the door opening again, and here's a chance to get established as a starter. In those days that's really what you wanted because a reliever wasn't making any money. You wanted to be one of those four starters.

"I pitched my first game against Atlanta and Aaron hit a home run in the eighth to beat me 3–2. Of course, everybody is saying afterwards, 'Good game, but nobody can fill Gibson's shoes; the Cardinals chances are diminished greatly.' Well, I went on to win nine in a row and we won the pennant."

Nellie precedes his analysis of the '67 Series with a jazzy story involving some teammates and him. It begins on the afternoon prior to Game One, as the Cardinals were working out at Fenway Park. "Now, I liked jazz, as did Gibson, [Curt] Flood, [Lou] Brock, (Orlando) Cepeda. The Modern Jazz Quartet with Milt Jackson was one of our favorites. We'd go to a lot of nightclubs. Well, Gibson came over and asked if my wife and I wanted to go to a party that night hosted by the wife of Bill Russell [the Boston basketball star]. Cannonball Adderley was performing along with his brother, Nat. And Cannonball was really hot at that time—"Why Am I Treated So Bad?"—and a lot of other great jazz songs. Gibson said they were gonna prepare soul food, and that Lou and Curt and their wives were going. I said sure, that I'd love to go.

"So we show up, and spent the whole evening at Russell's house; he wasn't there but his wife was a wonderful host, and there were some guys from the Celtics team—K.C. Jones, Wayne Embry, and a few others. When it came time to leave, K.C. yelled at us, 'Aw, the only reason we had you guys here was to get you full of champagne so we can kick your fanny tomorrow.' Well, the next day Gibson goes out and has a great game—strikes out 14, hits a home run. After the game, K.C. came down to the fence near us. Gibbie says, 'Hey, are we partying again tonight?' K.C. says, 'Oh no you don't. You guys live on that stuff!'"

After Gibson defeated Boston, St. Louis faltered in a Game Two that included several knockdowns of Cardinal players. "Our starting pitcher didn't protect our hitters that day, so our guys were pretty upset. But they never said anything to me about it. We went to St. Louis, worked out, and nobody said a word."

Given the start for Game Three, Briles was given an early message by a teammate. "I got the first batter on a popup. The ball went around the infield to Shannon. He was twenty feet away when he threw the ball back to me as hard as he could. Trying to say, 'Look, you better start doing something.' The next hitter makes out and the same thing—Shannon fired the ball back! It hurt! (Nellie winces.) So the next batter was Carl Yastrzemski and I hit him in the knee. Of course, the benches emptied, and I'm fined, and everything else. But let me tell you, there wasn't another knockdown for the rest of the Series. I went on to pitch a complete-game 5–2 win. I think that really gave us a shot of adrenaline. And for me, that game really was the launching pad. It really established me as a clutch performer, someone who could handle pressure. And that stayed with me my entire career."

There was more-immediate aftermath from his performance. "The next day, I went to my locker and there was a stack of telegrams that high (Nellie raises his hand over his head). I thought, 'Man, look at how many people are sending me congratulations.' Of course, they were all from New England and none of them complimentary (Nellie laughs.) I hit their fair-haired kid. They wrote things like, 'My son will never speak your name.' Or, 'We burned your baseball cards.' Some of them were very threatening and had to be turned over to the FBI. It didn't bother me, but they had to be taken seriously. When we went back to Boston, there was a guard with us. Of course, nothing happened."

With some exceptions, most notably the A's and Yankee teams of the seventies, championship ballclubs are characterized by exceptional team chemistry. That was the case with the Cardinals. Says Nellie, "The closeness of that club was phenomenal. Sure the guys were talented, but they always stuck together. In times of adversity, they'd offer encouragement and praise. And they'd always back each other up. That closeness was one of the very unique situations that I experienced in my 14 years. We still stay in touch today. Exchange family newsletters and Christmas cards. Even after all these years."

Asking Nellie to respond with whatever comes to mind, I mention some former Cardinals, beginning with Gibson. "Belly full of fire. Competitive. Intense. Accepted nothing but winning, had little time for those who made excuses. Could be tough on those who did."

Roger Maris, former Yankee rightfielder and home run record-holder who joined the Cardinals in 1967. "There's an interesting story about Roger. I came into a game that was one of his first with us. There was a runner at second representing an important run in the ninth. I could see Roger out of the corner of my eye, which meant he's in right-center. I motioned with my hand for him to move over because the batter was a lefty pull-hitter. So he did. I went into my stretch, checked the runner, and Roger's back where he was before. I'm thinking, 'Roger, what are you doing?' So I motion with my hand again and he moves over. I go into the stretch again, look over, don't see him, so I figure he's where he belongs. I threw the pitch and the batter rifles the ball into right-center. I know it's in there for a hit, so I run to the spot between third and home to back up in case the runner falls down or something and we have a play at the plate. As I'm running, I hear the roar of the crowd. I turn around to ask Shannon what happened, and he says, 'Maris caught the ball. Great running catch. We win.' I'm dumbfounded.

"We come off the field and I'm waiting for Roger to shake his hand, and he ran right by me. I'm thinking, 'Yeah, this is the Maris I've heard about—sulky and all that.' We get inside and he's at my locker. He says, 'I bet you're wondering how I caught that ball.' I said, 'Roger, there's no way you caught that ball.' He said, 'Let me tell you. I saw you throwing in the bullpen today. You really had the extra. And when you came into the game and started warming up, you still had really good movement. So when you moved me over, I moved but then I cheated back. And the last time, I didn't move back until you turned your head. I was gambling that you'd make your pitch, that he wasn't gonna pull you. One of the things you'll learn is that you'll never have to check Roger Maris.' I said, 'I'll never look again.'"

Former Giant first baseman and recent Cooperstown inductee Orlando Cepeda, who was also dealt to the Cards in a 1967 trade. "I would say he was the heart of that ballclub. MVP, .325 average, 100 RBIs. And he was a fun guy. He made that year fun for us. He coined the phrase

"El Birdos," kind of a bastardization of the name Cardinals. And that really became our trademark, our theme. And he kept us loose in the clubhouse. We had an old trunk in there, and every time someone made a bad play in the game, Orlando would get in there, jump out, and say, 'Who made the dumbest play of the game? Was it Zazu Pitts?' We'd yell, 'No!' He'd say, 'Was it Heinie Manush?' We'd yell, 'No!' He'd say, 'Was it Lou Brock?' We'd yell, 'Yeah!' Things like that kept us loose the whole year. We had intensity on the field but there was that element of fun, and Orlando was in the middle of it. I think he had the most fun that year than anyone."

Catcher Tim McCarver. "Tim was the smartest catcher I ever pitched to. Timmy loved being in command; knew how to be in command. His control of the game allowed me to focus on just throwing the pitches, and not have to worry about calling them. I had absolute, total confidence in the way he called the game."

Manager Red Schoendienst. "If you didn't like playing for Red, you didn't like playing for anybody. He afforded a veteran ballclub the latitude to play the way that each individual knew how to play. He didn't have to put on steal or hit-and-run signs for Brock or Flood. He didn't have "take" signs for Cepeda or Maris; just let them swing the bats. In actuality, there isn't a whole lot to do when you have McCarver, Cepeda, Javier, (Dal) Maxville, Shannon, Brock, Flood, and Maris. I mean, what is there to change? Other than rest guys once in a while. So Red's biggest asset was that he let us play and treated us like men. Didn't over-manage, didn't have overbearing rules."

Nineteen sixty-seven was arguably Briles' best season—a winner in 14 of 19 decisions, a 2.43 ERA, a victory in his first Series appearance. Yet, although his ERA was higher (2.81) in 1968 and he lost six more games, Nellie won a career-high 19 and might have realized that elusive goal of 20 had he been given the chance. With five games remaining, Schoendienst chose to bypass Briles in his final start. "We already had clinched the pennant. We were being talked about as one of the best clubs in history, and winning the Series again would have helped establish that. So I was told it would be better to rest. Looking back in a sort of selfish way, you think, 'Maybe I should have pushed a little harder.' That's probably my only regret about my career. That I didn't fight harder for myself. I was awfully trusting. Even later in my career, I probably should have been more forceful in pushing for opportunities."

Briles won 15 games in 1969, but tore a hamstring muscle in the spring of 1970 and pitched half the number of innings of the previous season. "But while I was injured, I was asked to visit hospitals and make a lot of appearances, which I was happy to do."

Nellie was not happy at the end of the season after receiving word from general manager Bing Devine that his salary was being cut in half. "I mean, how much money were we making then? Not much. So I said, 'No way, Bing. I pitched when I was hurt. Did all the things off the field you asked. I don't think I deserve a cut, especially after all the years I've performed well for the team.' So we weren't together on the salary."

After several weeks, Devine called Briles into his office, insisting that the matter be settled immediately. Nellie remained adamant in his refusal to take a cut, asking only the same salary as in 1969. "So he picked up the phone, dialed, and said, 'Hello, Joe? This is Bing.' He was talking to Joe Brown, the GM at Pittsburgh. He said, 'Nellie Briles is here in front of me. It's a deal.' He handed me the phone and said, 'Nellie, you wanna talk to your new general manager? You've just been traded.'"

Even though he felt betrayed and angry, Briles realized that Pittsburgh was a talented ballclub, had won their division, and needed pitching, while St. Louis was in the process of rebuilding. "Plus, you couldn't do anything about it. So on the one hand you don't want to leave, on the other there's the opportunity.

"I took the phone and introduced myself to Brown. Now, Joe, as I would learn later, tries to diffuse ticklish situations with some dry humor. I didn't know that at the time. His first words to me were, 'Nellie, is your fat ass in shape?' (Nellie laughs.) Well, I didn't want to hear that. I wanted to hear something like, 'Nellie, we're glad to have you, welcome aboard.' So I guess the pause that followed was an indication to him that he didn't say the right thing. He says, 'Nellie, give me your home phone and I'll call you when you get there.'"

Two days later, Nellie was still feeling uneasy about his baseball future when he got a morale boost while participating in the American Airlines Celebrity Golf Tournament in Phoenix. "There was another guy who was playing in that event who had won it the year before—Bill Mazeroski, my new teammate. He wasn't the regular second baseman at the time. Dave Cash had taken over. But he was still a real player's player. And he made me feel welcome immediately."

Briles was a content camper at the Bucs' spring training, but became frustrated during the season when used sparingly as a starter. He was given a regular turn in September and pitched effectively in helping the Pirates capture their division, prompting manager Danny Murtaugh to contemplate using him in post-season play. Asked to pitch a tune-up game in Philadelphia in the last week of the season, Briles reluctantly agreed, then pulled a groin muscle. Scheduled to pitch the third game of the National League Championship Series against the Giants, the injured

Briles was forced to sit out. "But Bob Johnson replaced me and pitched the game of his life against Juan Marichal."

Pittsburgh defeated the Giants in four games, and by the fifth game of the World Series Nellie had sufficiently recovered to be named the starter against Baltimore. "That game had a lot of significance for me. I hadn't pitched in two weeks. People were saying I couldn't pitch, that I hadn't thrown on the side, that I couldn't be sharp. And remember, it was a pivotal game."

With the Series tied at two, Briles tossed a two-hit shutout while contributing to the four-run offense with an RBI single. "That game is the highlight of my career. No question. Baltimore was heavily favored and had a great club. And I think Game Five was put in perspective by Earl Weaver before the game. Reporters asked how important it was. He said, 'Whoever wins will probably win the Series because then you only have to win one of two, and we're going home afterwards and that's a distinct advantage.'

"So I shut 'em out, and after the game the reporters run to Earl and say that it looks like the Pirates are gonna win. He says, 'No, no, no. You don't understand. We've won two in a row before. We have 'em on our own field.' Just spins it and spins it and spins it. Then they ask him what he thinks about me. He says, 'All I can say about Briles is I hate his guts. I hate his guts.'

"Well, to complete the story, six years later I'm playing for Texas. We're flying to California and, again somewhere over the Grand Canyon, I'm sold to the Orioles. I get to Baltimore around the eighth inning and the trainer comes in and asks, 'Nellie, are you okay to pitch? We're thin on pitching.' I say, 'Yeah, I'm fine.' He says, 'Well, as soon as the inning is over, Earl's gonna come in and you'll get your signals straight.' So I'm putting on my uniform and Earl comes in and says, 'You know, I still hate your guts from '71.' I said, 'Hey, Earl, it's great to be here.'"

Briles' career spanned from 1965 to 1978. He accumulated a record of 129–112 and an ERA (3.43) that would make most modern pitchers envious. Nellie talks with pride about the time period in which he played. "It was the beginning of modern baseball, with a lot of new parks. It was a time when the black ballplayer really came into his own. And look at the Hall-of-Famers from that era—black and white. It was an incredible period that produced so many stars.

"The sixties was an especially good time for baseball. There was expansion, but not to the extent that came later on. And baseball still wasn't sharing the athletic talent pool with other sports like it did later. In our time, if you wanted to make money as an athlete, you went into baseball."

Author (left) with Nellie Briles in his office at Three Rivers Stadium in Pittsburgh, Pennsylvania.

If Nellie has one disappointment in regards to his career it is never having made an appearance in an All-Star Game. "I thought I should have made it in '68, but Schoendienst picked Seaver over me. He said he couldn't take three of his pitchers and Gibson and Carlton were going. And that year was my best shot. I was always a second-half pitcher. Took me about 15 games before I got going."

Nellie finishes the interview talking about his work with the Alumni Association, which raises money for charities through banquets and golf tournaments. He graciously poses for photos, signs some baseballs, and thanks us for the opportunity to talk baseball. While exiting the parking lot, Lola and I take a last glimpse of Three Rivers Stadium, the Home of the Pirates for its 31st and final season, as it yields to PNC Stadium in 2001.

On the drive home via the Pennsylvania Turnpike, while we pass through tunnels burrowed into such charmingly-named mountains as Tuscarora, Kittatinny, and Squirrel Hill, the alternating darkness and sunshine are symbolic of a major leaguer's career. The indecision and doubt of a teenage amateur, the renewed confidence following the first pro contract. The apprehension of a minor leaguer, the elation following a big league debut. The frustration of a rookie benchwarmer, the satisfaction derived as a regular. The aggravating slumps, the gratifying streaks.

Although Nellie Briles' baseball journey did not end at the Cooperstown door, it contained sufficient sunshine to enable him to reminisce mostly with contentment today. "Baseball was really all I hoped it would be," he commented late in the interview. "To come out healthy, go through some experiences, play on some great teams, was terrific. I got to live my dream!"

Longfellow once wrote, "Look not mournfully into the Past. It comes not back again." There are, unfortunately, some former ballplayers who reflect with bitterness, as they dwell on insufficient opportunities, career-curtailing injuries, lost pennants, cantankerous managers, inadequate salaries, and unfavorable trades. The complaints are understandable, often justifiable, much more so than those offered by modern multi-millionaire athletes.

Yet, discontented old-timers should keep in mind that the ride down that major league road, however brief or laden with tunnels, is in itself a noteworthy achievement. For although millions have aspired to take the trip since the founding of the National League in 1876 and American League at the turn of the century, it has not been a heavily trafficked highway. Far better to have struggled on it than never having been allowed on at all.

Jon Matlack

Like all of our trips to visit with former ballplayers, the drive to the home of former lefty hurler Jon Matlack on the afternoon of April 25, 2000, is extremely pleasant. Patches of clouds decorate a dark-blue sky, while barns, silos, and grazing cows adorn the hillside that borders Route 12, the highway connecting Norwich and Binghamton, New York, where Lola and I had spent the previous two days visiting with her folks.

After an hour's drive, I spot a tan barn mentioned by Matlack as a landmark and pull into an adjacent driveway leading to the top of the hill. After exiting the minivan, we receive a warm welcome from the silver-cropped, still-physically-fit Matlack, a golden retriever and a terrier at his heels. Upon entering the charming rural home, we are led across hardwood floors to the living room, where Lola and I settle on the couch and Jon sinks into an equally cozy chair situated to our left as the interview begins.

Born on January 19, 1950, Matlack recalls growing up in West Chester, Pennsylvania, located approximately 40 miles southwest of Philadelphia. "West Chester was what everybody referred to back then as the end of the line—the train that ran from Philly stopped at Paoli, and if you went down Route 30 just a little bit further you ran into Exton. I lived five miles from Exton. It's very much built-up now but West Chester was a small town then. Had only one high school. There was West Chester Teacher's College, which is now a university, which gives you an idea of how the town has grown. Over the back fence where I lived was farm country; you could jump the fence and run through the corn fields."

Matlack's father was a plumbing and heating contractor who specialized in installing and repairing wells and pumps, while his mother "did what most moms did then, raise kids." The family of five lived in West

Chester until moving in 1955 to a house on the outskirts of town, where Jon lived until graduating from West Chester High School in 1967.

While growing up, Jon played Little League ball. He recalls the experience with fondness. "I was very fortunate that Little League started just about the time I was old enough to play. There were four teams when it began and, more importantly, it hadn't grown to the point where everybody was interested in winning. There was no pressure on you to perform. It was all about helping the kids learn the game. I wasn't influenced by that syndrome that so many dads have today—they want to relive their childhood through their kids playing Little League.

"Unfortunately, there are a lot of kids today who have to deal with that pressure situation. Even some of the coaches—and I'm not going to say all or even most—but some of them aren't helping the kids learn to develop their skills. Kids are learning to twist or utilize the rule system in order to better position the team to win." Jon offers an example. "The hitters are told to just take pitches because the opposing pitcher will probably walk you; his control usually isn't good enough to throw strikes."

Currently working as a minor league pitching coordinator for the Detroit Tigers, Matlack is particularly concerned about Little League pitchers, and believes instruction on the proper mechanics of pitching is vital, although admitting there may not be a single "correct" way to throw a baseball. "From my understanding, to throw a ball overhand is atypical of the way the body is designed. From what doctors have said about the way the muscle structure is and the way the joints work, the underhand softball motion is much more natural for the body than throwing overhand. So baseball goes against nature right from the beginning."

Matlack is convinced that throwing curve balls at a young age is potentially harmful. "Each individual has different physical traits and some will be less apt to break down than others. But there are things you can do to prevent that. I'd like to see youngsters prohibited from throwing breaking pitches. I have a strong belief that a lot of them become injured later on because they throw curve balls from that short distance of 46 feet. When they get older and have to throw curve balls from 60-feet, six-inches, the strain placed on the joints, ligaments and muscles—asking your body to throw the curve ball those extra yards—causes injuries.

"Some leagues have it where kids go from pitching from 46 feet to pitching from 54 feet before going to the 60-feet, six-inch distance, which is a good idea. But I feel the best thing is to wait for the body to develop. And I would much rather have a youngster who has developed a fastball over time by throwing it. I mean, that's the only way to develop it, by continually throwing it. It's the only pitch you can't teach. Curve balls, changeups, sliders we can teach in a relatively short period of time. So let the Little League coaches have kids concentrate on developing the fastball, which is the most important pitch anyway."

While playing for the New York Mets, Matlack was often asked to appear at awards banquets and year-end get-togethers for various leagues. At each appearance, Jon stressed the importance of allowing Little Leaguers to have fun, for coaches to teach fundamentals, and for parents to refrain from putting pressure on children to perform. "In visiting and talking with people at these banquets—the coaches or organizers from different areas—the single theme that came through was that kids reach a certain age and lose their interest in baseball; they burn out. A high school coach would tell me about how he saw a kid develop through the Little League and couldn't wait to have him on the team—he'd be drooling over him—and when the first day of tryouts comes, the kid doesn't even show up. And that's going on just about everywhere."

Matlack's father, a Little League coach, spent hours each day with Jon and his teammates teaching them the basics. The recipient of some forceful encouragement from his high school coach, Jon believes it was the right time to be pushed to perform, especially for one aspiring to play professionally. "I was very fortunate to have a wonderful coach named Charles Perrone. He had a very neat personality. Without yelling at you, he made you question whether you gave enough that day. Just by looking at you he'd be asking, 'Hey, is your work done?' Made you feel that you better go run another couple of laps. Made you want to give that extra."

Noting his teenage naïveté regarding baseball's scouting procedures, Matlack laughs his way through an anecdote that serves to underscore the point. "In my junior year in '66, we were playing a game and there were a bunch of guys behind the backstop watching with clipboards and taking notes. I asked the coach, 'What are all those guys doing back there?' He told me they were scouts. That didn't mean anything to me so I asked him what a scout was. (Jon laughs.) It gets worse. After Coach Perrone explained the scouting system, my next question is, 'What are they doing *here*?' And he told me they were looking at me and a few other players."

According to Matlack, the prospect of playing professionally was a "pipe dream," and he actually harbored the more practical hope that his pitching skills would lead to a college scholarship. "That idea changed when I was drafted in '67 by the Mets as the number four pick in the first round—Ronnie Blomberg was number one that year. I signed for *sixty-three whole thousand dollars*. And they would pay for my education after that. Pretty decent."

Jon attended the University of Pittsburgh, but transferred to West Chester College when his father was stricken with cancer. When he eventually succumbed, his son had not yet realized his goal of breaking into the majors. "But I honestly think that he always knew I would get there, even when I didn't know. Just some things he said a couple of times that makes me think so. Maybe it's just me wanting to have that feeling, but I really think he did always know."

"Both my mom and dad were always very supportive. They used to go to visit my grandparents in upstate New York and leave me home so I could play. Somebody would come by and pick me up, or I'd stay at the home of one of my teammates. That way I wouldn't miss any games. My grandparents didn't like that too much, the fact that I wasn't along for the visit, but baseball was my life and my parents were very good in the way they supported me."

After his father became ill, Jon set aside his educational aspirations. "It wasn't that I *had* to quit, but it's something I felt I had to do to help take care of the family, being the oldest child." Throughout his minor league career he maintained his desire to complete his degree, but always found obstacles. "Baseball kept throwing curves at me—we want you to play fall ball or go to Puerto Rico to play winter ball. So it was a catch-22—yeah, I wanted to go to school but I felt if I didn't follow-up on all the things they were asking me to do they wouldn't think as much of me as before or I might not develop as quickly. So it was put all your eggs in one basket and hope it turns out."

When the Mets drafted Matlack he was still playing American Legion ball. At the time, the major leagues and American Legion had an agreement that prevented draftees from signing until the end of the American Legion season. Matlack's minor league debut was therefore delayed. "My team wouldn't lose. We won our league, we won our district, we just kept going. By the time we got knocked out in the quarter or semifinals of the state tournament, it was August. I ended up signing on August 9th."

Shipped to the Double A ballclub at Williamsport, located a short distance from his West Chester home, the 17-year-old Matlack immediately became aware of two things—most of the players were older than him, and the overall level of hitting was appreciably better than any he had faced previously. "I get my hat handed to me in my first two starts. Got absolutely pummeled."

In the fall, Matlack was sent to Instructional Ball, where he worked alongside future major leaguers Nolan Ryan, Jerry Koosman, Al Schmelz, Jim Bibby, and Les Rohr. "Just a bunch of guys who threw the ball as hard as the dickens. And they were all huge. We took a picture down there by size, and out of 19 pitchers I was the tenth guy—nine guys bigger than me! At one point, I called my dad and said, 'You might have to send me a bus ticket home because I don't think I can throw with these guys.' If this is what it took to get into the big leagues—size and power—I didn't know if I'd make it."

Matlack skipped spring training tryouts in 1968 and returned to his studies at West Chester College, an option permitted by the Mets because he had attended Instructional Ball. Following the spring semester, he went to North Carolina and played Class A ball in the Carolina League. Jon attended his first spring training in 1969, but held no hope of making the club. "I might have pitched an inning. No question, there were a ton of guys that threw the ball very well. And even though I'm not totally blown away by the scene at this time, I still don't have that sense that I'm going to be okay."

When spring training ended, Matlack was promoted to Portsmouth and his solid performance that year helped the club capture the Triple A title. "It's interesting, every Met team from that year won. From the top all the way down through the farm system—the Amazin' Mets won the World Series, we won at Portsmouth, the Double A club won theirs, the A club won theirs—every ballclub! I would imagine that's very rare."

Matlack returned to spring training, then Portsmouth in 1970, and the pattern repeated in 1971. "By this time it's kind of like spinning your wheels—you spend a little time in spring training and you feel frustrated because you realize you're probably not going to make it. In your own mind you feel you need the chance, which you don't feel is ever coming. So that's sort of how I'm thinking when I'm back in Triple A in '71."

That July, Koosman pulled a muscle in his rib cage. The Mets put the southpaw on the disabled list and called up Matlack, instructing him to meet the team in Chicago. Two days later, Jon made his major league debut in the second game of a doubleheader in Cincinnati. Prior to the start, the rookie's nerves seemed uncontrollable. "I'll never forget, the clubhouse guy at Riverfront wanted to bill me for the carpet I wore out pacing back and forth. He'd yell, 'Will you sit down and relax?' That's how nervous I was.

"It was a day doubleheader so I'm pitching the late afternoon game. I can't begin to tell you who was in that lineup; it's all basically a blur. I think I was losing 2–1 in the sixth or seventh inning when they pinch-hit for me. Well, the Mets scored two runs and I'm in the clubhouse as the potential winner. I'm in the shower yelling, 'Yes! This is okay!' I was so confident because they brought Seaver in to wrap it up. It was near the All-Star break so he wouldn't have another chance to start again before the All-Star Game and he was rested enough to pitch a couple of innings. So I'm feeling pretty doggoned good. I mean, what better guy to pick me up and save it for me? And [Tug] McGraw backing him up if necessary. Lo and behold, Tony Perez hit his second home run of the game, and we lose 5–3. I don't get the loss but I don't get the win either."

Matlack appeared in seven games with the Mets that year, six as a starter, and although he failed to gain his first major league victory, his motivation was re-invigorated. "Getting that first taste of the majors, you understand very quickly that it's the only place to play. Not only because of the crowd and the conditions and the intensity of the game, but just knowing that it's the top level, that it doesn't get any better than that."

Following the 1971 season, Matlack was asked to play winter ball in Puerto Rico for manager Bill Virdon. "He was a very structured, disciplined, militant-type guy. At that stage of my life—21 years old—having that structure was very good for me. And Bill not only told you what to do in terms of conditioning, he went out there and did it with you. Stride for stride, push-up for push-up. Whatever we were doing, he was doing."

Matlack recalls meeting Roberto Clemente that winter. "He was a nice fellow. There were about eight Americans on the team and he invited us over his house, which I thought was a very nice gesture. Opening his house, making us feel comfortable, talking baseball. And he was very impressive. Not a huge guy, but well proportioned and obviously very strong. He used a maximum-dimension bat—as big and as heavy and as long as the rules say a bat can be. Huge. The handle was almost as big as the barrel of the bat. It was around 54 inches in length and weighed I don't know how many ounces.

"One day, he was talking to us about hitting and was handling this bat. The size and shape of it sort of intrigued me; I should have been listening to what he was saying. Might have helped me later. (Jon laughs.) Anyway, he set it down. I went over to pick it up. I couldn't get it off the floor. Here he was holding it and moving it around like it was nothing and I could barely lift it. That was very impressive to me."

While Matlack was pitching in Puerto Rico, the Mets were pitching a deal to the Angels that led to what today's historians rate as among the most notorious and lopsided swaps in baseball history—future Hall-of-Famer Nolan Ryan for third baseman Jim Fregosi. Jon explains why the trade did not seem so outrageous at the time. "Nolan was a great guy. Very, very personable. Hard-working. Threw the ball as hard as the dickens. But when he was with us he really didn't know where the ball was going when he threw it. Very little consistency in the ability to repeat pitches. He'd throw the curve for a strike, then in the next two or three there'd be no telling if it would be in the dirt or over the catcher's head. That was the big thing that changed when he got to California. He was finally able to control his stuff, and then the records just started to fall.

"I played for Texas, and after I retired I'd go back for Old-Timers' Day and Nolie was still pitching for the Rangers. We'd sit and chat. I'll have to remember to give him a call because I just read in the paper about his recent bypass surgery. I couldn't believe the big article they had in our local paper because we carry very little up here. It's a very tiny paper, but they had this big article with a huge picture. Apparently the surgery was successful and everything's gonna be okay."

Although the Ryan–Fregosi trade would prove to be a long-term disaster for the Mets, Ryan's departure provided an opening for Matlack. "I went to spring training sort of hoping I had a shot at making it. But I'm not really feeling a lot more confident. I got to pitch a lot, but I was never told anything and never had the feeling that I had earned anything, that I was gonna be okay, as we got close to the end of spring training.

"Now, the clubhouse at Miller Huggins Field in St. Pete is a big rectangular room with doors out to the field in the middle of one side of the room, doors leading to the street on the other side, the coach's office on one side, and the trainer's room on the other. And all around it are lockers. So you can see everybody's locker. Mine was right inside the front door, to the left. Well, it was very close to cut-down date when we came back from a road trip. As a matter of fact, I heard on the bus that there had been cuts that day. I walk in the locker room and quietly make like I'm taking off my uniform. What I'm really doing is looking around and counting lockers that still have clothes in them. If there were 25 and I'm still one of them, then I'm okay. I work my way around and get back to my locker, which is number 25. So I sort of go, 'Yes!' (Jon pumps his fist.) There's a voice behind me that says, 'That's right, kid. You made it.' It was Hodges. He had walked in the door, realized what I was doing, and just stood there and waited. I had no idea he was there. (Jon laughs.)"

Jon talks about the missed opportunity of playing for the widely respected manager who had led the Mets to its first pennant and world championship three years earlier. "A week later, we broke camp and went on our little tour with the Yankees. We were in West Palm Beach waiting to play the Yankees that night, with two or three more games scheduled to play after that along the Florida coast. Gil and some of the coaches went out to play golf and he fell over and died on the golf course. So, unfortunately, I didn't get to experience playing for him."

In his first season with the Angels, Ryan won 19 games, had a 2.28 ERA, and led the league in strikeouts (329) and shutouts (nine), while

Fregosi batted a paltry .232 with five homers and 32 RBIs. Critics derided Mets management for inane judgment, but fans' wrath was somewhat abated by the superb pitching of Ryan's replacement. Matlack won 15 of 25, threw four shutouts, and his 2.32 ERA was fourth-best in the league; his performance earned him Rookie-of-the-Year honors. "I wouldn't say I was surprised by my success. I guess winning Rookie-of-the-Year was sort of a surprise. The writers intimated I had a good chance to win but that talk was going over my head somewhere.

"What really turned my crank was the daily competition that I watched every day and got to participate in every fifth day—the psychology, the chess game, the game within a game. I was gearing toward a 'Take no prisoners, make no mistakes, win at all costs' mindset. That's what I was thriving on; everything else was just extraneous. I lived game-to-game, day-to-day. After I got a game under my belt, it was review it, take from it what was positive, analyze the negatives, try to make the corrections, and start looking in the paper to see who you're facing the next time—who's hot, who's getting hits, who's stealing bases—so that by the time I face them I've had four days to prepare."

By 1972, Rube Walker was in his fifth of what would be 14 years as pitching coach for the Mets. I ask Jon how much of an influence Walker played in his early major league development. "Rube said very little, but when he spoke you wanted to listen. Most of the time, all he'd do is remind you when it was your turn to pitch or that it's a good idea to throw more strikes than balls. But there were times when he had something on his mind—maybe he saw something you were doing wrong or thought of something you could do to improve. And I don't know if it was a change in his mood or what it was that gave you a clue, but you just knew that it was time to listen."

Matlack was assigned the locker separating Koosman and Seaver, much to the delight of the rookie. "I learned a lot from both of them. I'll give you an example. I started the 1972 season pitching out of the bullpen because they didn't need a fifth spot in the rotation in April; there were enough off days. So my first two appearances were out of the pen. I ended up winning a game in relief of Gary Gentry for my first major league win. Then I started and won, then I won again, and again, and again. I picked up the *New York Times* one Sunday and turned to the part of the Sports section that carried the pitching statistics. And right there at the top was Jon Matlack with a 6–0 record and 1.95 ERA. I said to myself, 'That can't be; gotta be somebody else.' Seeing me on top of all those others sort of knocked me for a loop. Before you could blink, I was 6–4 and my ERA had climbed up to 3.00.

"Well, I initiated a conversation with Seaver and he took the time to make a point to me. And that point was to accept any and all success that you have earned. If you don't believe you deserve it, you'll give it back. That's exactly what I had done. The subconscious mind had said, 'You don't belong here, son. Fix it.' At least that's the only explanation I have for it. And having coached now for 11, 12 years and seeing other guys going through the same thing, I think it happens a lot. They're doing well, then start thinking, 'Oh, it's just luck; I'm not supposed to be this good.' That's what that little man in your subconscious does unless you condition him to say, 'Hey, this is where we belong; keep fighting, we're gonna stay right here.' So Seaver's advice was a big help. It allowed me to get back on my feet and stop the slide of mediocrity I had been going through."

One of Matlack's pitcher-batter confrontations of 1972 remains among the most memorable of his career. Facing the Pirates in his last start of the season, Jon yielded Clemente's 3,000th and final hit. "It's early in the game. I had thrown five-consecutive fastballs. He fouled a couple off. So I've got him two-and-two and I'm thinking, 'If you drop the curve ball over the outside corner, you got him.' When I throw the pitch I'm instantly disappointed because I know it's not a strike, that's it's gonna be outside.

"So I'm thinking, 'Oh no, now it's three-and-two'—that's the instantaneous thought process because I knew this was a ball. I think initially it may have fooled him because he took his normal stride, but his hands stayed back. He was great at that. He must have recognized the spin and thought, 'Hey, I can do something with this,' and proceeded to one-hop the left-center-field wall with a pitch that wasn't even a strike. An interesting piece of hitting."

According to biographer Bruce Markesun, Clemente complained that there hadn't been sufficient press coverage during his quest to achieve the goal. Based on the sparse crowd of 13,000 at Three Rivers Stadium that day, and from listening to Matlack, Clemente's criticism may have been warranted. "When I gave up the hit, I had no idea it was his 3,000th. None. I'm thinking, 'What's going on around here? This is a stinking double.' The crowd is standing and cheering. The umpire's handing Clemente the ball at second base and I'm standing there with my arms crossed glowering at him like, 'Give me the baseball. We're trying to play a game here.'

"Anyway, somebody took a picture from the dugout of me with the umpire handing the ball to Clemente in the background. A couple of days later, that photo was sent to me in the clubhouse. It came from one of the clubhouse kids, but I'm assuming Clemente sent it.

"When you're going through the competition, trying to win a ballgame is all that matters in the world. Clemente's death just brings the importance of other things to the forefront very quickly. He was a great player, and from what I knew of him he was a dynamite individual. Baseball and the world lost that day."

During the next two seasons, Matlack accumulated an unimpressive combined record of 27–31, yet his ERA of 3.20 in 1973, and 2.41 in 1974 indicate his pitching effectiveness had not deteriorated. "Wins and losses don't always reflect the other numbers, and that was true for those two seasons. I guess I was frustrated to some degree, but my mindset was, 'Keep my team in the ballgame for as long as I'm out there.' I didn't have control over the outcome in any other way. So if I came away from a game and felt I had given everything and got beat 3–2, I still slept okay and could look myself in the eye while I was shaving and not think of slicing my throat. (Jon laughs.)

"It was that mindset that kept me floating those two years. Maybe not so much in '73 when I was pitching sort of like a yo-yo—good for a while and not so good for another period—but especially in '74 when I pitched great all year and still had a losing record. A guy did a statistical analysis once. I don't know if it's the same guy from Sports Data Network who now does all the stats for baseball. But he said that I was the best pitcher in baseball that year. I was 13–15, but if I recall correctly I lost eight games by one run and in 34 starts there were only three where I allowed more than three runs. He said that based on the average of runs scored by Cincinnati and Oakland that year, if I had played for them I would have been 31–3. Of course, it may not have turned out that way, but I found it really interesting."

Matlack was fortunate to have pitched a full season in 1973. Facing a bases-loaded seventh-inning situation against the Atlanta Braves on May 8th, he was trying to maintain a 3–2 lead when he was struck in the head by a batted ball. Jon displays exceptional recall of the incident. "Marty Perez is at bat. Two–two count. I throw a curve ball which is not a strike—right down the heart of the plate but low. He made an effort to check his swing. I thought he went too far and so did a few other people in the infield because they're yelling at the umpire, 'That's a swing!' He says no, and checks with the umpire at first base, Billy Williams, and he says no.

"So now it's three–two, and in an effort to get out of this mess, I went to overthrowing the baseball and landed too hard and lost sight of the ball as it traveled to the plate. So I don't pick it up when Perez swings. I can see him swing, hear the crack of the bat, but don't pick up the baseball.

Very eerie feeling. I finally pick it up when the ball was maybe as far away from me as the television is here [approximately eight feet away]. I was able to get my bare hand in front of it, and it tipped my fingers and hit the brim of my hat and hit me right there [Jon points to the middle of his forehead]."

"The ball caromed all the way to the dugout, so they told me afterwards. Ken Boswell got it. As for me, it was like somebody set a flash bulb off in my head. There was a bright flash and I thought, 'Wow, you got hit, better lie down.' And I just lay down and waited for the trainer. By the time he got there, I could look up and see my forehead—it had swollen up to that point. I had a 36-hour headache, but other than that I was all right. Well, except for the fact that I had a fractured skull."

In reporting the incident the next day, one newspaper compared it to the Herb Score accident of 1957, with pictures of Score and Matlack appearing side-by-side. Reading the article and learning of the Score tragedy for the first time made Matlack somewhat uneasy. "I thought, 'Wow, this is scary.' But I'm trying to tell myself that we got hit in different places. Score was hit in the eye and mine came off my forehead. So I'm kind of rationalizing why I wouldn't be affected psychologically like Score was. But I was worried about how I would react my next time out.

"Well, I pitched eleven days later. I had to wear a protective band on my forehead. Had to wear it for eight weeks until my skull had a chance to heal completely. The doctor said if I didn't wear it and got hit again, it would be curtains. I was a nervous wreck before the game. My concern was how I'd react if a ball was hit in my direction. Would I blink, flinch, would something I had no control of take place? I don't think there were any plays that I had to make that day, but there were numerous balls hit in my direction to short and second that never caused me any sense of ducking or blinking. Out of that experience, I knew I was okay. There was never another thought about it."

Matlack believes the likelihood of getting struck with batted balls and the potential for more serious injuries is greater for today's pitchers. "The ball is juiced, the hitters are stronger, the pitchers are throwing inside less frequently. Hitters are more dominant than they were in the sixties and seventies, for a number of reasons. Well, don't get me started on that subject. It's ridiculous what happens to the inside part of the plate and how wide they make the outside part. That leads to hitters' extension and an increase in balls going up the middle.

"As part of my job now, I sit behind the stands and read the radar guns. I've seen the gun pick the ball up coming off the bat instead of out of the pitcher's hand, and how a ground ball to shortstop is 106. What's a line drive gonna be? And you figure that by the time a pitch is delivered, a pitcher's distance is somewhere in the vicinity of 55 feet from home plate and by the time the hitter makes contact, the ball is actually in front of home plate, so that you're talking about 51 or 52 feet of actual distance between the struck ball and the pitcher, with the ball traveling at least 100 miles an hour. Not good odds."

One potential major league modification frightens Matlack. "What really is an issue is the aluminum bats they use in college. They better not think of using them in the majors, unless they are engineered to react more like wood. While I was playing, we used to play exhibitions against college teams and they would use their aluminum bats, but we pitchers had enough superior skill—location, velocity—so that we didn't really feel threatened by them. But give those bats to hitters with equal skill? Well, if they had ever legalized those things when I was playing, I would have retired."

In 1973, the Mets returned to post-season play for the first time in four years and met Cincinnati in the NLCS. The Reds prevailed 2-1 in the opener, with right-hander Jack Billingham besting Seaver at a pecked Riverfront Stadium. Seaver fanned 15 Reds batters, but solo home runs by Johnny Bench and Pete Rose provided the difference. "Seaver pitched a whale of a ballgame. I sat there and charted that thing. Made two pitches that—I'm not even gonna call them mistakes—but were maybe not quite where they should have been. Both were home runs. So I'm looking at the chart after the game, knowing I'm facing the Reds the next day. I'm thinking, 'This is about as good as it gets by a guy who's as good as any pitcher can be, and he still came up short.' It gave me a greater sense of resolve to not allow anything to stand in my way of winning."

That resolve translated into a brilliant two-hit, 5-0 shutout over a ballclub labeled "Big Red Machine" for its exceptional success in producing runs. The only safeties surrendered by Matlack were "seeing-eye" hits between short and third by part-time outfielder Andy Kosko. "Why couldn't he have been on the bench that day? (Jon laughs.) There are two things that stand out about that game. My family had come and they put them way up in the boondocks. We're talking third tier. Way up there.

"The other thing that stands out is something Rusty Staub told me during the game. Don Gullett, who is now the Reds' pitching coach, was pitching that day. As tough a lefty as there was back then. Well, Staub was the world's best at finding something a pitcher did to tip off what was coming. Early in the game he told me, 'I've got Gullett. I know what he's throwing. I'm gonna get him sometime today. Just keep the game close.' That kept me going all game long. Knowing sometime during the game Staub was coming through. We scraped up an early run, and I kept pitching and kept waiting. I'd get three outs, come into the dugout, figure out if Rusty was gonna bat that inning, and watch to see what happened. Then late in the game Rusty hit a three-run home run. He came into the dugout, came up to me and said, 'I told you! I told you!'"

The Mets spanked the Reds in Game Three, remembered today mostly for a bench-emptying brawl ignited by a hostile slide by Rose into shortstop Bud Harrelson. Charlie Hustle exacted revenge the next day in the form of a 12th inning game-winning homer, but Mets fans had the last laugh when their heroes took the series the following afternoon. "I think our ballclub was definitely motivated by the Rose slide and the fight that followed. Harrelson was one of the key figures on the ballclub, from somewhat of an inspirational leader to one hell of a defensive shortstop. He wasn't a particularly big guy and had taken a number of shots during the course of the season from guys trying to break up double plays. I think the fight with Rose was a situation that had gradually built up in Bud's mind; you know, he's thinking, 'I've had enough of this, this is the last straw.'

"The hard slide by Pete is just the way he plays all the time, regardless of the score or the importance of the game. I think if it had been anyone else, nothing would have happened. But Pete became the John Rocker of '73. They hated him in New York."

I ask Jon for his opinion of Rose's ban from baseball. "Before I give an opinion, I want to qualify it by stating that I am not as knowledgeable about the topic as I should be to comment on it. Having said that, at the time the rules were devised nobody realized that gambling was a disease. Maybe that should be taken into account. Look at the guys that have drug and alcohol problems. How many chances do they have to go through rehab and come back and play again? It's almost never-ending in some instances. If alcohol and drug users weren't considered people who are afflicted with a disease, maybe they would be banned for life as well. So I have a sense that the rule imposing a lifetime ban on players who gamble should be changed—not so much for Pete's sake, but because we now recognize that gambling can be a disease; and in recognizing it as a disease, we should put it on the same block as drug and alcohol abuse in terms of the way we treat and punish those who are afflicted.

"As for whether Pete should be in the Hall of Fame, hands down he has the statistics, but based on the letter of the law at the time Pete broke the rule, and the facts in the Dowd report, if the report is correct, I would say he doesn't qualify. His biggest problem may be that he still doesn't admit what he did."

It has been six months since the Rose issue resurfaced during the 1999 World Series, when NBC's Jim Gray rankled television viewers by displaying an aggressive, even contentious, posture in a pre-game interview with a seemingly beleaguered Rose. Matlack offers his thoughts. "There was no excuse for the way he handled the interview. To me, that was an absolute atrocity. I was sitting here watching it live, and I'm thinking, 'Please don't hit him, Pete.' I don't think I would have showed as much self-control. I know I wanted to hit him from here. That was ridiculous. Maybe there's a time and place for those questions, but that was definitely not the time and place—a celebratory atmosphere, in the middle of honoring the greatest players of all time, Pete being among them. Totally inappropriate. And it was like a vendetta, like, 'I'm going to force you to say something right now.' Just wasn't pretty."

With Seaver having pitched the decider against the Reds, Matlack was selected by Met manager Berra to start the opener of the World Series against Oakland. The lefty lost a 2–1 heartbreaker, with both A's runs being unearned. "Both were scored on a ball that Felix Millan catches every day of the week but that day didn't catch. And I allowed Kenny Holtzman, a pitcher who hadn't hit all year, to hit a double. That's something else that shouldn't have happened. Somehow he hit a ground ball between [Wayne] Garrett and the third base bag. But the loss wasn't devastating. It was more like, 'We're certainly not outclassed, we're certainly not overmatched. Let's go out and get them tomorrow.'"

The Mets rebounded 10–7 the next day, then lost another nail-biter in New York. Matlack started and won Game Four; he was removed from the game after eight innings despite holding a 6–1 lead. "I wasn't surprised or upset when Yogi took me out. It was a cold night in New York and we had the game well in hand. There's no reason to think that I should have stayed in."

Labeling Berra as "good people," Matlack claims he enjoyed playing for the skipper who had an easy-going, hands-off approach. "He left you alone, expected you to do your work. When he came to the mound, a lot of times he didn't speak loudly or clearly enough to make sense but you knew that if he didn't hold out his hand, you just said, 'Okay, Yogi,' and he'd go back to the dugout and you were still pitching. If he did put out his hand, you put the ball in it and you'd be the one going back to the dugout. He was the kind of guy who'd go, 'Here's the bats and balls, fellas, go play.' He wasn't a big strategist, didn't have a lot of complicated plays. He just wanted you to play sound, fundamental baseball and go out there and win."

I ask Jon to recall any amusing remarks or incidents involving Berra that might be classified as "Yogiisms." He mentions two. "I remember I needed to make a phone call in the airport, and back then you couldn't get a dial tone without putting a coin in the phone. I had no change and Yogi happened to be right there. I said, 'Yogi, got a quarter? I've gotta call my wife.' Something happened to the flight schedule so I wanted to let her know. My thought was that I'd get a dial tone, call her collect, and get the quarter back. Yogi gave it to me with the remark, 'I want this back!' Which I thought was kind of comical. (Jon laughs.)

"There was another time, we were coming from the airport late at night and Yogi hollers, 'I gotta take a leak. Don't let the bus leave without me!' I was sort of laughing about it because he's the manager. How the heck are they gonna leave without the manager? But I say, 'Okay Yog, I'll tell 'em.' So I go to the bus and yell out to wait for Yogi, that he went to the bathroom. So Yogi comes out and one of his pants legs is soaking wet. Just as wet as it could be. I say, 'Yogi, what happened?' I'm thinking maybe he missed or something, or maybe he tried to wash his hands and it splashed all over him. He says, 'You wouldn't believe this.' He tells me how he was taking a leak and this guy comes in and starts taking a leak next to him. And as this guy is standing there, he looks over and says, 'Hey, aren't you Yogi Berra?' And as he says it, he turns. I'll let you figure out the rest. (Jon laughs.) Is that a classic or what? Oh man!"

Jon reflects fondly on his times with the Mets and claims camaraderie among teammates was still strong at that time. "Would we all go our separate ways after a game? The game was gravitating toward that, but it hadn't got there yet. We spent a lot of time in groups—on the road, and sometimes at home. We'd go out to have a couple of drinks or a sandwich, go out to dinner, maybe go out on the golf course, maybe have a barbecue at home on an off day with wives and families, that type of thing.

"I think as the game progressed and salaries increased, guys developed entourages—agents, money managers. It's become a full-time job to take care of these million-dollar salaries, so there is less time to spend with other guys. I think the game has suffered because of it. I learned a tremendous amount sitting around Fisherman's Wharf in San Francisco with Cleon Jones, Don Clendenon, Seaver, Koosman, and Harrelson. Having a nice dinner, talking baseball after a game. I was young, sort of the low man on the totem pole, but was never excluded. I probably didn't have as much to say as everybody else, but I listened and picked up some valuable information. I don't know that guys today aren't getting it, but you don't see that happening as much now."

In 1975 and 1976, Matlack had a combined 33–22 record, but when his record sank to 7–15 in 1977 he suddenly became expendable. Wary of providing help to an adversary, the Mets looked to the American League and finalized a deal in December, sending Matlack to Texas in exchange for Willie Montanez. "I guess you can say the kiss of death was buying a house. All the guys told me, 'Buy a house and you get traded.'

"I bought a house up in Westchester—out in the country, four acres in the woods, just a wonderful spot, and it was about fifty miles from Shea Stadium. Well, we had a three-year plan to take this house and make out of it what we wanted, and we were able to do those things because I wasn't traded until three years later. So we add a fireplace, put a room in the basement, finish off a room over the garage that was adjacent to the master bedroom. Some of the work I did myself, some I hired out. The last project was a nice screened-in porch in the back. Well, I had just finished the second coat of paint on the porch and was down in the basement cleaning the brushes when my wife hollers down, 'Joe McDonald's on the phone for you.' When I heard that, there was some thought in the back of my mind that it might be about a trade."

A gray cat named Babe interrupts Matlack by leaping on his lap for some loving attention. Its purring is audible as Jon strokes it while intimating another reason for the Mets wanting to unload him that winter. "I had popped off during the season about wanting the club to do something to bolster us. It was a heat-of-the-moment thing and I probably shouldn't have said it. There were a couple of comments afterwards like, 'If you don't want to be here, we can always trade you.' My response was, 'That's not what I said. What I said was that I want to be here, but I would like to have a little help.' Anyway, I pick up the phone extension, not really knowing what it's all about but sort of supposing. He says, 'I have good news and bad news. The good news is that we've got Willie Montanez. The bad news is that we traded you to get him.'" (Jon laughs.)

Feeling tentative about playing in a different league with different hitters and a different style of play, Matlack adjusted quickly with 15 wins and a major league runner-up 2.27 ERA. Although his success faltered in the subsequent five years, Matlack reflects on his time in the junior circuit with satisfaction. "It was a good experience. Even though the National League style of play was much better, hands down, than the American League, I enjoyed my time in Texas. We had a decent ballclub. There was one year when we ended up a half-game out of first when the strike occurred."

Matlack's career ended following the 1983 season. "Was I released?" Jon echoes my question. "Oh boy, was I released. (Jon laughs.) It's just that there were so many notices—I got the phone call, I got the telegram, I got the certified letter. I don't know how many ways they're supposed to do it, but I got lots of them. Just didn't want me to miss the opportunity to get this wonderful news. What made it more weird is that it happened on Halloween. You know, nice trick or treat.

"I still had to be paid by the Rangers for another two years, but I tried contacting ballclubs the next spring. All I wanted was the minimum salary, which I think at that point was $40,000, if you can believe it. I contacted a few clubs and got a few responses like, 'Come to spring training; if we like what we see, we'll give you a contract.' I came back with, 'I've been in the big leagues for 12 years. I can still pitch. Give me a contract. The worst it's gonna cost you is $40,000.' Nobody was willing to do that."

Having served as player representative, Matlack believes lingering bitterness by the Rangers front office over his role during the 1981 strike led to off-the-field whispers in 1983 that would explain the lack of interest in the 33-year-old pitcher. "Somehow, I found out that the word on the street was my arm wasn't sound. I'm not sure how that rumor started, or if there ever was such a rumor. It's all innuendo, second-hand information, after-the-fact. But I have a strong suspicion that being involved as I was with the '81 situation had a direct bearing on that false rumor being spread.

"The thing that upsets me more than anything about that rumor is that during my players rep work in the '81 season, I went to Mr. [Eddie] Chiles, owner of the Rangers, and told him up front, 'This is the job that I have. It's gonna require me to do certain things. I'd be doing the same if I was on your side. I want you to understand that it's nothing between you and me. It's just something I need to do.' He gave me a song-and-dance about how he respected me for coming to see him, but I wonder now how much of that was legit. Again, nothing to base my suspicions on, no real feelings about it. I'm just saying that there's things that have come back to me over the years—people who have seen me at meetings that mentioned, gee, this was said or that it was him who said it. You put some of these things together and say to yourself, 'Maybe you can make a case for it.' Bottom line is it doesn't matter what the reason was. My career was over."

Jon talks about the turmoil of the early eighties that actually made him somewhat glad to be out of baseball. "There were some weird things going on. The commissioner was worried about drugs and player behavior and that kind of stuff. They supposedly had special squads of guys running around, keeping tabs and eavesdropping on players as they were out and about.

"One time, I was in the [Toronto] locker room when the Royal

Canadian Mounted Police came and put handcuffs on Fergie Jenkins and took him out for supposedly having some illegal substance in his suitcase that was seized by customs when we went into Canada. I never used to concern myself with what happened with my equipment bag or that it didn't have a lock on it when it was sent out, but it got to the point where I wanted to pack my own stuff and lock my bag because I didn't want somebody else putting something in it. So I can't say I was too disappointed when my career ended. I still liked the competition but some of the things that were going on were a little unsettling."

Following his retirement from baseball, Matlack remained in Texas, living on a ranch with wife Diane, "raising kids and horses." He supplemented his still-incoming Rangers salary and horse-selling income by working as a commercial real estate salesman. Jon became discontented in his new profession. "The more I got involved, the more I found that life in those areas was very gray. Baseball had been a very black-and-white existence. It was either fair or foul, a strike or a ball. There was no, 'It'll be a strike if you do this for me this time, it'll be a ball if you don't,' which was what I was finding in real estate—'Don't tell him about something that colors the value of the property; if he buys it, we'll slide you this over here or do this deal for you over there.' It wasn't really crooked, but it wasn't Kosher either. I was becoming very disgruntled. I wanted things to stand on their own merit; didn't want to feel indebted in any way or make my living saying, 'Okay, do this for me this time and next time I'll bail you out.'"

While involved in real estate, Jon maintained his interest in baseball, watching Rangers games on television with his son Danny, or taking him to Arlington Stadium. In doing so, Matlack perceived a decline in the skills of big leaguers. "I'd see guys doing things that I was taught not to do in A ball. It became apparent that maybe I had something to offer. I talked to Diane and asked what she thought about my becoming a coach. I told her we'd be taking a hit because coaching doesn't make much money, but if she didn't have a problem with it I'd like to give it a try. She said fine."

Matlack made inquiries, landed a job with San Diego, and remained in its farm system from 1988 to 1992, working in rookie ball in Arizona, Class A ball in Riverside, California, Double A in Wichita, Kansas, and finally in Triple A in Las Vegas the last two years. "Then the Padres had a change of ownership. The new people that came in swept everybody out, so I was fired."

The White Sox hired him immediately, and Matlack coached in Sarasota, Florida, in 1993, and moved with the Class A club when it transferred to Alexandria, Virginia, the following season. When Randy Smith and Steve Labratich returned to the San Diego front office in 1995, they summoned Matlack, who rejoined his former club in Las Vegas. Smith and Labratich moved to Detroit in 1996, and brought Matlack with them, where he was promoted to pitching coach of the Tigers. Jon lasted one year. "Existence at the major league level is ridiculous for a coach. You make nothing and get blamed for everything. You're allowed to make no decisions but you carry the load if somebody else's decisions don't look good."

Jon Matlack chats from his home in Norwich, New York.

In 1997, Jon was given the position he still holds today. "As the minor league coordinator, I have a lot more autonomy. Generally speaking, I run the pitching in the minors. I answer to a few people, but as long as I keep them posted with what's happening and which guys are making progress, they'll leave me alone to do my job. That's just the way I like it. Like it very much. Even got a business card! Exciting stuff!" (Jon laughs as he gives me a card.)

Jon says that encounters with former teammates or players are relatively rare these days, but on the few occasions they meet, it is just like old times. "It's kind of weird. I'll see them around once in a while, run into a guy at a BAT dinner or golf tournament who I haven't seen in five, ten years and (Jon snaps his fingers) there's the instant connection.

"For example, Seaver. I heard about his induction into the Hall and read about it in the papers. Hadn't seen or talked to him in quite a while. I thumbed through my phone book wondering if his number was still good. I called him up, he answered the phone, and we talked for hours. Just crazy the way things happen sometimes. You know, there doesn't seem to be any purposeful attempt to make contact with each other, but whenever contact is made, usually by happenstance, it's like no time has passed."

The ring of Jon's cell phone distracts our attention. After answering, he informs us that it was the high school coach of a young local prospect named Mick James with whom Jon had previously worked; the coach was inviting Matlack for another look-see. The conversation concludes with Jon's talking fondly of daughters Kristen and Jennifer, son Jonathan Daniel or "Danny," and Diane, who "has worked as a labor and delivery nurse for some time" and who had been called to the hospital earlier in the day for assistance with a childbirth. Jon leads us to his den containing baseball memorabilia. A half-hour later, he escorts us to our car, thanks us for coming, and invites us to return.

ON THE PHONE

For players living too distant to make in-person interviews feasible, or for those preferring conversations by telephone, arrangements were made accordingly. The conversations were generally shorter than in-person interviews—averaging a half-hour in length. In general, discussion focused less on personal history than on memorable events involving the interviewee, teammates, and opponents. Readers may note that some comments include reflections on ballplayers who met with tragic ends—Roberto Clemente, Thurman Munson, Lyman Bostock, Bob Moose, Don Wilson, Harry Agganis—while still active.

Enjoy.

Catfish Hunter

"When I signed with the A's in 1964 out of high school, Mr. [Charles] Finley asked me if I had a nickname," recalls 52-year-old Hall-of-Famer Catfish Hunter in March of 1998 from his home in Hertford, North Carolina. "I told him no. He said, 'What do you like to do?' I told him I like to hunt and fish. He kind of hesitated for a minute, and then he said, 'Well, when you were six years old, you ran away from home and went fishing. Your mom and dad looked for you all day and by four o'clock they found you. By then, you had caught two catfish and were bringing in a third one. Now, repeat it for me.' That's how I got my nickname."

Reggie Jackson and Hunter played together with the A's and later with the Yankees. "Reggie bothered some teammates by talking too much. But he didn't mean anything by what he was saying. When Reggie started talking in an interview, you could come back 15 minutes later, pick it right up, and never miss nothing. I always told Reggie, 'You're the Muhammed Ali of baseball. You can talk, but you can back it up. You can play baseball.'"

Hunter explains the origin of the feud between teammates Jackson and Thurman Munson. "After I signed with the Yankees, Munson had in his contract that nobody else could make more money than him. When Reggie came over, he asked Reggie how much he was making because he was supposed to be getting at least one more dollar than Reggie. Reggie would never tell him. Management probably told Reggie not to tell. That's the only reason Thurman and Reggie never got along."

Munson's strategy of indirectly reprimanding lazy Yankees reminds Hunter of former A's teammate Sal Bando. "Sal would do the same thing. He would come to me and say, 'How about getting on so-and-so on the bus trip today?' I'd say, 'What do you want me to get on him for?' He'd say, 'No, I'm gonna get on you. Then he will say something, and then both of us can get on him.' That's what Thurman would do. He'd get on somebody else, waiting for that one person to jump in, and that's when everybody would tell him what we thought real quick. We used to call it 'corrective criticism.'"

More Munson memories. "If Thurman didn't like you, he wouldn't say nothing to you. If he liked you, he would say everything about you—how bad your shoes look, how bad your necktie was, how you walked, how you slept—everything. Some of the young guys coming up would say, 'Why is he getting on me?' I'd say, 'He's not on you. He likes you. That's the reason he's talking about you.'"

In 1979, Munson was killed while flying his jet near Canton, Ohio. Hunter recounts how he learned of the tragedy. "I was at my home in Norwood, New Jersey. I was doing something in the yard, and my wife called me in and said that Mr. Steinbrenner wanted to talk to me. He told me that Munson died. When he hung up, I ran across the street to tell [Graig] Nettles about it. He said, 'Okay, what's the punch line?' He couldn't believe it either. Neither could Gene Michael. He lived near us, too."

On the day following his funeral, the Yankees won an emotional game against the first-place Orioles, with Munson's close friend and eulogist Bobby Murcer playing hero by driving in all five Yankee runs with a three-run homer and a ninth inning, game-winning, two-RBI single. Says Hunter, "The main thing is that we remembered afterwards what Munson did and what he meant to the Yankees, and how good a friend he was to us."

Hunter's first manager with the Yankees was former Pirate outfielder Bill Virdon. "Virdon was the type of guy who would take his shirt off and flex his muscles at you, and tell you to do this or do that. Which I loved. Personally, I thought he was a good manager. A lot of the other guys who played for him didn't like him. They said he thought he was better than the players. I would say, 'Yeah, but he's always got his door open. If you don't like something, he wants you to go in there and tell him.'"

As with any conversation with the tongue-in-cheek Tarheel, there are light-hearted moments. "One day, No-Neck Williams went to Virdon and said, 'Skip, why ain't I playing?' Virdon said, 'No-Neck, you can't hit a curve ball, and every pitcher today has a curve ball.' No-Neck said, 'I can hit 'em, Skip, I can hit 'em!' Virdon said, 'Okay, come out early tomorrow. We'll take a little batting practice and see.'

"Well, I'm always out at the ballpark early anyway, so the next day I'm shagging fly balls in the outfield and I see Virdon throwing to No-Neck. And, I'm telling you, No-Neck's rapping ropes everywhere. Then Bill stops, wipes the sweat off him, holds up the ball, and says to No-Neck,

'Curve ball.' He throws him eight-straight curve balls and No-Neck ain't even fouled one off yet. Everybody could die laughing. Couldn't believe it. Finally, Bill says, 'See, Walt. You can't hit a curve ball.' Walt says, 'Yeah,' and walks on into the clubhouse. He told me he was so embarrassed he didn't know what to do. But he still said, 'I know I can hit a curve ball. But Virdon's curve always comes in there spinning. I couldn't hit it to save my life.'"

Another Virdon anecdote. "I remember Sparky Lyle, Fred Stanley, and Ed Herrmann were gonna use a coffin to make a bar to put in the back of a van. And we had the coffin sitting right in the middle of the clubhouse at Shea Stadium. [Yankee Stadium was being renovated.] So we're having a meeting and all of a sudden, Virdon looks around and says, 'Where's Sparky?' Just like it was made in a movie, the top of the casket opens up—*squeeeak*. And Sparky's in there, with black stuff all under his eyes, and he sits up and says, 'You rang, Skip?' We all fell right down on the floor, laughing."

Yet another Virdon story. "Once, Pat Dobson was taken out of a ballgame and he didn't want to come out. He told a writer that the next time Bill Virdon comes to the mound, it was gonna take a tow truck to get him off, cause he wasn't leaving. The next day, we had a meeting. Virdon's walking around with no shirt on. Then he points straight at Dobson and says, 'And you, Mr. Dobson. It if takes a tow truck to get you off the mound, for sure, get one. But (pause) I (pause) don't (pause) think (pause) I'll (pause) need (pause) one! Do you, Mr. Dobson?' Nobody didn't say nothing, but I was laughing again."

Billy Martin took over the Yankee helm in 1975 and quickly gained Hunter's respect. "Martin was always one step ahead of the other managers because he knew what he was going to do before it happened. When it happened—bang—he made the move right away. He didn't have to ask anybody. That's the reason he won so many games."

Toward the end of the conversation, I inquire about Hunter's health. Three injections of insulin are required daily to control his diabetes, a duty performed since 1977. I casually ask about his ailing right arm and shoulder which forced him to a premature retirement from baseball in 1979 at the age of 33. A pause, then his altered tone, are clues that it is a worrisome topic. "I got my arm operated on last year and I was hoping I'd be able to pitch against my son in a high school game on Mother's Day this year," Catfish says. "But I've been noticing for the last month that something is wrong with my hand, that it feels numb. They say it may be a pinched nerve. I have to go back this week to find out if I need another operation."

It is no pinched nerve. By early November of 1998, doctors at Johns Hopkins Medical Center in Baltimore diagnosed Hunter's problem as the fatal amyotrophic lateral sclerosis, more familiarly known as Lou Gehrig's Disease, named for the player who, aware that he was doomed, proclaimed himself the luckiest man alive in front of 60,000 Yankee Stadium spectators. A paralyzed Gehrig died two years later.

Statistics provided by the Amyotrophic Lateral Sclerosis Association indicate that two out of every 100,000 Americans die annually from ALS, a rate comparable to that of the more notorious multiple sclerosis; that 300,000 living today will eventually die from ALS; and that life expectancy ranges from ten years following diagnosis to less than two. The most startling stat is the financial cost to families, which can reach as high as $200,000 annually. The drug Ritulek, developed early in the decade, prolongs life an average of three months. Other drugs offer hope, but are not yet approved by the FDA.

"In the clubhouse, they still had his uniform hanging in his locker," Hunter recalled about the game following Munson's death. "It was like we still didn't really believe that he was gone, that the first thing you know, he was gonna come back and be sitting there near his locker and start yelling at us or say something funny to us. It was unbelievable."

Tragedies are unbelievable, but they happen. So do miracles. I hoped there would be one for Hunter, but it was not to be. On September 9, 1999, less than one year following diagnosis, Hunter succumbed to ALS. Prior to the game against Boston at Yankee Stadium the next day, his former club paid tribute with a moment of silence. Longtime public-address announcer Bob Sheppard proclaimed, "Jim Hunter was more than a Hall of Fame pitcher. He was a Hall of Fame human being." Yankee ballplayers wore black armbands below the number five they had been wearing to honor Joe DiMaggio, who had passed away earlier in the year. Manager Joe Torre echoed the sentiments of all Hunter fans by stating, "We knew it was coming, eventually, but we didn't expect it so soon."

The world and baseball's loss is heaven's gain. Today, God is probably cracking up from one of Catfish's baseball anecdotes or homespun tales.

Fred Patek

The date: October 14, 1976. The setting: historic and newly-renovated Yankee Stadium. It is the top of the eighth inning in the fifth and final American League Championship Series. Exhilaration permeates the stands as over 55,000 spectators anticipate a glorious finish to the season, while pinstriped players are cautiously optimistic. In the visiting dugout, desperation displaces disquietude, as six outs are all that separate the Royals from a depressing flight to winter homes.

The flash of George Brett's bat ignites a dramatic mood swing as lefty reliever Grant Jackson's pitch sails into the right-field seats, scoring Brett and two teammates to tie the game. Not having witnessed a World Series appearance by the most successful sports team in history since 1964, Yankee fans lean back and anticipate the worst, while Royals players are aroused and upbeat. New York fails to score in the bottom of the inning, but mustachioed reliever Dick Tidrow forestalls doom for the Bombers with a scoreless stint in the top of the ninth.

Unprepared for a happy ending, fans are given one in a most unexpected and splendid fashion in the bottom frame as Chris Chambliss sends the first pitch thrown by reliever Mark Littell soaring above the outstretched arm of the leaping Amos Otis and over the right-center-field fence. As exuberant shrieks of acclamation reverberate throughout the ballpark, the Yankee hero battles his way around the bases past a gauntlet of backslapping trespassers and requires a police escort to the clubhouse. Meanwhile, despondency pervades the Kansas City bench as stunned players observe the mayhem on the field. To television viewers, one Royal is conspicuously grief-stricken. With his hands over his head, his face buried between his legs, Fred Patek sits sobbing.

Twenty-two years later, Patek reflects on the stadium conditions preceding Chambliss' epic blast, which remains the only home run to end a league championship series. "Just before the bottom of the ninth, there was a lot of commotion in right field," the 54-year-old former shortstop states from his Blue Springs, Missouri, home in March of 1998. "The game was delayed for about five or six minutes while they were picking up toilet paper, coke bottles, and all kinds of stuff. It was cold that night in New York, so Buck Martinez [manager] was yelling to Mark Littell, our pitcher, to take some warm-up throws while we waited. Well, it was noisy, and Mark can't hear out of one ear, so he didn't hear Buck. After the commotion, Mark throws the first pitch to Chris and he hits it out of the ballpark. I've often wondered, if Mark had thrown about 15 or 20 pitches to stay loose while we were waiting, well, maybe things would have been different."

Heartache followed the Royals for the remainder of the decade, as the Yanks defeated them in the two subsequent league championship series. Says Fred, "I think the loss to the Yankees in 1977 was the toughest for me to take because I really think we were the better club." The final standings support Patek's assertion. Kansas City won 102 games to outdistance runner-up Texas by eight games, while New York's 100 wins nipped second-place Baltimore by two. The Royals' top three pitchers—Dennis Leonard, Jim Colburn, and Paul Splittorff—combined for 54 wins, bettering the 46 by Ed Figueroa, Mike Torrez, and Ron Guidry. Kansas City's team ERA (3.52) was the best in the American League while the relievers combined for a league-high 42 saves. Although the Yanks hit 38 more home runs and had a team batting average (.281) that was four points superior, Kansas City led the majors in doubles and triples, and its 170 stolen bases were 77 more than that of their post-season rival.

The 1977 league championships again went to a deciding fifth and final game, played this time at Royals Stadium. The home team jumped to a 2–0 lead and held a 3–1 edge in the eighth when a Reggie Jackson pinch-single cut the lead in half. Still, the Royals were only three outs away from a World Series in the ninth when disaster struck again. "Paul Blair got the big hit to tie it up," Patek says. "Dennis Leonard, who throws real hard, jammed him with a fastball but Blair hit a broken-bat flair into right-center field." Mickey Rivers singled home the go-ahead run, Lyle breezed through the Royals in the bottom frame, and the Yanks had again whacked the Royals.

The 1977 Yankee lineup included Reggie Jackson, Lou Piniella, Graig Nettles, Roy White and Chambliss. Who did Patek most fear? "If I had to pick one that I didn't like seeing coming up in a clutch situation against us, it would be Thurman Munson. He was a good contact hitter, and a smart hitter. When there were guys on base, and the pitcher was ahead of him in the count, it seemed he would always get a base hit into right-center field to drive in a run.

"Some might have thought that he was too aggressive on the field, but I loved the way he played. I wish more guys played like that today. He came to play baseball the way you're supposed to play. All out. If you have any sense at all, you wind up respecting guys like that, and say, 'All right, go for it! Do it!'

"Munson would always talk to me every time I went to the plate. He'd say something like, 'Are you back up here?' I'd say, 'Yeah, and when I get on I'm gonna steal another base off you. You can't throw me out with that arm you've got.' He'd just laugh. We had a pretty good competition going between us. Whenever I'd steal a base off him, I'd get up, look at him, and laugh. And whenever he'd throw me out, he'd kind of stick his thumb up as if to say, 'Get outta there, I gotcha.' I really thought he was a super-neat guy. One of those type of guys that when you look back years later you say to yourself, 'Boy, I wish I had had the chance to play with him.' Or you say to yourself, 'Yeah, they beat us, but wasn't it great?'"

Although Patek's finest years were spent with Kansas City, his career began in Pittsburgh, debuting on June 3, 1968. He played shortstop until a mishap to the team's top star necessitated his shifting to the outfield. "Clemente got injured. I think he ran into a wall. We were short of outfielders, so I was asked to take over for Robby in right field. I wound up playing there for about three weeks until he got healthy, and he helped familiarize me with the new position by working with me during practice when I was shagging fly balls.

"Clemente had a real good sense of humor. And he was real good in the clubhouse. The players always had a lot of respect for him. Not just for his baseball skills, but also for keeping everybody loose. I always thought he was a leader that way as well. And of course, on the field, when he was hot, he could carry that ballclub. As for the stories about him being a hypochondriac, I never had the impression that Robby was one who tried to stay out of the lineup. And I remember him playing when he was hurt a few times. So I never thought that kind of criticism was ever warranted."

Never a home run hitter, Patek nevertheless belted a pair in the 61 games he played in his rookie season. "Memories are strange. You think about what happened like it was only yesterday, but it also feels like it was a lifetime ago. Like with my first home run. It came off Don Wilson in 1968. It was in Pittsburgh, and he threw me a fastball that was about belt-high, middle of the plate in. I hit it over the 406-foot sign where Bill Mazeroski hit his famous home run that won the Series in 1960. I hit it a long way."

Not bad for a singles hitter, especially considering it came against one of the hardest-throwing right-handers of the sixties and seventies. Fred laughs, "Yeah, he was pretty intimidating for a guy standing at the plate at five-feet, five-inches. Wilson really threw hard. He reminded me of Bob Gibson. He was tall and imposing and his fastball really got up there quick."

One of Patek's closest Buc teammates was former right-hand hurler Bob Moose, a reliable ten-year man for the ballclub. Moose is remembered for having thrown a no-hitter against the Mets a few days prior to New York clinching its first pennant, for having thrown the wild pitch that ended the 1972 championship series against the victorious Reds, and for his untimely and tragic death in a car crash in 1976 that occurred on his birthday. "Actually, Bobby and I started in the minors together in Gastonia, North Carolina. We lived together there and used to go out every night. I loved the guy, not only because our birthdays were on the same day, October 9. He was a character. Real energetic. Always had a smile. A great personality—outgoing and bubbly, and got along with everybody. And he was a good-looking Italian. You know, with the coal-black hair, dark skin and beard. I mean, a real lady-killer. He was one of those guys who, if a gal looked at a hundred guys in a group, he stood out."

Patek describes Moose's pitching style. "He was a control pitcher. He had good velocity on his fastball—a real heavy fastball that was hard to hit, and he had good movement on it and good location. He had a real good breaking ball and off-speed pitch, too. And he knew how to set up hitters. I don't know who ever taught or worked with him, but he had a real good head on his shoulders. He knew exactly what he wanted to do, and when you played behind him, you always knew he was going to be close to where he was trying to throw the ball. He didn't make a lot of mistakes that hurt him. And he didn't waste time on the mound, which is something I always liked in pitchers. It's difficult for infielders to work behind pitchers that are lethargic because it's hard to get any rhythm to the game.

"You could never tell by looking at him whether Bob won or lost. He did what he did on the mound, and when the game was over he'd forget about it, which I think was another asset that he had. He understood that on some days he was just going to get rocked. On those days, he'd just hope the hitters would make mistakes and let the men on the field do the job for him."

After three seasons with the Bucs, Patek was involved in a six-player swap in December of 1970. It was Clemente that broke the "bad news" to the native-born Texan. "I was playing winter ball in Puerto Rico. Robby was the manager. Davey Cash, Al Oliver, and I were sitting in the clubhouse playing cards. Robby came over next to me and put his leg up on the bench. He said, 'C'mon in. I need to talk with you.' So we went into his office. And it was almost like he was apologizing. He said, 'I have to tell you, I have some bad news. You've been traded to Kansas City.' Well, I was elated because I wasn't playing that much for Pittsburgh and I knew I'd have a better opportunity to play in Kansas City. I jumped up and started yelling, I was so happy."

Thus began Patek's tenure with Kansas City that ended with his trade to California in 1980—the same year the Royals captured their first pennant by defeating the Yankees in a three-game sweep. Although suffering his fair share of heartache, Patek today regrets nothing. He played during a decade of rising salaries. He played with likable and gifted teammates. He was a starting player in over 1,600 regular-season games. He participated in post-season play four times and with two different teams. Despite not possessing a World Series ring, Fred cherishes the memories of a 14-year major league career.

Vernon Law

Vernon Law has little difficulty in selecting his most frustrating pitching assignment in 16 major league seasons. Starting against the Braves in 1955 on only two days rest, the Pirate threw 18 innings—still the most by any hurler since Carl Hubbell's 18-inning shutout in 1933—yet merely earned a no-decision! "I was doing my sprints in the outfield before the game when I heard Murtaugh yell, 'Can you pitch?'" the 69-year-old former ace righthander recalls from his home in West Provo, Utah, in March of 1999.

Pitchers in those days rarely declined opportunities. Law was far from an exception. The Braves scored an early unearned run, but the score was tied at two by the fifth frame. "In the ninth, I was scheduled to hit and Murtaugh asked how I was doing. I told him, 'Skip, I'm fine.' So because I was a pretty good hitter, he let me hit for myself with the game tied." It remained even at two apiece in the bottom half of the twelfth. "It was my turn to hit again and Murtaugh told me, 'Vern, I better take you out.' I said, 'Skip, I'm fine. I'm getting them out one-two-three.' He said, 'Are you sure you're all right?'"

Vern reassured his manager, then worked another three innings. With the score still tied and Law due to bat in the 15th, Murtaugh faced a now-familiar dilemma. "He told me, 'Vern, I gotta take you out. If you ruin your arm, they're gonna run me out of town.' I said, 'Skip, now wait a minute. I've pitched this long, and I feel fine. C'mon. Let me win or lose this thing.' So I guess he felt sorry for me and let me stay in."

Bottom of the 18th. Same score, same situation. "Murtaugh told me, 'That's it. You're out of here. I don't want to hear anything. You've done more than you should have already. If you go on and hurt yourself, it's gonna be me, not you.' So I went into the clubhouse.

"Well, Bob Friend took over. He gave up a run and we trailed 3–2, but we scored two runs in the bottom of the 19th and Bob got the victory. But that's been my story in baseball."

Law relates another hard-luck saga. In 1959, reliever Elroy Face won 17-straight games, two shy of the major league mark for consecutive victories in one season set by Rube Marquard in 1912 (Hubbell won 24-straight from 1936–1937). Face triumphed 18 times that year, also a still-standing record for firemen. According to Law, seven of Elroy's wins might have been his had he been the recipient of a little more hitting support. "Three of them came in a row. In one game, I went seven innings with the score tied and Murtaugh took me out for a pinch-hitter. Elroy relieved me, pitched two innings, and got the victory. The next time out, I went eight innings with the score tied. We had men on first and third with one out. Again Murtaugh used a pinch hitter for me and the batter hit into a double play. Face relieved and got the victory.

"In my next start, we had the bases loaded with no outs, and I said to myself, 'There is no way I'm gonna lose this sucker.' Well, the pinch-hitter popped out, the next batter hit into a double play, and that was it for me again. Face relieved, pitched one inning, and got the win.

"The next day, I threw batting practice. Normally, the pitcher doesn't touch the ball the day after a start. I got out there and started firing, just cutting her loose. Murtaugh didn't say anything to me. He just let me work it off."

Bad breaks notwithstanding, Law had many satisfying moments in the majors. He was among the Pirate celebrants after Mazeroski's blast in the '60 Series and probably had as much to do with Pittsburgh taking the world championship as any teammate. Despite pitching with an injury, The Deacon was the victor in Games One and Four and was pulled in the sixth inning of Game Seven with a 4–1 lead. "Murtaugh had his mind made up when he took me out," Vern recalls. "He knew I had pitched the whole Series on a bad ankle and might have thought I was losing a little on my fastball. I felt strong, but there was no changing his mind.

"But when Murtaugh and I were standing on the mound together, Don Hoak [Buc third baseman] came over. I'll never forget what he said to me: 'Deacon, when you walk off here, you hold your head up. You did a good job for us.' I appreciated that because I was feeling bad, being taken out. I always wanted to finish what I started. Maybe that's because I had no success with relievers coming in to save me.

"Today, not many want to stay in for the full nine. I know I couldn't pitch the way they handle these pitchers. If I'm pitching a good ballgame and the manager comes to the mound in the seventh to take me out, I'm just not giving him the ball. I'd probably be fined more money than I made."

Law injured his ankle prior to the '60 Series, a result of horseplay on the team bus following the pennant-clinching victory against Milwaukee. "During the Series, I couldn't push off on the rubber. I had to use my arm more to get the velocity I needed. It put a strain on my shoulder and I tore the rotator muscle."

Law's impairment persisted for three seasons. "I would rest for ten days, go out and throw five or six innings, but then I couldn't throw again. Finally, about two-thirds into the 1963 season, Murtaugh told me that I should quit because I've had too good a career to try to just hang on. I told him if I wasn't going to have a chance to pitch anymore, I might as well retire.

"I went home and kept working on strengthening my arm. I built it up so that I was strong enough to make a comeback. I called Joe Brown, our general manager, and told him I had every intention of coming back and that if he wanted to give me a contract, fine. If not, I wanted my release so I could sign with someone else. He gave me a 25 percent cut and took a chance with me. At first, it still hurt for me to throw but I stuck with it. And in 1965, I had my best year in major league baseball. I could have won every game that year if I had gotten just a little more support. I started the season losing my first five decisions and my ERA was slightly over 1.00. I went 17-9 and had a 2.15 ERA and won Comeback of the Year Award. To be able to come back and pitch effectively after they said I was through—well, let's just say that was the most satisfying part of my career."

Law remembers teammate Clemente. "There was a lot of prejudice during the 1950s. Black ballplayers couldn't stay at the Warwick Hotel with us or eat in the same restaurant. Roberto didn't let the racism interfere with his playing but it must have bothered him. I heard him being interviewed by Bob Prince once. They were discussing the 1960 season. He said that he never wore his World Series ring because he felt he should have won the MVP that year instead of Groat. I was shocked to hear that. But I guess it really hurt Roberto. Throughout his career, I don't think he felt he ever got his just due.

"Maybe Roberto didn't get the accolades that Mays and others did because he wasn't a desirable interview for newsmen. He didn't speak English very well. But his overall talent was exceptional. He was an adept hitter, he had a great arm, and he could run the bases very well. He was as fast going from first to third as most players who were considered speedsters. And could he run fly balls down. He chased a lot of my mistakes. He made so many clutch catches for me. He would run at full speed with his back to the infield and make an over-the-shoulder catch, then make a great throw back to the infield. He was just very impressive."

Law disputes Clemente's reputation for being temperamental. "Roberto was moody at times, as I suppose we all are. Maybe he had a tendency to show it more than most people. But he certainly wasn't a recluse. Just the opposite, he was outgoing. He had an infectious smile, and a great sense of humor. He liked to pull practical jokes on teammates, particularly Joe Christopher. If you ever have the opportunity to talk to Joe, you'll find out exactly the kind of humor Roberto had. But Roberto got along with all his teammates. You couldn't help but like him. And you knew you had a friend in Roberto."

Known for having an erratic relationship with Murtaugh, Clemente nevertheless liked playing for the Irish skipper, as Law tells it. "Danny gave Roberto more leeway. He let Roberto room by himself, which was unheard of then. Roberto was a bit of an insomniac and that's why he preferred being by himself with no one to disturb him while sleeping. Murtaugh let Roberto plan his own workouts. It's not that Murtaugh was showing favoritism, but he really knew his players. Some needed to be pushed, others needed to be let alone. Murtaugh was my favorite too, even though he took me out of some ballgames that I thought he shouldn't have."

Vern addresses Clemente's notoriety for hypochondria. "It's hard for me to say whether there were times Clemente could have played when he chose to sit out, because he gave so much all the time. But there was a time one season when we were in the heat of a pennant race and he asked out of the lineup for a series against Houston. For what reason I didn't know, and it wasn't for me to ask. Maybe he just wasn't feeling well. He hadn't been hitting Houston pitching very well that year, and there were some comments made in the press about that being the reason for Roberto's not playing."

Law comments on Clemente's death in 1972. "I was coaching at Brigham Young University here in Provo when I heard about the plane crash. His death says a lot about Roberto. He didn't have to be on that plane, but he wanted to give hands-on help."

Prior to coaching at Utah's prestigious university, Law coached a couple of seasons for the Pirates. One of his pitching protégés was a competitive Pennsylvania right-hander named Bob Moose. "There are people blessed with exceptional talent, and there are those who have the desire to excel and make do with what they have. I think Moose falls into the latter category. He knew what he had to do to win. He wasn't overpowering. He had to pitch to spots, to use the changeup, and pitch to hitters' weaknesses. And he was a bulldog-type pitcher. He battled you tooth and nail.

"Moose and I got along very well and he had no problem with listening to my instructions and advice. He even pitched a no-hitter when I was the coach. Of course, during the game I just shut up and let him do his job. The thing about the Moose no-hitter is that there was not one tough play. All the plays were routine."

Vern praises Moose's work ethic and attitude. "He was a regular guy and got along with everybody. He worked hard and did what was asked of him without any complaints. I think he took care of himself enough off the field to be successful on. He didn't blow his chance for a good career like some players I've known."

The interview ends with Law's comments regarding Mazeroski's credentials for the Hall of Fame. "I'm kind of upset with the way they put people in. There are some who deserve to be in there and aren't, and some who are in that don't belong. Maz should be there. He probably saved as many runs with his glove as he drove in. He won the Gold Glove so many times, and he was a good clutch hitter. He was a grind-out ballplayer, and he worked hard at his game."

Law may never make it into Cooperstown, but his penchant for completing starting assignments along with his laudable comeback from a calamitous and presumed career-ending injury by themselves make his lifetime achievement in baseball meritorious. His views regarding current athletes are worth noting. "Sometimes when guys get to the big leagues today, they forget whence they came. They can't handle the money, fame, and position as a major league ballplayer. They become too independent, and they think they can get away with anything."

And that's the Deacon speakin'.

Clem Labine

The fifties are known for being a time of tranquillity and innocence. Entertainment provided by the new medium of television diverted our attention from the nuclear nemesis and racial injustice. We loved Lucy and roared at Ralph Kramden, while Ozzie and Harriet served as parent role models, and the Lone Ranger assured that good ultimately overcomes evil.

And no matter how vehemently Kruschev threatened, Americans still had their national pastime. Baseball supplied the All-American boy in Mickey Mantle, and offered black stars like Willie Mays and Hank Aaron as proof of racial equality, on the ballfield at least. Patriotism was perpetuated with pre-game playing of the National Anthem during telecasts. Broadcasts of World Series games, still played in the sunshine then, were heard in thousands of homes, offices, and stores throughout the country, and through transistor earphones by students seated inconspicuously in the rear of classrooms.

If political and social reform was at a standstill during the fifties, baseball offered some change with integration (although many teams were slow to accept blacks and Hispanics) and the exodus to the west by two of New York's most revered franchises—the Dodgers and Giants. For numerous citizens, however, the century-old sport embodied all that was right with traditional values, and justified political, social, and legal conservatism. Considering the upheaval of the subsequent decade, it is understandable why many of today's Americans over the age of fifty recall with affection the serene fifties. Similarly, considering the revolution in baseball during the sixties and beyond—expansion, artificial surfaces, domed stadiums, the designated hitter, free agency, arbitration, relief specialists, pitch counts, radar guns—it is not surprising that many old-time players and longtime fans refer to the fifties as the finest period in the sport's history.

For five of those glorious years, the World Series meant a Subway Series between the Yanks and Dodgers—the Bronx Bombers vs. the Boys of Summer. And in each season leading up to those climactic clashes, and in several championship games, Brooklyn's Clem Labine played a significant role. Yet, much of the discussion with the 72-year-old former pitcher in March of 1999 centers on his 1960 stint with the Pirates, and on former teammate Clemente. "I didn't really get to know Clemente as well as some of the other Pirates," Labine remarks from his home in Vero Beach, Florida. "But I know he was very vocal in fighting for the people of Puerto Rico, as Jackie [Robinson] had been in fighting for black players. Roberto felt there were a lot of great ballplayers in his country that weren't being recognized or weren't given a chance.

"For the two years I was there, it was hard to get close to Clemente. He would be invited to parties after games, but never attended. But it's not like he disliked his teammates. And he showed a good sense of humor in the clubhouse—hiding your shoes or playing other practical jokes. Joe Christopher was one of his targets. But Joe was kind of easy to egg on."

Labine had been a successful hurler with the Dodgers for ten seasons before being traded to the Tigers (he learned of the swap while pitching a game in Los Angeles), then the Pirates in 1960. I ask how he fared facing Clemente. "I was a low-ball pitcher and didn't give up too many homers to Roberto. I would say I had moderate success against him. But I remember one game in particular that I started against the Pirates. It was a doubleheader and Sal Maglie pitched the other game for the Dodgers. Anyway, I gave up six hits in the ballgame and Clemente got three of them.

"Clemente was a Berra-type hitter. He could hit the pitch out of the strike zone and hit it with a lot of power. He had a unique batting stance and stride. He would step in the bucket once in a while but had great bat control."

Labine selects one modern ballplayer he believes is most comparable to Clemente. "Sammy Sosa. And as good a ballplayer as Sosa is, I would have to say that Clemente was better. He had everything you looked for in a player—ability to hit, run, throw, and he was a good base-stealer. He could get that extra base for you. He was the spark of the ballclub, and a very unselfish player."

Labine doesn't recall any prolonged antagonism between Clemente and manager Murtaugh, teammates, or the press. "For the time I was there, Clemente and Murtaugh got along very well. Of course, I was there at a very good time—in 1960 when we won the Series. Everybody got along then. There might have been a few harsh words between players once in a while, but no major problems.

"Clemente tolerated the press most of the time, but not always. He was a pretty fiery guy but he wasn't the type of person who got all over a reporter for writing something bad about him, like the time they claimed he was sitting out due to injuries that didn't really exist. But for the time I was there, he gave 100 percent all the time."

Labine played for three teams in 1960—the Dodgers, Tigers, and Pirates. The final move to Pittsburgh in June was fortuitous, as he shifted from a club under .500 to one bound for the Series. Appearing in 15 games, all in relief, Labine won his only three decisions while notching an equal number of saves and posting a 1.48 ERA. "It is so different being with a contender than playing on a second-division club. When you're in the chase towards the end of the season your adrenaline is really going through you."

Clem underscores the role played by Murtaugh in steering the Pirate ship toward the flag. "Danny was a very good handler of men. He knew when to give and when to take. But he was the boss on the field and was an old-school manager. He wasn't afraid of his job. He had you play the game the way he wanted it played."

A member of five pennant winners with the Dodgers, Clem notes one similarity between the 1960 Pirates and those Brooklyn teams. "We came from behind so often. We could be down seven runs in the seventh inning and we would come back. So it wasn't the type of club that would quit. That's why I wasn't surprised when we came back against the Yankees in the seventh game of the Series."

During the Series, Labine caught the flu and hurled ineffectively in three relief outings against New York. He decided to rest in the clubhouse during the deciding seventh game, but then changed his mind. "As sick as I was, I left the clubhouse and sat in the bullpen. In Forbes Field, the Pirate bullpen was right near our clubhouse anyway. I knew it was going to be the end of the Series either way and I wanted to watch. That was a good play on my part because I got to see Maz's homer. Like everybody else, I ran toward home plate and started celebrating."

Neither the world championship with Pittsburgh nor the Brooklyn World Series victory in 1955 top Labine's list of greatest achievements. Nor his being a member of six pennant-winning clubs. Nor does his *major league high* 56 victories in relief during the decade of the fifties. Nor his 62 appearances and 47 games-finished in 1956 (both are Brooklyn club records). Nor his 10–0 victory in Game Two of the Dodgers' three-game playoff with the Giants in 1951. Nor his 1–0 ten-inning whitewash of the Yankees in Game Six of the 1956 Series. Not even his being walked twice in one inning in a 1954 game or his three homers as a Brooklyn batter during the 1955 season, anomalies for one regarded as among the worst-hitting pitchers in history. "I would have to say my most satisfying accomplishment was making it to the major leagues. It was what I had dreamed of all my life. Most of us trying to make it had many doubts.

"Remember, at that time we used to come to spring training and there would be 200 pitchers. You used to have to wait in line for an hour to get fed. So your odds of making the big league club were not too good. When you finally make it, and are recognized later by your peers as being a decent ballplayer, it's a thrill."

Among the first pitchers to be recognized as a relief specialist, twice leading National League firemen in victories and saves, Labine nevertheless served as an occasional starter, accumulating a 14–11 career record. "I loved being a starter. And I wouldn't think of looking to the bullpen for help. That would be the last thing on my mind.

"If there is one modern pitcher who reminds me of myself more than anyone it is Orel Hershiser. When I saw him for the first time, I fell in love with him, if you'll pardon the expression. He had that great sinking fastball, and that good curve ball—and a good neck as they say, a bulldog's. He didn't look around for help.

"Everything is so different today. I look at pitchers give up the ball so easily, or see them start looking in the fifth inning when there's a chance for a victory. It's unbelievable. Modern pitching strategy is such baloney. I know they can do wonders with arms today, and I think the care given to pitchers' arms is a good thing. But the coddling is so ridiculous. What I wouldn't give to be a closer today. Go out, pitch one inning, and get a save. Closers in my day were from the seventh inning on. Saves are so much easier to get today."

Not particularly impressed with the assortment of pitches used by modern moundsmen, Clem explains how some are merely variations of those thrown by his contemporaries. "They're not so different. For instance, the split-finger fastball that everybody uses—well, Elroy Face's forkball was practically the same kind of pitch. And he had a lot of success with it."

Following the 1961 season, the unprotected Labine was drafted by the expansion New York Mets, a ballclub notorious for assimilating fading stars during the first half of the decade. Joining Labine were such accomplished old-timers as Gil Hodges, Richie Ashburn, Gene Woodling, Gus Bell, Don Zimmer, and pitcher "Vinegar Bend" Mizell. Labine pitched in mop-up relief for three games, then retired. "I got out because everything started to become the same. Going to the ballpark wasn't a thrill anymore. Even with the bases loaded in a crucial situation, it just wasn't the same—I had done it so often before. I could have hung around a few more years, but I didn't want to do that. For me, when the excitement of competition leaves you it's time to leave the game. But if I hadn't left when I did, the hitters would have made sure I got out sooner or later."

Virgil Trucks

In the twentieth century, twenty major league pitchers threw two or more no-hitters. Among that elite group, only Johnny Vander Meer (1938), Allie Reynolds (1951), Virgil Trucks (1952), and Nolan Ryan (1973) tossed a pair of no-hitters in the same season. Trucks came close to a third two times in 1952, spinning a one-hitter and two-hitter for the Tigers. Labeling the pair of no-hitters his ultimate achievement, the 80-year-old Birmingham native now residing in Punta Gorda, Florida, nevertheless selects a 1938 game with Andalusia of the Class D Alabama-Florida League as his greatest baseball thrill. "It was a fantastic ballgame," Virgil comments in a March 1999 conversation. "The game went on the ticker tape and I still have it in my scrap book."

Playing in front of a home crowd, Trucks held the opposition hitless through nine. His counterpart was attempting to do the same as Virgil led off the bottom of the inning. "I got a clean single, and then I was sacrificed to second," the no-hit virtuoso explains. "I went to third on a wild pitch, and scored on another wild pitch. I won 1–0, pitched a no-hitter, and got the only hit and scored the only run of the ballgame. I was young and just starting out as a pitcher so, of course, it was the biggest thrill of my life." The masterpiece was also the apex of one of the most remarkable seasons by any minor league pitcher, which featured a 25–6 record, 450 strikeouts, and two no-hitters.

Three years earlier, Trucks was a raw 16-year-old outfielder playing amateur baseball with his father and two brothers in Birmingham. His first taste of professional ball came the following year with the local Stockum Pipe Corporation. "I was a pretty good hitter. I played sandlot ball for them. You were paid a salary but you also had to work eight hours a day. I was paid about $20 a week to work in the pipe shop and play ball. We played every Saturday. They had quite a few good players on that team.

Today, those guys could probably make it in the big leagues with no problem."

Trucks attracted major league interest. "A scout for Detroit named Eddie Goosetree spotted me and offered me a $100 contract. My dad had to sign for me because I wasn't 18 years old yet." Virgil stuck with Stockum until it was time to report to the Tigers' camp. "One day, a guy came to me while I was at work in the factory and offered to pay $25 a week and free room and board to play ball three days a week for his club. So I went to the manager of the Stockum ballclub and asked for a $5 raise. He said no way, so I said goodbye and joined the Shawmut Alabama club. It was part of the Carolina Textile League. The manager there converted me to a pitcher. I won ten and lost one that year."

At the close of the season an umpire from the Textile League who resided in Andalusia, situated about 20 miles north of the Florida–Alabama line, informed the local ballclub of the pitching prospect. Andalusia contacted Trucks, requesting he join the team for the playoffs. "They had won the second half of the season and Union Springs had won the first half. They said they would pay my expenses to make the 200-mile trip. They also told me they'd pay me $35 for every game I pitched. So I pitched the opening game of the series and I won 5–0. Then I pitched the final game and won 3–0."

With the victorious conclusion to the series came another offer from Andalusia—$500 to play the entire 1938 season. "Well, I had never seen that much money in my life so even though I had already signed with Detroit, I signed a contract with them.

"Later, the owners gave us an outing for winning the playoffs. It was at Fort Walton Beach, Florida, which was nothing more than a few cottages scattered along the shore. That night, the owners were playing poker and I was watching. They kept dropping chips on the floor. I would pick them up and they told me to put them in my pocket. By the time they were finished, I had two pockets full of chips. They told me to take them over to the cashier. I dumped them on the table and started walking away. The guy said, 'Wait a minute. You got some money coming.' There were $85 worth of chips. So I guess that was my bonus for signing."

Virgil was concerned about having signed two contracts—one with Andulusia, the other with Detroit—and even contemplated going to jail. "I didn't know what to do, just being a kid and all. I thought about going back to play semi-pro ball and wait for them to come arrest me. Well, at that time they had a minor league baseball commissioner. (Frank) Shaughnessy was his name. I went to see him and he said, 'Well, you come back to see me in two hours and I'll tell you who you belong to.'

"Two hours later, he told me that my contract was with Andalusia. I said, 'Well, how could that be? I signed with Detroit first.' He said that Detroit had pigeonholed my contract and that Andalusia had actually sent the contract first. So Detroit wound up buying my contract from Andalusia for $10,000 and agreed that I would stay with Andalusia for the rest of 1938."

Trucks played a couple of seasons in the Tigers farm system before his first serious shot at the majors in 1941. "I went to spring training but they had a lot of pitchers—Bobo Newsom, Tommy Bridges, "Schoolboy" Rowe—so they decided to give me more experience. They farmed me to Buffalo after spring training and brought me back later on that year." His major league debut was also his sole appearance that season. On September 27, Trucks pitched two innings in relief and despite fanning three, was ineffective, yielding four hits and a pair of runs.

Yet, Detroit was impressed with the fireballer, who received another big league opportunity in 1942. While earning a salary of $450 a month, Trucks accumulated a 14–8 record, two shutouts, and 91 strikeouts, while posting a 2.74 ERA. Following a 16–10 mark in 1943, Trucks, like numerous ballplayers affected by the military draft, was out of baseball for the next two seasons and returned to the Tigers in time for the 1945 Series. Virgil recalls, "The Tigers didn't win the pennant too easily that year. If they had lost to the Browns at the end of the season they would have had to play Washington in a playoff."

The Fall Classic featured the Bengals and Cubs, both known for having masterful moundsmen, dependable defense, and seasoned skippers. By 1945, Cub manager Charlie Grimm was in his ninth of what would be 19 years at the helm, while the Tigers' Steve O'Neill had six of 14 managerial years under his belt. "I enjoyed playing for O'Neill. He was a nice person, a kind guy, not the type to get on you for any mistake you made."

O'Neill started Trucks twice. Virgil squared the Series by going the distance in Game Two, as Hank Greenberg's three-run rocket off Hooks Wyse was the difference in the 4–1 victory. He had the ball and a 1–0 lead in the potential Series clincher in Game Six, but the Cubs erupted for four in the fifth frame and eventually won in the twelfth. The Tigers' Hal Newhouser received ample support two days later and coasted to a 9–3 decider, as the Motor City earned its first world championship in ten years.

In his 17 years in the majors, the hard-throwing righthander with the apropos sobriquet "Fire" accumulated impressive career stats of 177 victories, including 20 in 1953, 35 shutouts, over 1,534 strikeouts and a respectable 3.39 ERA. In 1949, he won 19 games, had a third-best 2.81 ERA, and led the league in strikeouts and shutouts. Following his trade to St. Louis in 1953, he put together his only twenty-win season, notching five for the Browns before being shipped to Chicago later that season where he won another 15. In 1954, Trucks's trim 2.79 ERA, 19 victories, a league-best five shutouts, and third-best 152 strikeouts, one short of his career high, did little to indicate that the 35-year-old was slowing down. In his final four years, however, he was mainly used in relief, finishing his career with the pennant-bound Yankees of 1958.

Besides O'Neill, Trucks played for nine other managers. He recalls two. "Paul Richards was one of the smartest managers I ever played for. He was always thinking ahead of other managers. I only played for Casey Stengel for half a year, but I wouldn't say he was a great manager. At that time, he was old and he really left the pitching to Jim Turner, the pitching coach."

Having pitched throughout the 1940s and most of the 1950s, Trucks faced several of baseball's all-time great hitters. His choice as toughest? "I've said it time and again, and there's no doubt in my mind today, that Ted Williams is the greatest hitter I ever faced. The best all-around player? I would have to flip a coin between Joe DiMaggio and Mickey Mantle. They could throw, they could run, they could hit, they could do everything that an all-around ballplayer was supposed to do. Of course, I can only evaluate based on who I pitched against, so I'm not taking anything away from Mays or Aaron or any of the National League ballplayers."

I ask Trucks to compare some of the old ballparks in terms of being easier or more difficult for pitchers. "I would have to say that Tiger Stadium was a good ballpark for a righthander to pitch in. There weren't that many good left-hand hitters when I came into the league. It was like Comiskey Park in Chicago where I had some good years. I was a fastball pitcher, so I would rely on my best pitch wherever I played. Fenway Park wasn't the most pleasurable place to pitch, but it still didn't bother me too much. I didn't think about the ballpark. When it was my turn to pitch, I pitched."

Among Trucks' many roommates throughout his career was Dick Wakefield. The lefty-swinger was a promising outfielder when he joined the Tigers in his first full season in 1943. "Wakefield was the first big bonus ballplayer. He could have been another Ted Williams if he had concentrated. He had a great batting stroke and a lot of potential. The only thing about him was that he was a lazy ballplayer, and I know because I roomed with him for seven years."

Detroit's sizable investment of $52,000 appeared justified after the rookie led the league in hits and doubles, but after another successful year in 1944, Wakefield's production and motivation steadily decreased. According to Trucks, the Tigers made a final attempt to rekindle the spirit of their once-coveted prospect by hiring baseball veteran Dick Bartell as a coach in 1949. "Bartell was probably number one in the country for being a bench jockey. Back in those days, guys like Bartell and Ernie Bonham didn't bench jockey because they didn't like you. They did it to try to upset you and make you lose your concentration. They don't bench jockey anymore today. With the kind of money they make, I guess they feel it doesn't matter. There's no profit in it.

"Well, anyway, the Tigers hoped that if Bartell could get on Wakefield a little, he would liven up. But it just couldn't be done."

Tall and muscular, Wakefield had occasional power but never surpassed a dozen home runs in any of his nine years in the majors. "There weren't many power hitters in the American League during my time. Very few Williamses, DiMaggios, Mantles. Hitters didn't try to hit the ball out of the park all the time. Today, you can be five-foot, five and weigh 145 pounds and hit it as far as the 200-pound man. Of course, that has to do with the smaller strike zone, the ball being livelier, the bats being lighter. And you can't knock batters down. If you do, the umpire warns you and then you can't pitch the way you want to. In my day, I dusted off a few and never had any problems with batters bothering me afterwards. That's the way the game was played. I wasn't afraid of any of them. If I hit a batter, that was just too bad.

"Somebody once asked me how long it would take to pitch a ballgame today. I said about five hours. He asked me why it would take me that long and I told him, 'Well, two hours I'd be pitching and the other three I'd be fighting.' Let's face it, if a pitcher can't pitch inside, there's no reason to pitch, because if you have to pitch to a hitter's power you're not going to have too much success."

How would Trucks handle Mark McGwire? "I'd jam him. I wouldn't let him just stand up in the middle of the plate and hit anything he wanted to hit. Pitchers are probably afraid to throw close because of his size, but that wouldn't bother me. If he's big enough to hit, he's big enough to take what I can put out."

One modern hurler impresses Virgil more than any other. "Greg Maddux is the smartest pitcher in baseball. He knows what he can do and what umpires can do for him. Umpires can mean a lot to a ballgame and to a certain pitcher. Maddux knows that the umpire is going to give him a pitch off the outside corner, so he pitches there."

Frank Tanana

For one year, he bested the best. For the remainder of his career, he was no Nolan Ryan. Just Frank Tanana, regarded today as one of the most productive strikeout artists in baseball history.

Any ballclub would settle for having the best fireballer on its roster. During much of the seventies, the California Angels had the top two in Ryan and Tanana. From 1974 through 1977, Ryan took the strikeout crown three times, with Tanana winning in 1975. Their combined number of strikeouts for the same period (2,136) is the highest by any duo for a four-year span. Their combined 588 in 1976 is the third highest season total in baseball history, behind Ryan–Bill Singer in 1973 (624) and Sandy Koufax–Don Drysdale in 1965 (592).

Although Ryan was clearly the superior thrower, Tanana's individual stats are nonetheless impressive. During the four-year span, the southpaw averaged 229 strikeouts per season, attaining a career-best 269 in 1975. His ERA was below 3.00 three times (to Ryan's two), and his 2.54 in 1977 led the league, as did his seven shutouts. His 180 Ks in 1974 ranks eighth on the all-time list for American League rookies. He peaked with a 17-strikeout performance against the Rangers on June 21, 1975, fanned 15 Minnesota batters nine days later, and whiffed 15 in a ten-inning game against Oakland on September 6, 1976. His career total 2,773 Ks ranks second on the all-time American League list for southpaw pitchers (behind Mickey Lolich) and sixth among all A. L. pitchers (behind Ryan, Roger Clemens, Walter Johnson, Bert Blyleven, and Lolich).

While Ryan continued gathering Ks in the two subsequent decades, reinforcing his claim to greatness, the effectiveness of Tanana's fastball abated. Hurling merely 90 innings in 1979 after averaging 259 innings-pitched the previous five years, at 26 Tanana was considered by some a washed-up mop-up man as the 1980 season began.

Frank speaks candidly from his home in Farmington Hills, Michigan in March of 1999. "It's true, I had to pitch a lot of innings with the Angels," the 45-year-old asserts. "I'd go 12, 13 innings. It was ridiculous and it shouldn't have been done." He qualifies his criticism of managerial decisions by accepting much of the blame for his arm problem. "When you're young and feeling strong, you say, 'That's okay. Give me the ball.' You feel that you can go out there every day.

"And maybe I was being overworked, but I wasn't taking care of myself off the field. That had something to do with the injury, and it also interfered with the healing process afterwards. I guess if I have any regrets about my career that would be it. Still, I feel that every day I went to the ballpark and put on a uniform, I loved being there. And every time I toed the rubber, I gave it my best."

Accustomed to blowing away batters, Tanana made a dramatic adjustment to accommodate his impairment. He became a junk specialist, rarely throwing fastball strikes while mesmerizing hitters with change-ups and slow curves. The modification resulted in less stress on the arm and another dozen seasons in the majors. In 1980, he rebounded with 223 innings-pitched in 32 appearances, all but one coming as a starter, and though he never quite reached the workhorse level of the first five years, Tanana averaged 215 innings-pitched from 1980 to the time of his retirement in 1993. Tanana acknowledges, "I was fortunate to be able to make the transition from power to finesse pitcher."

A 21-year man, Tanana had more major league starting assignments than any other hurler who never won twenty. He also holds the unique but quirky distinction of playing twenty seasons without ever making a plate appearance, a streak broken when he became a National Leaguer for the first time in 1993 as a member of the Mets. Frank recalls other, more distinguished achievements. "The game I struck out 17 batters was a lot of fun. That's an individual kind of thing and one I'll always remember. The other two are more team accomplishments. In 1979, the Angels won their first division ever and I pitched the game that clinched it. It was against the Royals in September. The celebration that followed was a lot of fun, and the fact that I had been hurt all year, never gave up on the season, and battled and worked hard to get healthy, then pitched and won the clincher, well, it's just a really fond memory. The game ended with Rod Carew throwing the ball to me, and I stepped on first base for the out.

"In 1987, I won the last game of the season with the pennant up for grabs. It had all the pressure and suspense and notoriety of a World Series game. There was national television coverage. We were playing Toronto, who we had chased all year. We started the season with 11 wins and 19 losses and went on a tremendous streak and ended up winning 98 games. Toronto won 96 that year. So that last game was the culmination of an incredible season. I was fortunate enough to beat Jimmy Key 1–0 that day. Larry Herndon hit a home run in the second inning that just barely cleared the left-field screen at Tiger Stadium. And again, I was involved with the final play. The ball was hit back to me, I underhanded it to Darrell Evans, and the celebration began. I would have to say that was my career highlight, not only because I went the full nine at a time in my career when I wasn't throwing many complete games, but because it was more of a team accomplishment than an individual one."

Games having special significance brought out the best in Tanana, exemplified by his division and pennant-winning performances. Tanana recalls other instances. "I had success in games where new stadiums were being opened or closed. In 1976, Seattle opened their dome and I shut them out. When Chicago opened their new Comiskey Park, I started and beat them. And when Baltimore's Memorial Stadium closed down, I pitched nine innings and won that ballgame. It seemed the more people in the stands, the better I pitched."

With the exception of the Astros' Bob Knepper, Tanana was Ryan's teammate for more seasons than any of the tall Texan's pitching partners. Complementing his 100-miles-per-hour Express was Nolan's notoriety for delivering occasional brushbacks, making already-nervous hitters more jittery. Tanana offers a relevant anecdote. "I remember Nolan hit Thurman Munson in the head one day in Anaheim Stadium. He was being roughed up pretty good in the game, and came inside with one of his fastballs. Thurman was unable to get away from it and the ball hit him in the helmet. I don't recall if he stayed in the game. It might have been a glancing blow. I've seen Nolan hit a few people when we were teammates, and if he got them solid, they didn't stay in the game."

The story reminds Tanana of his uncanny success against Munson, a .292 lifetime hitter and the 1976 American League MVP. "Thurman is one of the few hitters I remember how I did against. I think for the first 32 or 33 times up against me, he went hitless. That's pretty amazing for a hitter of his stature. Of course, Thurman caught me early in my career when I was overpowering. And he was the kind of hitter who liked to dive into the ball. Those kind didn't do too well against me. I'd bring it right in on them. They were easier for me to get out because they went right into my strength. The guy who bailed out would be a little more successful if he could guess with me. For sure, not all the outs Thurman made were strikeouts or weak ground balls. No doubt, he hit some line drives right at people. But for some reason, he couldn't find the hole against me.

"I remember speaking to him about it at the All-Star Game in San Diego in 1978. He was the one who brought up the fact that he hadn't had a hit off me. I smiled and said, 'I had no idea. You gotta be kidding.' So he called me a few names, and we laughed.'"

Tanana recalls Munson's competitiveness. "Thurman was intense. He was a chatterer, hustler, in-the-dirt type of player. You could tell he really enjoyed the game. He showed up to play all the time—a day-in, day-out kind of guy. I didn't get to bat during my career until I played with the Mets, but I heard about how Thurman used to try to get into your head when you came up to the plate. How he would do anything to distract you. That must have been a challenge for hitters, trying to focus while Munson was throwing dirt on your shoes, or chattering about where to go to eat after the game, or asking how's the family—doing or saying anything so he could get you out."

In 1978, the Angels signed free-agent Lyman Bostock, a talented outfielder in his fourth year in the majors, having hit .282, .323, and .336 in previous seasons with Minnesota. Tanana evaluates the skills of his former opponent and teammate. "Lyman was a line-drive, up-the-middle-type hitter. He could hit with some power but was definitely not a power hitter. He'd drive the ball in the alley or up the gap. He was a good all-around hitter, and hit lefties and righties about the same, maybe righties a little better. When I faced him, I approached him the way I approached any lefty batter. You get them out by first making him very conscious of the inside pitch. I would work hard to bust batters in on the hands. You know, saw off their bat. Then I'd come back with a fastball or breaking ball away.

"Lyman was really coming into his prime when he joined our ballclub. But he also came in with a lot of pressure after signing a new contract with a new team. He pressed so hard and was doing so poorly the first month. He was a proud young man and wanted to do so well that when he didn't, he felt just awful about it. In fact, if my memory serves me correctly, he even made an offer to Mr. [Gene] Autry [owner] to give back some of his salary. Of course, Mr. Autry didn't take him up on it."

Bostock turned things around in 1978 and by late September was among the top ten hitters in the league. Then, on September 23rd in Gary, Indiana, Bostock was a backseat passenger in a car when he became the fatal victim of a mistaken-identity shooting. In a case of justice denied, the killer was subsequently judged to be legally insane, spent a few months in a hospital, and was released. "We were in Chicago when Lyman was killed. I went to get some breakfast and heard the news in the hotel lobby. It was a tremendous shock. The reality of death can hit an athlete hard. We act and think like we're invincible. I know I never had that close connection with death before.

"We played that same day. It was tough, but that's the nature of the game. You do what you have to do. The game goes on. But it was very quiet in the clubhouse before and after the game. Very somber."

According to Tanana, Bostock was missed for more than his on-the-field contributions to the team. Labeling him a fun-loving extrovert who enjoyed music, Tanana adds, "He was a competitor, a great guy to have in the clubhouse. Racial things didn't matter to him. Some players have trouble with people from other races. Lyman wasn't that way at all. He was an Angel who put the uniform on, played hard, and pulled for his teammates.

"Lyman never coasted when he played and was constantly working on his game. But that can be said of a lot of major league players then and now. When you reach that level, the top of your craft, well, nobody gets there without working hard. And when they make it, they strive to be the best they can possibly be as a major leaguer. The really good ones settle for nothing less."

Having played for many managers during stints with the Angels, Red Sox, Rangers, Tigers and the Mets, Frank foregoes evaluating them, explaining, "We didn't go very long with managers, for whatever reason, so it's hard to make a determination of their ability on such a short time." He makes an exception by citing Angel skippers Norm Sherry and Dave Garcia as being solid baseball men who gave their lives to the game and paid their dues, while defending them for failing to win a division title. "They didn't manage a long time either, but I would have to say they both knew the game strategically, were good tacticians, and did as good a job as they could. Sometimes, managers can get a little overwhelmed with the responsibility, and other times they're just not given enough time. Or control. Ballplayers know whether or not a manager has a lot of authority over decisions being made. There's a much better feeling in the clubhouse if he does. I have my doubts about whether Norm and Dave were given that free rein."

During the batting barrage of the 1990s, Tanana's effectiveness waned, leading to his retirement following the 1993 season. "There's no doubt in my mind that the ball was juiced up. When I was younger, hitters wouldn't think of trying to hit one out of the ballpark going the other way. An opposite-field home run was rare. Towards the end of my career, even Punch-and-Judy hitters would hit balls out the other way. Also, the strike zone changed. Umpires discouraged pitchers from throwing inside. Whether it was a conscious effort to prevent hitters from being hurt, I don't know. But it did become more difficult to get an inside strike at the end of my career. And the outside strike became wider. It's like the umpires took two inches from the inside corner of the plate and in their mind extended it outside. I would have had a tough time winning early in my career, even as hard as I threw, if the strikes were being called the way they were later, because the inside corner was my bread and butter."

Today, Tanana remains involved with major league baseball. "Well, I go down every year to the Fantasy Camp that the Tigers put on. Also, I work with Baseball Chapel, a ministry that offers a worship service on Sunday in each ballpark. I work here with the Tigers in that capacity."

Would Tanana's lifetime stats be markedly superior had he remained injury-free throughout his entire career? Assuredly, his strikeout totals would have improved, in light of his averaging 7.3 Ks per nine innings during the pre-injury years. Nonetheless, at the onset of the new millennium, Tanana will be listed among the top 100 big league pitchers of all time in appearances, victories, innings-pitched, and shutouts. He will place 15th in total strikeouts, and *third* among lefthanders (behind Steve Carlton and Lolich). Consider, too, that these impressive rankings were attained after hurling most of his career with a bad arm that necessitated a major alteration in his pitching strategy and technique.

Not a bad career for a pitcher who was no Nolan Ryan.

Jimmy Greengrass

It is a pleasantly warm and clear evening in Chatsworth, Georgia, in March of 1999 as 72-year-old former outfielder Jimmy Greengrass describes the terms of his first professional contract from a rocking chair on the front porch of his home. "I was offered $150 a month plus $1.50 a day meal money for the road. I still have that contract hanging on my wall. Every time I start feeling sorry for myself I go in there and take a look and say to myself, 'Well, things have been worse.'"

At the time of the offer, Jimmy was a sure-handed third baseman in high school and on other local teams in Addison, New York, located about 60 miles south of Buffalo. "I played pepper every day since I was five years old. It made me a pretty good fielder." One of his pepper partners, Paul Wildrick, wrote to the Yankees in the spring of 1944 extolling the skills of his fellow jock. After observing Greengrass in several games, New York scout Paul Krichell made an offer Jimmy couldn't refuse, but his mother could. "I was 16 years old so my mom had to sign for me," Jimmy explains. "She was against it at first. She wanted me to graduate with my class in 1945. I had to swear to her, the postmaster, the principal, all the teachers, the coaches, the chief of police, the minister, and everybody else in town that I would come back and graduate with my class the following year."

Jimmy played third base that summer at Wellsville, New York, part of the Pony League. "They had hand-me-down pants for minor leaguers in those days. They handed them down from the big club all the way down through the minors until they got worn out. And guess whose pants I got to wear? Joe DiMaggio's. They were his old road pants. They had his name stitched in there in red. I wish I had them now."

True to his word, Jimmy returned to Addison in the fall to finish his final school year. Following graduation, he returned for another season at

Wellsville, then surprised everyone by enlisting. "I was supposed to play in Binghamton in 1946. The manager there was Lefty Gomez. I went in the service instead and I never bothered to notify the Yankees.

"So I was at Camp Lee, Virginia, in the summer when, lo and behold, here come the Binghamton Triplets to play an exhibition with our camp team. I was in boot camp the day they came but I read in the paper that the Triplets were in camp. Well, even though I was restricted to the training area, I waltzed over to the ballpark. When I got there, I went up to Lefty and said, 'Hi, Lefty.' He started yelling at me, 'Greengrass, you sorry rascal. You're supposed to be with me.' Well, wouldn't you know it, General Gramm, a four-star general, heard Lefty yellin' and came over. He said, 'Lefty, do you know this man?' Lefty said, 'Yeah, he's the best third base prospect in the Yankee organization.' The general looked at me and said, 'Son, be in my office at eight o'clock in the morning.' I thought I was going to be court martialed."

An apprehensive Greengrass returned to the barracks, where he was confronted by an enraged commanding officer. "The C.O. started yellin', 'What have you done, Greengrass? The general's staff officer called and said he wants you in his office at eight sharp tomorrow morning.' So the next morning, my C.O. took me over there personally. The general invited us into the office, but then he dismissed the C.O. I thought, 'Oh, boy.' Then the general said, 'Jim, I'd like you to play on our baseball team. You want to go try out with them?' I said, 'I sure do.' Boy, was I relieved."

After being honorably discharged in 1950, Greengrass rejoined the Yankee organization, which sent the 22-year-old to their minor league club in Muskegon, Michigan, where he played shortstop, the outfield, and even pitched for two years. Jimmy jokes, "I never found out whose idea it was [to make him a pitcher]. I would have punched him in the jaw." After hitting .379 in 1951, the righty swinger moved up a notch to the Triple A club in Beaumont, Texas. Manager Harry Craft put an end to Greengrass' pitching career. "He was the first to put me in the outfield permanently. He knew I could field and throw. And I loved it out there."

In 1952, Jimmy was sent to the Reds organization in exchange for righty sidearmer Ewell Blackwell. It wasn't until 25 years later that Greengrass learned of the circumstances leading to the trade. "Casey Stengel told me the story at an Old-Timers' Game in 1977 in Cincinnati. It was the only time we ever talked.

"Toward the end of the 1952 season, the Yanks were in a pennant race. Stengel wanted to get Blackwell to win four ballgames. Well, Gabe Paul [Reds general manager] and Rogers Hornsby [manager] were at Tulsa with the Reds farm club playing our Beaumont club. My first time up, I hit a double, the next time up I hit a home run, the next time up the guy hit me with a pitch. I ran to first base. I would have gone to second if that second baseman hadn't looked around at the last second. Well, Hornsby saw that and said to Paul, 'That's the guy I want, right there.'"

Included in the August 28 swap for Blackwell were Greengrass, Yankee reliever Bob Nevel, minor leaguer Bob Marquis, and $35,000. Jimmy flew to Boston, where the Reds were playing the Braves in a twi-night doubleheader. "I joined the team at about the seventh inning of the first game. They had the uniform ready for me and I put it on and went out there.

"I was sitting on the bench when Rogers Hornsby saw me. He said, 'Come here, son.' I went over to sit by him and he said, 'You ready to play?' I answered with probably the greatest statement that I ever said in my life. I said, 'Hell yeah, that's what I came here for.' Rogers just smiled and said, 'Well, you're pinch-hitting in this game, and you're playing the next game. So go find a bat.' And who was pitching out there? Warren Spahn. Well, I tell you, I had the rabbit knees—going to bat for the first time in the majors, and against Warren Spahn! But Rogers said to me, 'Hey Jim, it's easier to play in the big leagues than the minors. The lights are better, the field is better, the pitchers have better control. Why hell, even the coffee tastes better.'"

Arguably the greatest right-hand batter in history, Hornsby gained notoriety as a manager for his lack of diplomacy with front office executives and players. Greengrass offers a different perspective. "Rogers Hornsby? I loved the man. And I think he really liked me. I was his kind of player. I was a hustler and I loved to play. The thing I saw in Rogers in the two years I played for him was that he would get on players who wouldn't hustle, who wouldn't play up to their ability. Those are the ones who complained about him being a tough manager.

"The only thing he said to me in the way of criticism was that I was curling my bat behind my head before I swung and that it was making me late on the fastball. He said that's why I was hitting the ball to right-center when I could be pulling it. So he asked me if he could shout out to me from the third base coach's box if he saw me doing it. I said, 'Sure, it wouldn't bother me a bit. I didn't even know I was doing it.' You know, they didn't have the films and all the other stuff they have today. Well, I'm up at bat and all of a sudden I hear him yell, 'C'mon, hold that bat straight up!' Well, it woke me up and I hit that ball good."

In the early 1950s, the Reds were still playing in Crosley Field; the historic ballpark was not replaced by the symmetrical, carpeted Riverfront Stadium until 1970. Built in 1912, Crosley is still remembered today for having hosted the first night game in major league history (1935). "Crosley was the best ballpark in the world. The field was immaculate. The Swabbs [father-and-son groundskeepers] would take good care of that field. You couldn't find a pebble, or even a lump of dirt on the grass."

Crosley's outfield was notorious for its steep incline, making the fielding of fly balls adventurous. The slope was particularly acute in left field. "You'd run up a bank to get to the wall. I had to learn to play there." He had a manager more than willing to teach. "Every day in Cincinnati at ten o'clock in the morning, I was out at the ballpark and Hornsby would run me up and down that embankment one hundred times. Then he'd stand with a bat at shortstop and hit line drives up against the wall and I'd have to field them. But I learned to play that embankment well."

Greengrass had a memorable first two weeks in the big leagues, finishing the 1952 season with five homers and 27 RBIs in 17 ballgames. In his first full season in 1953, he made the *Sporting News'* All Rookie Team by hitting 20 homers, becoming the first Reds' rookie to gather 100 RBIs (Mike Piazza would be the next National League rookie to match the feat in 1993), and joining Gus Bell as the first Cincinnati outfielders in history to accumulate 100 RBIs in a season since Cy Seymour's 121 in 1905.

Jimmy's sophomore season was equally superb, as he connected for 27 homers and 95 RBIs while hitting .280. But the Queen City's rising star plummeted toward the end of 1954. "I'll tell you how it happened. I went sliding into second base in a game in Pittsburgh. I was trying to break up a double play. Curt Roberts was the second baseman. He went up in the air to get the throw, and instead of coming down with his spikes and chopping me up, he tucked in his spikes. But he hit my right leg solid with his knee. Purely unintentional. It was just another bump as far as I was concerned.

"Two weeks later, it swelled up like someone had put an air hose in me. It kept getting sore and I had to keep working it out. It was getting tougher and tougher for me to play. Finally, Dr. Harry Rogers, the old Braves' team doctor, is the one who figured out that I had crushed a vein and got phlebitis.

"The next year, I went to spring training. My leg was still bothering me and I got off to a bad start. We were in Pittsburgh and Birdie Tebbetts, who took over as manager of the ballclub, called Andy Seminick, Glen [Gorbous] and myself up to Gabe's suite across from the ballpark and told us we had been traded. I was really surprised because I was hurt at the time. The Reds told the Phillies that I was 100 percent. When the Phillies found out, they were pretty upset. But I told Mr. [Bob] Carpenter

[Phils' president], 'Nobody asked me if I wanted to be traded. If you had talked to me, I would have told you about my leg problem. Get on the phone, or let's get on a plane and go over there, and I'll tell them they're liars.' Mr. Carpenter, who was a great man, said, 'Look, you're the guy we wanted in this deal and we're going to get you fixed.' He sent me to Johns Hopkins Hospital. They diagnosed the case and I stayed off my leg for four weeks."

Jimmy's 1955 stats fell dramatically. Playing in 107 games for Cincinnati and Pittsburgh, he managed merely 12 home runs and 38 RBIs, while his batting average dropped 26 points. Of more concern was his leg problem, which wasn't going away. "I went to spring training the next year and the trainer had me run in the surf and do other things to try to get that leg going. It got a little stronger but it never did respond. When I played for the Phillies in 1956, I still couldn't push off my right leg when I was hitting. I was hitting balls solid that were going only 320 feet that used to go over 400.

"The Phillies organization stayed with me. I played in the Coast League for them and had some good years. Scouts would come see me once in a while and the first thing they'd say is, 'How's the leg, Jim?' Even before saying hello. But I knew I didn't have a prayer of making it back. There were so many ballplayers and so few jobs in the majors then. Now, they have so many teams I can't even count them."

One of Jimmy's Cincy teammates was slugging first baseman Ted Kluszewski. Six-feet, two-inches, 225 pounds may not be unusual measurements for today's burly ballplayers, but in the early 1950s Kluszewski dwarfed most of his peers, as did his hitting stats: a lifetime .298 average, three consecutive forty-homer seasons, four-straight 100 RBI seasons, a string of five seasons batting over .300, league leader in homers (49) and RBIs (141) in 1954, and one of five players in history to smash 40 or more homers in a season while striking out fewer than 40 times, the *only* player to do it three times. Presently, he is the *only* non–Hall-of-Famer to reach the .300, 30-homer, and 100-RBI plateau in one season four times.

Klu's hulking size was matched by a good-natured disposition. "Ted was a great big honey bear," Jimmy laughs. "I only saw him get mad but one time. We were in St. Louis. We used to have those knock-down, drag-out affairs there. Every time we played them, they'd knock us down. So we got into a knockdown contest. Harvey Haddix was pitching for the Cardinals. Well, Gus Bell comes up and cranks one out of the ballpark.

So Klu comes up and Haddix gets the sign from the bench to knock him down. Haddix gives this look like, 'What are you talkin' about? He's bigger than a pine tree. You want me to knock him down?' So old Harvey winds up and throws one right at Klu.

"Klu never flinched. He just stood there and the ball hit him right on the side and bounced all the way back to the mound. Klu just turned around, very slowly, took his bat—it looked like a fence post; you know, he had a 48-ounce bat—and raised it up with his right hand and shook the ground with it. The bat shattered. The veins in Klu's neck were swelled up and red, and he walked down to first base very slowly. He never said a word, but he had that glare about him. One that commands respect. Haddix looked at him and took off for left field."

Kluszewski wore shirts with sleeves cut extremely short, exposing extraordinarily massive biceps. As legend has it, this was done to further frighten already apprehensive hurlers wary of Ted's power-potential. Greengrass offers a different explanation. "That wasn't his idea. They [the ballclub] had to do that because if they didn't he was all bound up in the shoulders and couldn't swing the bat. They designed it that way for him. They would tailor-make your uniform then. They'd do it in spring training. I think it was the Spalding Company that would come down and get your measurements and make your uniforms."

One year, Jimmy played second base in winter ball and was befriended by San Juan teammate Roberto Clemente. "What a ballplayer. He had great speed, and could hit the ball like a rocket anywhere. He stood way back in the batter's box. Rogers Hornsby liked that about Clemente because he used to do the same thing. Clemente would stand in the back corner on the outside, away from the plate so he stepped into everything. You couldn't throw him a ball away from the plate and get him out because he could reach them all. He could bust that inside ball, too. He didn't take a big stride, but he was always moving into the ball so when he hit it, he hit it with everything in his body.

"And what a shotgun for an arm. There was a time I saw him throw a guy out in San Juan that you couldn't believe. He must have been out there about 370 feet by the wall when he caught it. He turned and fired that ball to home on the money. The runner was trying to tag from third and Clemente must have thrown him out by ten steps. He did that a lot against big-league clubs, but not against us. The Reds players didn't take any liberties with him. We knew he'd gun us down.

"One day in San Juan, there was a fly ball hit into short right. I was going out and Roberto was comin' in, and the ball dropped. Nino Escalera, the first black player for Cincinnati, was the manager. When I got to the dugout, Nino was all over me. 'Ay, Jimmy. Get out of the way next time. Let him take it.' Roberto came over and said, 'No, no, no. Not Jimmy's fault. My fault.' So we became great friends."

Greengrass also remembers Clemente for his deceptive humor. "You look at him and you say, 'Oh, Roberto's not gonna do anything.' But he'll pull some kind of practical joke on you—put some other guy's pants or hat in your locker. Nothing too serious, but just to have some fun. He never picked on me a whole lot, but he liked my name. But a lot of people liked it. I remember when they'd announce my name in the Polo Grounds: 'And now coming to bat, number 23, Jimmy Greengrass.' And the fans would just go crazy over there."

Playing four days a week in Puerto Rico, Jimmy and Roberto would relax on off days by going fishing. "I remember he hooked a big barracuda off the beach. He took that barracuda from near our hotel probably a full mile down the beach, across the coral rocks, to near a big hotel where they had a casino. He never gave up on that thing. He went in and out of the water, onto the rocks, until he landed that barracuda. I was with him at the start, but I wasn't at the end. When he went across those rocks I said, 'I'll see ya.' I just sat up there by the other hotel and watched him bring it in.

"They had good food in San Juan. Roberto and I used to eat a dish that I really liked. It had some kind of beans and pork in it. And we used to drink sugar cane syrup. It was supposed to be good for the bowels."

The constraints of major league baseball prevented the friendship from enduring. "In those days, they didn't like it for ballplayers from different teams to socialize. You might run into a ballplayer at a spot where you'd go if you wanted to have a snack after a ballgame, before you turned in and went to bed. But they had curfews and all that good stuff. And you had to abide by them, too."

When he retired from baseball in 1956, Jimmy immediately sought different employment. "I went to Lockheed Aircraft and a guy named Roger Thornball interviewed me. He knew me as a ballplayer. After we finished talking about my career he asked me, 'What do you know about airplanes?' I said, 'I only know two things: how to buy a ticket and how to fasten the seatbelt.' He said, 'Great. That means we can train you.'"

Greengrass worked at Lockheed for ten years before a layoff ended his factory work. "I was glad to be out of it. I was used to being outdoors so working inside all those years wasn't fun. We had a big party to celebrate my leaving." He then obtained a job as deputy sheriff in Chatsworth, holding the position for 20 years.

Jimmy's work history spans more than forty years. If his tenure in baseball was abbreviated, he's not kicking. It's been a full and rewarding life.

Bill Virdon

Bill Virdon was in his fourth full year with the Pirates when the team won the pennant in 1960. Like former teammates Friend and Labine, Virdon today recalls the team's never-say-die attitude throughout the season, and during the Series against the Yanks. "When we were trailing 7–4 in the eighth inning of the final game, I was thinking we still had a chance," the 67-year-old former centerfielder comments from his home in Springfield, Missouri, in April of 1999. "I think everybody else in the dugout was thinking the same thing."

Virdon describes his at bat during that eventful frame, which proceeded Gino Cimoli's leadoff single off southpaw Bobby Shantz. "Shantz was tough on lefty hitters and he was tough on me, so I didn't like facing him. But he hung a curve ball and I hit it hard, but it was right at Kubek. I said to myself, 'Uh-oh, perfect double-play ball.'" The infamous bad hop ricocheted off the throat of the Yankee shortstop; Kubek was removed from the game. "So instead of two outs, nobody on and the Series practically finished, we have two men on, no outs."

The other crucial play of the inning involved Jim Coates' mental mistake on a Clemente slow roller, as he failed to cover first base. "It wasn't an easy play and it's hard to criticize him. But Clemente reached on a play he should be out. It turned out perfect for us. A couple of batters later, Smith hits a homer that was probably more important than Mazeroski's. So we end up scoring five runs in an inning that we might not have scored any. That just gives you some idea how things went for us that year."

Virdon rates the Yankees the better ballclub in 1960, but adds, "You don't have to be the better club to win the Series. And we did the things that we had to do to win it. We weren't what you would call outstanding, but we were a bunch of guys who liked to play hard and we got the job done when it had to be done—got an out or a hit when we needed it. Everybody contributed—the Groats, the Hoaks, the Mazeroskis, the Stuarts, the Clementes, the Skinners. The pitching staff wasn't the best in the world but they all got the job done when they had to."

Eleven years later, Virdon would again experience the thrill of a world championship in Pittsburgh, this time as a coach working for the same manager who had led the club in 1960. "Murtaugh was by far one of the most underrated managers. I don't think he had a shortcoming. He didn't over-manage and he was a good strategist in that he always seemed to use the right people at the right time in game situations. He read players, read their abilities, and put them in situations where they could succeed. He was one of the better people that I've ever known in the game. I'm a little prejudiced because he was responsible for me staying in the game and getting into management. He really set me up as far as managing the Pirates. So maybe it's not fair to ask me."

Virdon is referring to Murtaugh's retirement following the 1971 championship season, which led to Virdon's first of 13 seasons as manager. His ballclub breezed through the regular season, winning the Eastern Division by 11 games, its 96 victories the most by any team in baseball, but the Bucs' hopes for repeating as world champs were abruptly eradicated by Sparky Anderson's Reds in the championship series. With his team trailing 3–2 in the final frame of the final game, Cincy superstar Johnny Bench delighted 50,000 Riverfront Stadium spectators with a game-tying homer. Two singles and two outs later, Pirate reliever Bob Moose hurled a wild toss, handing the Reds the flag. "If he gets that curve over, we probably win the game. He had thrown Hal McRae a couple of curve balls, and McRae had swung and missed, so Moose had two strikes on him. He just tried to do a little bit more with the next one, throw the curve a little sharper, and he just held onto it a little bit too long and the winning run scored."

Some might suggest that Moose should have come back with a fastball after throwing two consecutive curveballs, but Virdon doesn't second-guess the reliever's pitch selection. "Bob was actually a curve ball pitcher. That's not to short-change his fastball, because it was decent, but his curve was his best pitch, his out pitch. He was very effective with it." Nor does Bill second-guess his electing to go with Moose with the pennant on the line. "He was a gung-ho guy and wasn't afraid of anything. I'd just as soon have him pitching out there as anybody. Everyone on the ballclub liked him because they knew he would give you all he had."

For the Pirates, the Cincinnati victory was a bitter ending to a magnificent season. "In the clubhouse, there was a lot of disappointment.

I sincerely believe we had a better club in '72 than we did in '71 when we won it all. We won our division by a big margin in '72. We just got beat in the playoffs."

Virdon's first year as manager corresponded with Clemente's final season. As his teammate, coach, and manager, Virdon had observed the All-Star right fielder in action for 17 consecutive seasons from 1956 to 1972—virtually Clemente's entire career. "Clemente was one of those people you looked for if you're managing or trying to put a club together. Every aspect of his game was outstanding. There wasn't anything he couldn't do. His throwing really impressed me. I remember a play he made at the Astrodome. I was coaching at the time. He went back to the fence at full steam, jumped with his glove over the fence, banged into the wall, and came down with the ball.

"Maybe Clemente was somewhat of a hypochondriac but I think he always played when he was able. All you have to do is look at the number of games he played. And he wasn't the serious type like some people think. Maybe that was the case early in his career when he was struggling a little to get his feet on the ground. But after he established himself, he was more carefree and fun-loving, a happy-go-lucky guy. He had a knack of telling stories and keeping us in stitches. I can remember sitting and laughing at a lot of his stories."

What about Clemente's alleged uneasy relationship with Murtaugh and some teammates? "I don't remember him having any real big problems with anybody. He was a bit of a loner. Maybe that was more because of us than him. But later on, he fit right in with the ballclub.

"I don't think he and Murtaugh were ever too close. Early on, Clemente was a bit of a complainer and Murtaugh didn't like that. Like any good manager, Murtaugh was trying to get the most out of his ballplayers. His approach to Clemente wasn't to pat him on the back like some others might do. I think Murtaugh got as much out of him as anyone would have. And he always had as much respect for Clemente's ability as anybody, and was glad to have him on the club."

And Clemente's purported resentment over not being selected as the MVP in 1960? "He might have felt that he had as good a year as Groat and should have gotten it, but I think that's a normal situation. I don't condemn him for that. He didn't dwell on it as far as I know and it certainly didn't affect his performance on the field. My feeling is that Groat was probably as responsible as anybody in the National League for leading his ballclub that year."

Virdon again took the Pirate helm in 1973, but jumped onto the Yankee ship in 1974 and guided the club to second place, a mere two games behind Baltimore—the closest the team had come to post-season play since its pennant-winning season of 1964. Bill's tenure in the Big Apple would be brief, but today he recognizes a particular pinstriped player as exceptional. "Thurman Munson was one of the best people I managed in my career. He was a leader and helped our club in that respect. The one thing I remember about him more than anything is that he was one of the best at getting hits and RBIs when it meant something. He had that ability to reach back and get the run in more than other people. And he had excellent ability at calling a game. His only defensive shortcoming when I was there was his throwing. He had hurt his arm."

Bill contrasts the Yankee backstop with rivals Bench and Fisk, all of whom the former American and National League manager had the opportunity to observe in action. "I mentioned his long suit [clutch RBIs], and I would put him ahead of the other two in that respect, and that's going some. Bench I considered one of the best I ever saw because of his all-around ability. Munson didn't have the power that the other two had. So I would rate Bench the best I ever saw, and I would have to say Munson was next, even though he didn't play as long as the other two."

Munson's inclination to intentionally distract hitters is addressed. "He did it good-naturedly," Virdon justifies in referring to the catcher's chattering and soiling of batters' spikes, explaining that it was merely part of his personality to do anything to help the club win. "And he would get on his teammates if he saw they weren't giving 100 percent. They couldn't argue with him because he gave everything he had all the time and he wanted them to do the same."

In 1975, New York was playing .500 ball two-thirds into the season when owner Steinbrenner replaced Virdon with fan-favorite Billy Martin. Well respected as a strategist and disciplinarian, Virdon was immediately hired as skipper of the Astros. While completing the season with Houston, Virdon observed the work of nine-year veteran pitcher Don Wilson. "He had an impressive fastball. I wouldn't compare it with Nolan Ryan's. He had a good curve ball and he knew how to throw strikes and when not to. He had a knack for pitching."

Unfortunately, Virdon did not have further opportunity to see the ace righthander in action. That winter, an intoxicated Wilson returned home late one night, parked in the garage, and fell asleep in the still-running car. His death, and that of his five-year-old son, who also died of carbon monoxide poisoning while sleeping in his bedroom above the garage, shocked the baseball world and focused attention on the still-lingering issue of alcohol and drug use among athletes. Virdon comments in retrospect, "Drinking was somewhat of a problem during my days as a player and manager. The reason for that is the nature of the game, all the time you have on your hands. I really think a lot of guys soothe their aches and pains by drinking. Others drink because they can't handle the pressure. I think the situation has improved some. More people are aware of the dangers. And with all the money out there, players are also aware that they are jeopardizing a lot more now than they used to."

In 1979, the Virdon-led Astros fell two short of the Reds in the fight for the flag, then won its first division title the following season. In the division series, Houston battled Philadelphia to a fifth game, which again resulted in heartbreak for Virdon. Playing at the Astrodome, his team held a 5–2 lead in the eighth when the Phils put five on the board. Houston answered with two to tie in the bottom of the inning, but lost on an RBI double by Garry Maddox in the tenth.

Three years later, Virdon shifted to Montreal where he managed his final two seasons. In his 13 years as manager, he accumulated an impressive win-loss record of 995–921; his win total ranks among the top thirty on the all-time list of managers with a winning record. "I was lucky in my career. I was fortunate to have players that were very capable. And in almost all the years I managed, I had a closer. I really think that's the important thing to have on a club—someone who can close it out after your team busts their tail to get ahead late in the game."

Like many old-timers, Virdon is disgruntled by the manner in which the economics of baseball have affected player performance. "Long-term contracts have hurt the game. It's almost impossible for a human being to give the most of his ability every day when he knows he has several years playing time locked up. It shouldn't be that way. You're supposed to play 100 percent no matter how long your contract is. That's what you said you would do when you signed. I'm not blaming anybody for the long-term contracts. I'm just saying it's human nature to slack off, and long-term contracts take the pressure to perform every day off of players."

Bill is enjoying his retirement, somewhat thankful that his work as manager is behind him. "Managing has changed. It's harder to discipline players today. You fine them $1,000 and they bring in cash. Years ago, if you fined someone $100 you got their attention. I'm not saying you can't have discipline on a ballclub, but you have to find a different way."

Sparky Anderson

In 1998, the Yankees compiled 114 wins, establishing an American League record that was two short of the major league mark set by the 1906 Chicago Cubs. The team lost only 48, leaving them with an astounding .704 winning percentage. The pinstripers finished 22 games ahead of the Red Sox, whose admirable second-place record of 92–70 would have been good enough to capture four Eastern Division flags since divisional play began in 1969. The Yankees breezed through the Texas Rangers and Cleveland Indians in the divisional and championship series, and swept the Padres in the World Series.

In a year when sluggers Mark McGwire and Sammy Sosa were being compared with Babe Ruth, and Roger Clemens with some of the greatest pitchers, it was inevitable that debate would surface over whether the 1998 Yankees deserved the title of greatest team ever. Contrasts were made with the 1906 Chicago Cubs, whose slick-fielding double-play combo of Tinker, Evers and Chance helped win 116 games; with the 1961 Yankees, which included Mickey Mantle, Roger Maris, Yogi Berra, and Whitey Ford; and with the Oakland A's of the 1970s, led by the incomparable Reggie Jackson and the unflappable, smooth-throwing right-hander Catfish Hunter.

Contrasts were also made with the Cincinnati Reds of the 1970s, the Big Red Machine that produced five division titles, four pennants, and two world championships from 1970–1976. It was a club that boasted the best catcher in baseball in Johnny Bench, a two-time home run champion and three-time RBI leader; the league's top second baseman in Joe Morgan, known as much for his elbow-twitching batting style as for his sure-handedness in the field that led to five consecutive Gold Glove Awards; Tony Perez, the power-hitting Cuban with the closed stance who averaged 104 RBIs per season from 1969–1976; the Hit Man, Pete Rose, who from 1970–1976 had four of his major-league record ten 200-hit seasons. The team peaked in 1975 when it won 108 games, 20 more than runner-up Los Angeles, then dismissed the Phils in three-straight in the championship series and outfought the stubborn Red Sox to take the World Series in seven games.

With comparisons being made between the Reds of the 1970s and the 1998 Yankees, I ask 65-year-old Sparky Anderson, Cincy manager from 1970–1976, to do the same. "Last year the Yankees had the numbers, but no one can tell me that they were the best, simply because they didn't have the chance to play with some of the great teams of past eras," Sparky argues from his home in Thousand Oaks, California, on an April morning in 1999, a year prior to his induction into the Hall of Fame. "It's impossible to give a right or wrong answer. But that doesn't mean we can't talk about it. We should keep arguing about it in restaurants or beer joints or at the office. That is why baseball is so different from all other sports—because of its history."

Anderson's contribution to baseball history began with a one-year stint as second baseman for the Phillies, followed by a season as coach for San Diego in 1969, then 26 years as major league skipper—nine with the Reds and another 17 with the Tigers, which included a world championship in 1984. It made him the only manager to win a World Series in both the National and American leagues. Anderson won more games and had a better winning percentage than any other skipper except for Connie Mack and John McGraw.

Some are born to lead. "When I competed as a player, I think everybody knew how much I loved the game. I played as hard as anybody could play, and the one thing I cared about was winning." Anderson singles out former Tiger Kirk Gibson as having the same kind of attitude. "There's a player who will probably never be a Hall-of-Famer, but one thing I can always say is that he only cared about winning. He never thought about going 0–4 as long as the team won."

A remark that a scout once made to him comes to mind. "Paul Florence had snow-white hair like me and worked for Houston for years. I was managing St. Petersburg in the Florida State League in 1966. He called me over to the screen one day and said, 'You know something, some day you're going to be a major league manager because you can manage.' And I think people recognized that in me."

What was it that people recognized? "I don't like to use the word 'communicate' because, to me, that word is used so much. But I had a way of understanding the players who were, I guess you could say, on the bubble. You know, the ones who were thinking, 'Will I make it, will I not make it?' Maybe it's because I was that way and understood. But for some reason, I understood the stars as well."

Not everything about managing came easily to Anderson. "The most difficult part was not being able to tell the truth. I made a rule with myself that I would never use a player in the paper to pay for a mistake. Not to be able to tell the truth and always keeping it inside—I think that was the hardest to do. But you have to do it if you want to keep a relationship where you can always discuss things with a player. Once you expose him, take the clothes off a person, you will never get them back on. You've embarrassed him, and therefore you have nothing in common any more."

Anderson remembers a humorous moment that occurred at the onset of the 1975 World Series. "We had quite a bit of rain in Boston and had to find a place to work out. Tufts University offered us their facilities and Harvard offered theirs. And it was nothing against Tufts and nothing against Harvard, but I just wanted to have a little fun with them. I made the remark, "You know, we're going to use the field house at Tufts because I just don't quite feel right about being a 'Hahvad' man."

Sparky pays tribute to one of the game's all-time greats. "Everyone talks about Mays being the greatest. I never got to see Mays in his prime so I can't make a judgment. But I can honestly say that the greatest *opposing* player I ever saw was Bobby Clemente. I always called him Bobby when I visited him in Pittsburgh. He was such a funny guy. I'd tease him and ask, 'Bobby, how are the sportswriters doing?' He'd joke back in broken English, 'Spahky. Deez sportswriters. I kinnot stand dem!'

"Bobby could do more things than any player I've ever seen. I used to coach third base for Preston Gomez in San Diego. Once he told me, 'Now, I want you to know about Clemente cause he'll play a game with you. If we have a man on first, and there's a base hit to right field, he'll pretend to be loafing in on it. The moment you start your wave for that runner to come to third—look out, there's gonna be an explosion.' Well, sure enough, I don't know what inning it was, but the situation came up. And he put me in his trap. And I did it. And let me tell you, my runner was about two-thirds of the way to third when the ball arrived. I came into the dugout and Preston was laughing. He said, 'What did I tell you?' But that was Roberto. There wasn't anything he couldn't do."

During the 1976 Series between the Reds and Yanks and later while managing in the American League, Anderson observed the work of New York catcher Thurman Munson. "Munson was what you'd label a tough guy. He wasn't a power thrower, but he was one of those guys that knew how to get rid of a ball. Offensively, he was one of the game's great hitting catchers. I'm not talking about hitting thirty, forty home runs, but he could hit. I remember in the World Series, our people who scouted him said that he could hurt you with power if you tried to come inside on him. So we pitched away most of the time and he wound up hitting over .500."

Notwithstanding Munson's heroics, the Reds swept the Yanks in the Series. A key factor was Cincy's success in neutralizing Mickey Rivers, a .312 hitter during the regular season. In each at bat, third baseman Rose played extremely shallow, preventing the speedy lefty from dropping a bunt. It was a dangerous gamble, since Rivers was adept at slapping the ball the opposite way. "Before the Series, Pete came to me and said, 'I want to get right on top of this guy and make him hit.' I said, 'You want to get what?' He said, 'I want to get right on top of him.' I said, 'If you want to get right on top of him, go ahead. It won't be me there.' So throughout the Series he played in, and it was the funniest thing. It just psyched out Rivers so much."

Anderson hasn't finished talking about Rose. "The time has long passed when Pete should have been inducted into the Hall of Fame. Let me tell you, it comes down to a very simple point. And I'm not a lawyer and am not going to pretend to be one. But I have enough common sense to understand this. Just show me, and I'll go along with you, one piece of evidence that says Pete Rose did something wrong or illegal—*as a player*! Maybe there is evidence, although much of it may be innuendo, that he could have done something wrong as a manager. I don't know. But is Pete Rose qualified to be elected to the Hall as a manager? I don't think so. But doesn't he have the right to be voted in as a player? Unless you can show me what he did wrong as a player, then he deserves to be eligible. There are two different issues here."

One former Reds player who made it to Cooperstown is Johnny Bench. The 12-time All-Star was inducted in his first year of eligibility in 1989. "I've already said that deciding who is the best is something you can't do, but that's with the exception of Johnny Bench. His case is unarguable. And I'll explain it to you from a man who saw most of the great ones—Casey Stengel. He came up to me one day and said, 'Shotgun.' That's what he used to call me. 'You will never live long enough to ever see anyone behind the plate like that young guy you got. He is the best I have ever seen, the best you have ever seen, and will be the best that anybody else ever sees.' Now remember, Casey has seen Berra, Dickey, Cochrane, he's seen them all.

"And I can honestly say that no one has ever played their position—including Ozzie Smith, Willie Mays, and so on—as Bench played his. He never even had to work at it. It was just automatic. He had hands like a shortstop and vision like a cat. They did a test on him at a Kansas City school once, checking his peripheral vision and all those things. The doctor said, 'I've never seen anything like this guy.' We used to see Bench do things and we'd say, 'My gosh. I've never seen that.' And Alex Grammas, my coach, would say, 'Yeah, and you never will again until he does it.'"

Sparky sympathizes with the plight of modern players, a rarity among old-timers. "One of the things that bothers me is the way they're always talking about salaries." He uses the case of Kevin Brown as an example. The hard-throwing righthander was the ace on the pennant-winning Padres of 1998 before signing with the Dodgers as a free agent during the winter. "Today, I pick up the paper and read about how Brown gets beat by San Diego and how he gets booed over there. Well, that's fine. Getting booed is part of the job, and Brown handled it well. I watched him as he went to the dugout. Not once did he make a move. Looking straight ahead, a professional all the way. But in the article, they have to put in the fact that he's making $105 million.

"I'd just like to know why they have to be reminded of their salary all the time? Who gave them the salary? No player to my knowledge can sit down, fill out his own contract, and send it to the commissioner's office without it being sent back void because it didn't have the owner's name on it. If the owners want to pay these salaries, why are we blaming the players? But the moment it appears that they're not doing good enough on the field, you read or hear about their salaries. This goes on for six, eight months."

Still not finished. "People tell me that players aren't like they used to be—that players in the past would play for nothing. Well, let me tell you, that's the biggest myth going around. I got news for you. Players in the past were playing ball because that was the easiest way to make $150 a month rather than working in the coal mines. So that stuff is a lot of malarkey. And if the players today aren't the same kind of guys as in the past—is the world the same today? I can honestly say that when I talk to a player and think about when I started, they are so much more intelligent today. They want to know why. They are very inquisitive. And I like that. Because if I, the manager, can't answer their questions, what am I doing running the club?"

Having managed in Detroit for 15 years, Anderson is somewhat saddened by the imminent closing of Tiger Stadium, scheduled for the end of the 1999 season. "For one thing, it reminds me that I'm getting old," he laughs. "But you know, it all stays in your memory. I can shut my eyes and see Tiger Stadium and go through the tunnel and up the walkway. I can see where the restrooms are, where the phones are. They used to tell me, and I never believed before now, that when you get old, that's when your memory gets *sharp*. So the new stadium is wonderful because life is about moving to the next step."

Despite his liberal views on baseball, Anderson is critical of some aspects of the modern game, including thin-skinned umpires. "The fans have always come to see the Leo Durochers, Casey Stengels—managers who would put on a show. I managed against Leo at his latest time, and even then I loved watching him go at the umpires. There's nothing wrong with digging a hole at home plate. The groundskeeper will come out, fill it up, and we're ready to go again. And what's wrong with throwing your hat? Earl Weaver, my god. You mean to tell me he wasn't an attraction? And Billy Martin. Everybody talks about how he got into trouble here or there. But Billy did so many great things for the game, it's unbelievable. Fans wanted to see Billy. And Tommy Lasorda. People just loved to watch him manage. He helped fill the seats. I'm not saying everybody can be a Durocher, Weaver, or Martin, but if there is one, then let him go. Because that's one of the reasons fans enjoy going to the ballpark."

Sparky is enjoying his retirement and would not consider another managerial offer. "I think everybody has to know when they're done. I just could not go to bed at night knowing I'd have to get up in the morning, go to the ballpark, and sit around all day waiting until game time. If I could go from my hotel room and go right to the dugout dressed and ready to manage the games, I'd do it. But all those hours just sitting around in the clubhouse, I just couldn't do it anymore."

It is baseball's loss that the colorful Anderson no longer occupies a major league dugout. No longer can we delight in his meticulous arguments with arbiters, or observe his slow walk to the mound where Captain Hook would extend an opened right hand to the pitcher, expecting the ball to be placed as gently as if it were an egg. But we can still enjoy and appreciate his commentary. For that, he will always be amenable. As Sparky would say, talking baseball is what makes the game so great.

Dick Williams

In Dick Williams' 21 seasons of managing in the majors that included six first-place finishes, which was his most exciting? "Well, if you're just talking about the season and not including the World Series as part of the year, there's no question in my mind that the 1967 season was the most exciting," the 71-year-old resident of Henderson, Nevada, replies in April of 1999. "The Red Sox hadn't won in 23 years. They were known as the Country Club. We were a 100–1 shot and won the thing on the last day of the season. Remember, that was when we had one division—a ten-team league—so it was tougher in those days."

Williams, who currently works as advisor and scout for the Yankees, selects Opening Day of 1967 as his most memorable of 3,023 games at the helm. "It was my first game as manager. We played the Chicago White Sox and Eddie Stanky was managing. And we won the game. I love Stanky. He's a good man. My son's a pitching coach today for the Tampa Bay Devil Rays and he played for Stanky at the University of South Alabama." (Eddie "The Brat" Stanky died shortly after the interview.)

Williams singles out Carl Yastrzemski for his contribution to the team's success that year. "I played and managed in both leagues so I saw a lot of great players. I never watched a player who had a year like Yastrzemski. Running, throwing, fielding, hitting, and hitting with power. He deserved to win the MVP and Triple Crown that year."

The Red Sox battled the Cardinals in the 1967 Series before falling in Game Seven in Boston. "We just had too much Bob Gibson against us," the St. Louis native states. A month later, the rookie skipper was named Manager-of-the-Year, and though he recaptured the award with the A's the following decade, he asserts that "winning it in 1967 was more exciting."

Williams' baseball experience began as a player, signing with the

Dodger organization after his high school graduation in 1946. "They called them the Brooklyn Dodgers; I called them the Branch Rickeys. Before I got to the majors, Rickey had lost out on a power struggle with O'Malley and he moved on to Pittsburgh and later to St. Louis. Rickey was a real baseball man. He had worn a uniform. O'Malley never did. Rickey had been on the field and played on some winners and losers. So I learned baseball from Rickey in my years in the minors with the Dodger organization. He was strong on fundamentals and I was brought up that way. I guess you could say I patterned my managing a little after him, even though I think you manage more to your own personality."

The outfielder made his major league debut with Brooklyn in June of 1951. "Then in 1952, I separated my shoulder diving for a ball in St. Louis and I wasn't able to throw very well after that. I became a utility ballplayer. But I still played 13 years in the majors." During his National League stint, Williams observed the skills of several superb players of the 1950s. "I saw Hank Aaron break in. If they had let him run, he would have been an outstanding basestealer as well. But they didn't want him to get hurt. And Jackie Robinson. I would have loved to see Jackie at age 21. He was 29 when he broke in. And Willie Mays. Well, he was just Willie Mays. Just outstanding."

His playing career over by 1964, Williams secured a managing position the following year with Boston's minor league club in Toronto. By winning the Governor's Cup in two successive seasons, he caught the attention of the Boston front office and was appointed Red Sox skipper for the 1967 season. "Dick O'Connell was my first general manager in the majors and I just think the world of him to this day. I was not a Yawkey man. He said I was too tough on the players but I must have grown awfully smart after he fired me [in 1970]. I went to Oakland and won all three years."

From 1971 to 1973, the Williams-led A's won three division titles, two pennants, and two world championships, while gaining notoriety for perceptible discord among owner, manager, and players. In retrospect, Dick mentions nothing negative about his former A's athletes. "Reggie Jackson was like my son. I loved him. He played hard for me. I thought the world of him offensively and defensively. He was one of a group of great players. The captain was Sal Bando. He was my main man. My pitching leader was Catfish Hunter. Reggie would try to voice his opinion, too.

"I loved all those guys on that ballclub. [Gene] Tenace. [Dave] Duncan. [Joe] Rudi. [Bert] Campaneris. Dick Green. [Ken] Holtzman. [Vida] Blue. [Blue Moon] Odom. [Rollie] Fingers. You have to remember, we were world champions for two-straight years, and the year before we won 101 ballgames but lost to Baltimore in the playoffs. After I left, they won another world championship and then won a division title the next year. And you know, one year we only had one guy who hit over .300. I think it was Reggie. Everybody else was hitting .275, .285, .295. No one you'd call superstars, but we had great pitching and defense and we played as a 25-man unit. And we won."

Irked by the lack of respect shown his former club by baseball commentators who laud Cincinnati as the team of the 1970s, Williams argues, "They talk about the Big Red Machine, but our club was much better. We beat them in the Series without Jackson and [Darold] Knowles. We won three in a row and five-straight division titles. But all we hear about is how great Cincinnati was. Have them just check the records."

The Reds' abundance of superstars, including future Hall-of-Famers Bench, Morgan, and Perez, should-be Hall-of-Famer Rose, and slugging standout George Foster, may explain the club's enduring glory. With the exception of Jackson and Hunter, Oakland was composed of capable but not overly talented players who relied on all-around effort to win ballgames. Williams likens his former ballclub to the most successful team of the 1990s. "We played the game the way it should be played. Execution. Fundamentals. That's what you're supposed to strive for. That's what Joe Torre has done with the Yankees. I was with them all spring last year and he got them to play good hard-nosed baseball—what I call National League baseball. They would do the little things that it takes to win."

Describing his association with A's owner Charlie Finley as "a long-distance relationship—we played in Oakland and he worked in Chicago," Dick characterizes his former boss as "demanding," while noting that "we did most of our stuff by phone until we got into the playoffs and World Series—which he had never accomplished until I got over there." Implying that Finley unwittingly bolstered his managerial position through constant interference, Dick explains, "The players were never mad at me, they were mad at the owner. But Charlie did a lot of good things for a lot of players. He took care of them."

Williams praises his former adversary for having an innovative mind and sound fiscal judgment. "Finley had all those promotions for the fans—Family Nights on Mondays, Hot Pants Day, Mustache Day. You know, silly promotions. And actually, he didn't do too much advertising. He ran a skeleton crew in the front office. And he was wise enough to get out of it before the salaries got high. When he sold the club, he warned the owners, 'Whatever you do, don't let the players have arbitration.' And that's been one of the reasons why the salaries have escalated. Charlie was a lot smarter than people give him credit for."

Following his World Series victory in 1973, Williams left Oakland. "I resigned. Charlie didn't fire me," he emphasizes. "Finley wished me well and told me he wouldn't stand in my way. So I signed a three-year contract with the Yankees. We had a press conference announcing the signing, and we were going to play the next two years at Shea Stadium [Yankee Stadium was being renovated].

"Then John Clayborne, who worked for Charlie, told him he should get some compensation for me. So Charlie changed his mind and asked for compensation. When the Yankees said no, Joe Cronin, who was the lame-duck [American League] president, blocked the deal, even though Houk had left the Yankees with a year to go on his contract and they let him go to Detroit."

Deciding to sit out the 1974 season rather than honor the final year of his Oakland contract, Williams worked for multi-millionaire and entrepreneur John D. MacArthur until approached with a managerial offer on July 1st. After reimbursing Finley $100,000, Angels owner Gene Autry signed the coveted skipper to a three-and-a-half year deal. "I never felt very comfortable with any owner, but I loved Gene Autry. He was never able to win anything when I was there or when anybody else was there, but he was a tremendous man. He let his baseball people run the show and treated his employees wonderfully. He was a baseball fan and was around the ballpark all the time. He put a lot of money in that ballclub and wanted badly to have a winner. They came close a couple of times but could never quite make it."

Still, Williams' tenure in Anaheim was a stormy one, characterized by conflict with front office executives (General Manager Harry Dalton in particular) and with players. Three sixth-place finishes led to his dismissal in the autumn of 1976. "Dalton did the firing," Williams stresses. "Autry felt bad letting me go. But then I went to Montreal and was there for five years and turned the franchise around."

It is no idle boast, as the bottom-berth Expos improved to fifth place in Williams' first year, to fourth in 1978, and to second the next two seasons before winning the second half of the split-season in 1981 despite the controversial manager being sent packing prior to Montreal's defeat of the Phils in the playoffs and loss to the Dodgers in the championship series that year.

Impressed with the Expos turnaround and hoping the controversial but successful skipper could do the same for his last-place team, fast-food mogul and Padres owner Ray Kroc immediately signed free-agent

Williams to a multi-year contract. The acquisition yielded benefits three years later in the form of the first division title and pennant in the history of the 16-year-old franchise. The Padres lost the Series in five games to the Tigers, as Williams again saw too much Gibson—Kirk Gibson this time—as he belted a pair of home runs in the clincher.

Despite his success in San Diego, Williams was fired during spring training of 1986 following a disappointing fourth-place finish the year before. "Ray Kroc died and Joan Kroc, a lovely lady, didn't know anything about the game. Her son-in-law [Ballard Smith], who had screwed up a hockey franchise, a basketball franchise, and probably would have screwed up any other franchise they would have bought, took over as president. So he paid me off and after two managers, [Steve] Boros and [Larry] Bowa, Jack McKeon took over as both manager and general manager, which is what he wanted to do for a long, long time."

Two months after his departure from San Diego, Williams headed north to Seattle. "George Argyros hired me, and I figure he's one of the smartest businessmen around. He bought out his partners for a grand outlay of $13½ million (1981) and sold it for $76 million (1989). And he didn't spend a nickel on players." The unpopular owner's tightfisted approach did little to improve the ballclub, as futility and frustration characterized Williams' final years as manager, which ended with his dismissal two months into the 1988 season.

Described by critics as an arrogant and contentious leader, Williams offers no apologies today for his style, insisting he would do nothing differently if given the chance. "I've been with six different clubs and I've turned, I'd say, five of them around. They were losing clubs, hadn't won in a long time. I may have gotten on people's nerves in the front office because I was demanding and wanted to do things my way. But it paid off. The results were there and the statistics show it." Those stats include a 1571–1451 record, seven seasons managing ballclubs with 90 or more victories, six first-place finishes, three pennants, and two world championships. If winning is an indication of a manager's ability, the record books support Williams' claim.

Experts have cited 1979 as Williams' most successful season, as the Expos bettered its win total of the previous year by 19 and finished only a game behind the first-place Pirates. Dick concurs. "I still feel one of the better jobs I ever accomplished was up at Montreal, even though we never won a flag. The year before I got there, they lost 107 ballgames. By my third year, we won 95. The next year, we won 92. And we were doing it with a bunch of kids. We had some veterans sprinkled in, but this was a club that was mostly youngsters."

There was one aspect of managing that Williams found distasteful. "I never liked the DH. Finley and Cal Griffith thought of that. It was their baby. Naturally, I had to go along with it, but I liked it when the pitcher had to come to bat. You know, the strategy involved—the flip-flops and all that. Without the DH, there was more for a manager to do."

Turning attention to the modern game, Dick discusses the impact of the 1998 season on baseball's resurgence. "I thought what McGwire and Sosa did last year was terrific. You have to remember, too, that there were four players who hit 50 or more home runs. And, I'm partial because I work for them, but I think what the Yankees did—winning 114 games and going ahead and winning 11 more in the post-season—was great also. The season certainly did bring baseball back and I think it will get back to where it was before that infamous strike."

Known for stressing defense and mental alertness while managing, Williams isn't satisfied with today's brand of ball. "It's totally different today. Everybody is swinging at the end of the bat trying to hit it nine miles. Teams don't advance runners like they should. To me, it's not a team sport anymore. Players are bigger, stronger, richer certainly, but they don't play the game as before. I wouldn't even attempt to manage today. The player and agent are running the show."

That Williams' managerial career has concluded is probably for the best. His in-your-face, get-involved style is obsolete, not befitting the model modern manager, who prefers diplomacy to candor, leniency to accountability, mechanical methods to subtle strategies. Provide most of today's helmsmen with a few power hitters, several five-inning starters, a closer, some stat sheets, and he is content. For Williams, it would not suffice.

Hector Lopez

In the 1994 book *Baseball with a Latin Beat*, author Peter Bjarkman explains the Yankees' 1953 decision to bypass talented but flashy Puerto Rican–born Vic Power as the franchise's first black ballplayer. He writes, "The Yankees would wait for the soft-spoken American black Elston Howard [Bjarkmans adds in parentheses: "whose role would be largely to understudy Yogi Berra"] and then for the hardly more charismatic Hector Lopez, lead-footed and lead-fisted infielder from Panama. Neither Howard nor Lopez could 'carry Vic Power's glove' according to most knowledgeable scouts hovering around the American League scene."

According to Bjarkman, Yank executives spurned Power for no other reason than his flamboyant style of play and less-than-humble personality. Bjarkman's point was that black and Hispanic ballplayers were expected to act in a restrained manner so as not to draw attention to themselves, and that Power's inclination for one-hand snatches on the field and light-skinned women off the field worked against his playing in pinstripes. Bjarkman quotes Power's comparison of himself and Howard, presumably as further proof that Power should have been the Yankees' obvious choice. Power says, "There wasn't much competition because he didn't have the numbers." (Bjarkman adds in parentheses: "Nor did Howard ever match Power's hitting totals in the big leagues.")

In eagerness to support his argument, Bjarkman misleads readers by suggesting that Power was the vastly superior player among the trio. In fact, all were well-regarded prospects in the early fifties. Certainly, no one familiar with Howard's first three major league seasons would take seriously the notion that he was brought up merely for the purpose of having a soft-spoken minority on the club who would give Berra an occasional breather. On the contrary, so impressed were the Yankees with Howard's hitting ability that he was used in the outfield in order to accumulate sufficient at bats until the time came when Berra relinquished the backstop position.

A comparison of careers justifies the Yankees' judgment in selecting Howard and Lopez over Power. Howard was a catcher, Power a first baseman, making a defensive comparison difficult. Howard nevertheless notched two Gold Glove Awards in his 14-year career and would have won more had exceptionally gifted backstops Earl Battey and Bill Freehan not been contemporaries. No such formidable defender posed a serious challenge for Power while grabbing seven consecutive Gold Gloves until 1965, when slick-fielders Joe Pepitone and George Scott began their domination of the remaining decade.

Nor do statistics support Bjarkman's claim that Power was a more productive batsman than Howard. Both batted over .300 three times, but Howard peaked with a .348 mark in 1961 while Power's best was .319 in 1955. Despite accumulating nearly 700 additional career at bats and hitting in ballparks more batter-friendly than expansive Yankee Stadium, Power had 41 fewer home runs; he never hit as many as 20 in a season, while Howard had three consecutive 20+ seasons. Although Power gathered more lifetime doubles, Howard had more triples (50 to Power's 49) and more RBIs (762 to 658). Power's batting average exceeded Howard's (.284 to .274), but not his slugging percentage (.411 to .427).

Finally, Howard won the MVP in 1963 and was a strong contender in 1958, 1961, and 1964 while competing against the likes of Berra, Mantle, and Maris. Power was never seriously considered, and the obvious argument in his defense—his never playing for a contender—can be countered by the fact that he played several years for capable Cleveland clubs that might have challenged for the flag had their first-sacker overachieved with the lumber.

Perhaps the mellowness of Howard and Lopez made them more attractive choices for the conservative New York brass, but to infer that it was the sole reason for their selection is invalid. Bjarkman labels Lopez as "lead-footed," but fails to acknowledge Power's never having swiped more than nine bases in a season. And despite Power's more alluring surname, it was his sole slugging advantage over Lopez. While Kansas City teammates from 1955–1958 (peak years for Power, according to Bjarkman), Lopez and Power had nearly identical homer totals, while Lopez's career mark exceeds Power's despite 1,400 fewer at bats largely accumulated in the most spacious of ballparks. Had Lopez remained with Kansas City or played with ballclubs other than the talent-laden Yankees, he, like Power, would have played regularly throughout his career, and almost certainly would have been among the top sluggers in the league. Surely, executives for a franchise renowned for its success must have seen something in Lopez other than his aversion for calling attention to himself.

Elston Howard passed away in December of 1980 at the age of 51. Seventy-one year old Hector Lopez today lives in Hudson, Florida, located approximately 40 miles northwest of Tampa, where he works as the Yankees' minor league hitting instructor. "Ellie was a great ballplayer and great man," Hector says in our conversation of March 2000, nearly twenty years after his former roommate's death. "He was probably my best friend on the Yankees. When we were on the road, most of the time we'd get up early, have breakfast, and then go to a movie. At that time, you could go to the movies at ten o'clock in the morning. But before we went, we'd stop in a department store so Ellie could get a tie. He was always buying ties. Then we'd go to the movies for a couple of hours, have lunch, and go back to our room to rest up before going to the ballpark."

In Jim Bouton's controversial 1970 tome, *Ball Four*, the pitcher-author disclosed the risqué antics of teammates and spewed disparaging comments about players, managers, and baseball executives. Bouton's revelations revolutionized the baseball book industry, as authors and biographers shifted emphasis from on-the-field activities to off-the-field affairs and personality assessments. (It is an approach that some today, admittedly a minority, consider a literary setback rather than progress.)

Recently, an anniversary edition of *Ball Four* was published featuring a new epilogue in which a retrospective Bouton defends the book for its candor while claiming that no one suffered any lingering harm from it. It should be remembered, however, that while writing *Ball Four*, Bouton completely disregarded the feelings of acquaintances, a transgression for which he has apologized to no one. And yet, Bouton still wonders why many of his targets remain offended. He just doesn't get it.

Commentary in *Ball Four* included subtle yet scathing criticism of former teammate Howard; Bouton implied his being both a hypocrite and an Uncle Tom. In his sequel, *I'm Glad You Didn't Take It Personally*, Bouton suggested that Howard had the opportunity to exact revenge about a year after publication of *Ball Four* when they crossed paths in the corridor of the football Giants dressing room. The duo merely exchanged greetings.

Perhaps Howard was already aware of the damage he could cause. When I ask how well the duo got along as battery mates, Lopez responds by recalling an incident that occurred at West Point. "The Yankees used to play exhibition games against the army cadets every year. We were down there once and Bouton challenged Ellie to a boxing match. I don't know exactly how it came about, but the next thing you know they were in the ring. Ellie knocked him out. I guess Bouton was sorry he was running his mouth."

Lopez talks about his own baseball experience. Born in Colon, Panama, in 1929, Hector played ball in junior high and high school, but the notion of someday becoming a big leaguer did not arise until age 18 in 1947. "The Yankees and Dodgers came down to Panama for spring training. After watching them, that's when I really started thinking about playing professionally."

Hector played semi-pro ball for the next four years, signed with the Kansas City A's in 1951, and made $250 a month playing for its Class C club in the Canadian Provincial League for two seasons. In 1953, he was promoted to Williamsport of the Eastern League, made the jump to Ottawa of the International League in 1954, and finally got his big break at age 26 in 1955. "I was playing for Columbus and was called up by the A's (in mid-May). Lou Boudreau was the manager. The next year was my first full year in the majors and that's when I moved to the United States permanently."

Lopez had two hits in four at bats in his major league debut in Boston. Playing regularly at shortstop and third base, he finished the season with a .290 average, 15 home runs, 68 RBIs, and followed up with another fine season (.273, 18 HRs, 69 RBIs) in 1956. Lopez's playing time was curtailed in 1957 with the arrival of Yank castoff Billy Martin in June, but with The Kid's trade to Detroit in 1958 Hector returned to full-time duty and produced 17 homers and 73 RBIs.

Lopez's most noteworthy achievements with the A's were a three-homer game on June 26, 1958, at Municipal Stadium and a 22-game hitting streak in 1957. "For the moment, I don't recall the name of the pitcher who stopped the streak," Hector says. "A Cuban pitcher, I think. May have pitched for the White Sox. Might have been [Sandy] Consuegra."

Hector's four full seasons with Kansas City would mark the only years playing as a regular. It was also a time when discrimination of blacks and minorities was prevalent in the mid-western town. "Playing in Kansas City was a very, very difficult experience. A lot of things you couldn't do, a lot of places you couldn't go. It was very trying. Things didn't open up until around '61 or '62. Until then you had to stay in certain sections of town. Vic Power, Harry "Suitcase" Simpson and I would room together."

In late May of 1959, the A's and Yankees swapped third basemen, with Hector going to the Bombers for Jerry Lumpe. "Harry Craft was the manager and he was the one who told me. I was really happy about it. My mother was living in Brooklyn at the time so I would be able to see her more. My father was still living in Colon. He saw me play a lot of ball in Panama but he never saw me play in the majors except when the game was on television."

As a Yankee fan during the early sixties, I recall Lopez being a proficient opposite-field hitter. According to Hector, he had been a pull-hitter with Kansas City, taking advantage of the short left and left-center field dimensions at Municipal Stadium. No such benefit for right-hand hitters existed at Yankee Stadium, where the distance from home plate to left-to-center field walls ranged from 400 to 460 feet. "When I met Casey [Stengel], he mentioned, 'Son, you gotta hit the ball to the opposite field. It's too big a park to try to pull the ball.' That's when I started developing my stroke to right field."

What was it like playing for The Old Professor? "Casey never did much talking to the ballplayers. What I remember most about him is that he never called a player by his name. He'd always say, 'You! Grab a bat!' or something like that. Ralph Houk would always talk to you like a man, call you by your name, talk things over with you before he did something. He was what we called a player's manager."

The most prominent of Yankees during Lopez's tenure with the club from 1959 to 1966 was Mickey Mantle. "He was the leader of the ballclub, even though he never said much. Everybody respected him because he played hard all the time and he always wanted to win. There were so many times when we were down two or three runs when Mantle would give up trying to hit home runs and would bunt the ball just to get on base and start a rally. He led by example."

In 1960, Hector was the Yankees' regular right fielder and he responded with a solid .284 average in 408 at bats. But his playing time reduced that of Elston Howard, who was removed from the outfield and platooned with Berra at backstop. In 1961, the Yanks were committed to Howard as the regular catcher, with Berra and Blanchard spelling him occasionally. In order to give Blanchard and Berra additional playing time, Casey alternated them and Lopez in right field. Hector's plate appearances dropped in 1961 and 1962, and only Mantle's knee injury in 1963 enabled replacement Lopez to again accumulate over 400 at bats. From 1964 to his final season in 1966, he averaged only 228 at bats per season.

Still, Hector had some memorable moments in pinstripes. "One of my greatest accomplishments was my performance in the 1961 Series. I drove in seven runs, which tied a Series record at the time. Had a triple, home run, and double. Had five hits in nine at bats, something like that."

Only one other achievement comes to mind as being more significant. "Just being able to play in the big leagues for as long as I did at the time that I played is something I'm proud of. There was a lot of competition, a lot of great players during the fifties and sixties. Plus the fact that there weren't many black ballplayers at that time. Especially in the American League. So I guess you can say I made the most out of my opportunities."

Lopez recalls some of the formidable pitching opponents he faced during his career. "I guess the toughest for me was Dick Radatz. When he was pitching in Boston, that left field wall didn't do me any good. But there were other tough pitchers for me. Whitey Ford and Bob Turley, before we became teammates. Herb Score before he got hurt. Mike Garcia and Early Wynn. The American League had some pretty tough pitchers. Even some relievers. I remember Narleski and Mossi were a pretty good combination."

After the Yankees gave up on Lopez, he went to an Anaheim spring training tryout in 1967. Failing to make the Angels' roster, he decided to play Triple A ball in Hawaii, hoping a big league ballclub would bring him up during the stretch drive. Although Hector put up impressive numbers, the call-up never came. The Hawaii franchise moved to Buffalo in 1968, where Lopez put together another solid season but again failed to attract major league interest. Opportunity finally came in 1969, though not in the form Lopez had expected. "The Washington Senators hired Ted Williams as manager. He came down to spring training and saw me trying out. He said, 'Hector, what the hell are you doing here?' I told him, 'Ted, I'm just trying to make a living like everyone else.' He said, 'How about a job managing?'

"So I managed the Buffalo Bisons that year. It's funny, everything that's ever been written about me, all these stories, and no one's ever mentioned anything about my managing at the Triple A level. I never understood that. If I wasn't the first black ballplayer to manage at the Triple A level, I must have been one of the first."

Unfortunately, Hector's managing position lasted only one year. He decided it was time to get out of baseball. "I got a job working for the Hempstead Department of Parks and Recreation as a Recreation Specialist. Used to give baseball training for the kids in the town. Did that for twenty years." He returned to baseball in the early nineties as manager of the Yankees' Tampa farm club, which was part of the Gulf Coast League. "After that, I became a Yankee minor league instructor in Tampa, which I still do today. I work with players at the minor league complex, helping them with hitting and playing the outfield and infield. It's a year-round job so I'm pretty busy most of the time."

Hector discusses what he perceives as the biggest change in the game today. "It hasn't changed much except for the use of middle relievers.

Starters go five, six innings, and they're out of the game. The set-up guy comes in and pitches until they get to the closer. Those things didn't happen in my day. That's about the only big change since I played. That and the fact that the players are bigger and stronger."

At the time of the interview, much of the baseball conversation in America focused on controversial remarks made by Atlanta's John Rocker in a *Sports Illustrated* article published the past winter. Rocker made what were deemed invective comments about New York City, its residents, and its minority groups. At first, the lefty reliever claimed the right to freedom of speech but later apologized for his imprudent outburst; he was nonetheless fined and suspended by Commissioner Bud Selig and continued to be the target of criticism and abuse by the media and fans alike.

Lopez is sympathetic toward the beleaguered pitcher. "I think Rocker made a mistake and paid for it. They should forget about it and let him go on with his job. From what I heard him say on television, it sounds like he's sorry for what he said."

Does his forgiving attitude extend to Pete Rose and his banishment from baseball? "I don't think Rose should be allowed back, but he did a lot for the game and he earned a chance at being in the Hall of Fame. He has the stats to prove it."

Hector harbors no bitterness today in regards to his years as a part-timer. "I never regretted playing for the Yankees. I know I could have played regularly for most other ballclubs, but look at all the chances I had to play in the Series (1960–1964). And I got two World Series rings (1961, 1962)."

Hector may have lacked flamboyance but he understood the merit of being a team player—and reaped the rewards.

Ralph Houk

The 1961 Yankees: Maris breaks Ruth's homer record with 61. Mantle smashes 54. Catchers Berra, Blanchard, and Howard combine for 64 home runs. The Yanks set a major league record for team homers with 240. Whitey Ford wins 25. Luis Arroyo notches 15 victories and 25 saves, both league-leading relief stats. The ballclub wins 109 games, outdistancing runner-up Detroit by eight games. The Bombers take four of five from the Reds in the Series.

A dream team having a dream season? No problems? No pressure? Eighty-year-old former manager Ralph Houk remembers differently as he speaks from his home in Winter Haven, Florida, in April of 1999. "In 1961, I was replacing Casey which was a rough job. Casey was such a great guy and a friend to all the writers in New York. I was never a big star during my playing career so I guess it kind of surprised a few people that I was named manager. I wasn't afraid of taking the job. It's just that replacing Casey put some pressure on."

That pressure intensified when the Yankees entered September tied for first with the Tigers. "Then we had that big series with them in New York. That was the series Yogi made a real good play in left field to throw [Al] Kaline out at second base trying to stretch a single into a double. So we won that series and Detroit kept on losing and we kept on winning and we ran away with it in the final month."

Houk's playing career consisted of utility duty for the Yanks from 1947 to 1954. "I was a platoon catcher in my rookie season. Aaron Robinson was catching against right-hand pitching, and I was catching against lefties. Yogi was playing part-time in right field. He was hitting so great that they had to get him in the lineup every day. So Yogi took over behind the plate, and about all I did after that was break in Yogi's glove."

Houk managed three years for the Yanks' Triple A farm club in

Denver, then returned to New York and coached for Stengel from 1958 to 1960. The Old Professor delegated much responsibility to his coaches, which was all right with Ralph. "It was great working for Casey. And, of course, it became my job to eat dinner with him on the train trips. Crosetti, Dickey, and Turner said, 'Now it's your job, Ralph.' So I would sit there with him until he was through."

Prior to obtaining the Yankee position in 1961, Houk was tempted with other offers. "In 1960, Kansas City was looking to hire me. Parke Carroll was the general manager and I knew him quite well. And Kansas City was my hometown. So that was the only offer I was really interested in. I came close to accepting. Then after the Yanks lost to Pittsburgh in the Series, Roy Hamey [Yanks' GM] came to me and said, 'Don't take that KC job yet.' Soon after, they called and said there would be a press conference in New York announcing my hiring. I was glad then that I hadn't taken any other job."

The big story of 1961 was the M&M quest to surpass Ruth's seasonal homer mark of 60, set in 1927. Maris succeeded, his 61 round trippers remaining the major league mark for 37 years until surpassed by Mark McGwire's 70 and Sammy Sosa's 66 in 1998. I ask Houk how Maris, who died of cancer in 1985 at the age of 51, would have reacted to McGwire's sensational season. "Roger would have pulled for McGwire. That's the kind of guy he was. He wasn't concerned about the record at all when he broke it. He was happier when players on the team did something to win ballgames than he was when he hit a homer.

"There is no question that Maris belongs in the Hall of Fame. Not only because he was the first to break Ruth's mark. He was a great baserunner and would do anything to win a ballgame. Many times he'd give up the chance for a homer to try to bunt the man over. And on top of that he was an outstanding right fielder with a great arm. I remember the Series against San Francisco when he made the key play in the last inning that helped us win the seventh game."

Ralph is referring to a ninth inning threat at Candlestick Park in 1962. The Giants trailed 1–0 with two outs and a man on when Willie Mays lashed a drive to the right field corner. Maris hustled to the ball and fired it back to the infield preventing baserunner Felipe Alou from scoring. Right-hander Ralph Terry then retired Willie McCovey on a frozen rope to second baseman Bobby Richardson, giving New York their 20th world championship.

How impressed was Houk with Big Mac's season of '98? "I didn't really follow McGwire's chase. I was never one who gave much thought about records but I think they're all going to be broken anyway. The ballparks are different now. The pitching has thinned out. You don't have the strong minor league system that you used to have. So really, it's gonna be a lot easier to break records than it used to be. I think Roger's record was a lot tougher to achieve than McGwire's."

Asked to compare the '98 Yankee ballclub with his great team of '61, Ralph, like Sparky Anderson, believes it's difficult to compare teams from different eras, but gives his club the edge nonetheless. "Naturally, I would feel that way," he admits. "But we had an outstanding bench. We had good catchers. We had great outfielders in Maris, Mantle, and [Hector] Lopez. We had a great third baseman in Boyer, a great second and short combination in Richardson and Kubek. And you had Skowron at first. Then we had Whitey, and Terry had a great year, and we had the best relief pitcher in baseball in Arroyo. You know, that's pretty tough to beat."

After winning pennants from 1960 to 1964, the Yankees fell on hard times. With Houk upstairs at the general manager's position, and former Cardinal skipper Johnny Keane at the helm, the Yanks finished a dismal sixth in 1965. Houk replaced Keane early in 1966, but his return couldn't prevent the aging ballclub from finishing in the cellar for the first time in fifty years. With the exception of the 1970 team, which finished in second place with 93 victories (Baltimore won 109 that year), Houk's ballclubs were marked by mediocrity from 1966 until his final season in 1973. "When you don't have the players, it's hard to win. It's that simple. Anybody can manage when you have the talent. You make the move according to the kind of players you have."

I ask Ralph to assess some of his former Yankee players. Not surprisingly, the discussion begins with Mantle. "He gave more of himself than probably any player I've ever known. Mantle just wanted to win. He'd hit a home run or two and we'd get beat and you'd have thought he had a bad day. He'd strike out three times and we'd win and you'd have thought he had a great day."

By 1967, his legs deteriorated from chronic bone disease, Mantle received a reprieve from Houk. With no designated hitter rule that would keep Mickey's bat in the lineup and his body on the bench when the team took the field (Yankee Ron Blomberg became the first-ever DH in 1973), Houk converted the center fielder to a first baseman, a position that required less running. The strategy succeeded, as Mick endured for another two seasons. Thirty years later, Ralph has second thoughts regarding the move. "Mickey told me, 'That damned first base is the toughest place I've ever tried to play in my life.' You gotta remember, you gotta play off the bag, on the bag, off the bag. It's not easy if you've never worked at it before. And it probably put a lot of pressure on him. So I'm not sure that was the greatest idea.

"There are so many Mantle memories. I remember the time in Baltimore when he ran into a fence and got hurt. I remember thinking to myself, 'Well, there goes the pennant.' But he'd rise to the occasion after coming back from an injury. I'll never forget a game in Cleveland. We were three runs behind in the late innings, maybe even the top of the ninth. We had the bases loaded and I put Mantle in to pinch-hit. He hit the ball out of the park and we went ahead, but we blew it in the bottom of the ninth. Losing that game killed me. Sometimes, you remember the losses more than the wins."

In the winter of 1968, after experiencing his most unproductive season as a regular with stats showing 18 home runs, 54 RBIs, and a .237 batting average, Mantle called it a career. "Mickey was still a good ballplayer compared to the major leaguers at that time," Ralph maintains, "but he probably did the right thing. I had talked him out of it the year before, but couldn't do it again."

Mick's replacement in center field was fellow Oklahoman Bobby Murcer. Almost immediately, Yankee executives touted the lefty-swinging slugger as the next Mantle. It was an unfortunate comparison that put pressure on the 23-year-old, but Murcer responded with eight solid, if not spectacular, seasons as a pinstripe regular that included a .331 average in 1971 and 33 homers in 1972. "Bobby was a guy who could do a lot of things. He could run. He was a tough ballplayer. You know, go in hard at second to break up double plays. He'd give you that 120 percent. And he was a winner. He didn't play for himself. A lot of players I see today look like they're more interested in doing good for themselves than for the team.

"I'll never forget a game when Bobby was a rookie. We were playing in the old ballpark in Seattle. Bobby was playing shortstop early that year, and in this game he was nearly killing people in the stands with his throws. So I made a joke out of it and told him, 'Let's see if we can save a few lives. Let's try playing you in center field.' So I put him there, and he did a fine job."

Another Yank during the Houk reign was first baseman Joe Pepitone, known as much for his temperament as for his talent. Ralph compares his bad boy of the sixties with New York's problem child of the nineties, Darryl Strawberry. "Joe was a kid who came from a tough neighborhood in Brooklyn. He had a lot of ability. At times, he was a little bit of a problem, but it wasn't with drinking or drugs or any of that stuff. I'd call him in and talk with him. He'd listen and we'd straighten things out.

So far as I'm concerned, we didn't have a problem. Joe and I got along great. But I couldn't put up with someone like Strawberry. He just wouldn't be on my ballclub. From what I read, Joe appears to be a better guy than Strawberry."

I remind Ralph of a game in 1966 that best exemplifies the frustration felt by players, managers, and fans from 1965 to 1975. The Yankees were playing the league-leading Orioles in the opener of a doubleheader at the stadium. Trailing by two in the bottom of the ninth, the Yanks had two on and two out when switch-hitter Roy White, one of a handful of productive Yankee batters that year, drilled a drive destined for the lower row of seats in right. Outfielder Frank Robinson, traded from Cincinnati the previous winter and who would finish the year as a Triple Crown winner, made a last-second lunge and toppled into the stands. Disappearing from view for several seconds, Robinson emerged with glove held high. Umpire Hank Soar ruled the ball caught and Baltimore the victor, precipitating a stormy but futile protest by Houk. "I remember the game and I'm positive Robinson did not catch that ball. And I think that rule ought to be changed. If you catch a ball and fall into the stands, I think it's gotta be called a home run. I mean, who knows whether it was caught or not? Only Robinson, and he's not telling. When I ask him, he just grins at me. That's almost the same as telling me he didn't catch it."

Catcher Thurman Munson began a brilliant ten-year career under Houk's leadership in 1970. "The thing that impressed me most about Munson was his improvement. He was an outstanding hitter as a kid, but he had to learn to catch. He developed the quick-release throw. And he became just like Yogi. Yogi knew how to catch according to his pitcher. He remembered all the hitters' weaknesses and knew how to run a ballgame from behind the plate. Munson was the same way. He became a great catcher, and I give [coach] Jim Hegan a lot of the credit for that. He was more or less Munson's instructor when he was young."

Along with Murcer, White, and Munson, Sparky Lyle and Graig Nettles played under Houk's tutelage; all five went on to make key contributions to Yankee pennants in the late seventies and early eighties. Yet, Houk's adeptness in handling players is rarely acknowledged by modern evaluators of managers. "Patience. With young players, you have to have that. You have to treat them the way you wanted to be treated when you were a kid. Let them know what they're doing right as well as what they're doing wrong. And never embarrass them. Try to bring them along as slow as you can and let them know you're behind them all the way, even when they're going bad. During slumps, I'd try to let them work their way out of it. If you sit them out, I think they become more worried."

Following numerous losing seasons, and with rookie owner George Steinbrenner intruding in on-the-field activities, Houk decided to leave New York. "George told me, 'Ralph, you're making a big mistake leaving here. I'm gonna go out and spend money for ballplayers and we're gonna have a winning team.' Well, he did what he said he'd do. He got Hunter and Reggie Jackson. And they became winners." Most people today assume Steinbrenner and Houk separated on bad terms, but Ralph claims otherwise. "I never had as much of a problem with George as was written. When I left, I had a year to go in my contract. They weren't going to let me go. A lot of things developed from that."

Houk managed in Detroit for five years, then another four in Boston. Not once did his team reach post-season play. Ralph has no regrets. "It was great working in Detroit and Boston. I couldn't have been treated any better. They tried to keep me in both places, and that's good when you can leave and they want you to stay. You see, I decided to retire after my last season with Detroit. I was out of baseball for two years. Then Sully [Haywood Sullivan] kept talking to me. And Yawkey wanted me, too. Well, we had family that lived around the Boston area. So I took the job. They treated me wonderfully. In fact, they gave my wife a Cadillac when I left.

"Lee MacPhail [Yankee general manager] was a good baseball man and I enjoyed working with him. We were real close. When I left Boston, his son was the general manager in Minnesota. They finally talked me into coming up there to be vice-president. But I didn't stay in town. I went up there maybe once a month and we'd talk about the players and other things. That was [Tom] Kelly's first year as manager. I went to spring training with him for two years. Finally I said, 'Hey, I'm getting out. This is it, period.' And that's when I got completely out of baseball."

Houk explains why he didn't consider other managing offers. "The traveling is really what did it. When you get older, the traveling gets to you. You play a night game, take a plane to go to the next town, get there early in the morning. Then the phone rings, and you've got to answer it. It's usually the press and you've gotta answer their questions. So it gets to be a job more than fun.

"I haven't really missed baseball, although sometimes when you watch the games you miss the competition. And the game itself is still great."

With 33 years of major league service as player, coach, and manager behind him, Ralph is enjoying his retirement. "I live on a golf course. I had a bad back, but I just got it operated on in Winter Haven about six weeks ago. A specialist worked on some pinched nerves on my spine. He must have got it all cleaned out because I'm sure feeling better. So it looks like I'll be playing golf again in a couple of weeks. Then I have a boat in Everglade City not far from here and I go fishing a lot over there."

I wish Ralph luck with his recuperation and thank him for his time. It was his pleasure, he responds, adding that he found me "easy to talk to" and "more knowledgeable than some others I have spoken to." It is the supreme compliment for a fan that regards Houk as his all-time favorite manager. Who could forget the long black cigars tucked in the side of his mouth; his preoccupation with pebbles while observing the game from the top step of the dugout; his wanting to be the first to congratulate Roger, Mickey, Elston, or Bobby for belting one out; his kicking dirt and flinging his cap while arguing with umpires; his being the first on the field at the outbreak of a brawl; his being known as a player's manager, and the Major?

Along with Weaver, Williams, Martin, Lasorda, and a few others, Houk was among a dying breed of skippers who wore their hearts on their sleeves. How different from the prototypical modern manager—hidden in the dugout with face buried in stat sheets, wary of offering constructive criticism to temperamental players following bush-league mistakes, fearful of approaching imperious umpires following blatantly incorrect calls.

Heaven forfend the implication that today's brand of baseball is dissatisfying. Fans must remember that all aspects of the game—including player output and managing techniques—are superior and preferable to that of the past. Let us remain ever so grateful.

Index

Aaron, Hank 9, 78, 117, 161, 169, 196
Adderley, Cannonball 117
Adderley, Nat 117
Agganis, Harry 145
Agyros, George 199
Aikens, Willie 100
Alabama-Florida League 166
Ali, Muhammed 147
All-Star Game 13, 45, 68, 114, 117, 123, 129, 130, 174, 192
Allard, Brian 101
Allison, Bobby 31
Alomar, Roberto 71
Alomar, Sandy 71
Alou, Felipe 209
Alou, Matty 89
American Association 8, 22
American League 21, 33, 45, 107, 124, 140, 152, 170–171, 173, 187, 189–191, 198, 201, 206
American League Championship Series (ALCS) 59–60, 151, 189
American Legion 21, 59, 62, 69, 112, 128
amyotrophic lateral sclerosis (Lou Gehrig's Disease) 150
Anaheim Stadium 173
Anderson, Sparky 185, 189–194, 210
Aparicio, Luis 30, 61
Arlington Stadium 106–107, 142
Armstrong, Louis 30
Arroyo, Luis 208, 210
artificial surface 33, 68
Ashburn, Richie 164
Atlanta Braves 35, 36, 91–94, 105, 117, 134, 207
Autry, Gene 174, 198

Bair, Doug 99
Ball Four 203
Baltimore Colts 18, 50
Baltimore Orioles 18, 32, 52, 122, 152, 173, 187, 197, 210, 212
Bando, Sal 91, 147–148, 196
Banks, Ernie 68
Barber, Steve 31
Barchiachini, Reno 72
Barlick, Al 88
Bartell, Dick 170
Baseball Assistance Team (BAT) 143
Baseball Chapel 176
Baseball Network 108–109
Baseball with a Latin Beat 201
Bauer, Hank 44, 77, 79
Beckert, Glenn 89
Bell, Gus 164, 180–181
Bench, Johnny 78, 94, 136, 185, 187, 189, 192–192, 197
Benedict, Bruce 94
Berra, Dale 2–3, 49–58
Berra, Larry 50, 58
Berra, Tim 50, 58
Berra, Yogi 8, 30, 44, 49–55, 57–58, 80, 105, 138–139, 162, 189, 192, 201, 205, 208, 212
Bibby, Jim 128
Big State League 8
Billingham, Jack 136
Binghamton Triplets 178
Bird, Doug 90
Bjarkman, Peter 201–202
Blackwell, Ewell 178–179
Blair, Paul 152
Blanchard, Johnny 205, 208
Blomberg, Ron 127, 210

215

Index

Blue, Vida 196
Blyleven, Bert 171
Bockman, Eddie 62, 113
Boggs, Wade 41, 44–45
Bomback, Mark 56
Bonds, Barry 18, 54
Bonham, Ernie "Tiny" 170
Boros, Steve 199
Bostock, Lyman 145, 174–175
Boston Braves 179–180
Boston Celtics 77, 117–118
Boston Post 23
Boston Red Sox 18, 20–22, 25–27, 38–39, 41–42, 44–45, 47–48, 118, 150, 175, 189–190, 195–196, 213
Boswell, Ken 135
Boudreau, Lou 35, 204
Bouton, Jim 203–204
Bowa, Larry 59–71, 86, 199
Boyer, Clete 44, 81, 210
Boyer, Kenny 116
Branca, Ralph 13–15
Branzell, Joe 99
Brecheen, Harry 22, 30, 81
Brett, George 151
Brideweser, Jim 75
Bridge on the River Kwai 56
Bridges, Tommy 168
Brigham Young University 159
Briles, Nellie 111–124
Brissie, Lou 76
Brock, Lou 117, 120
Brokaw, Tom 79
Brookens, Tom 100
Brooklyn Dodgers 8–9, 13–16, 22, 59, 77–79, 106, 161–163, 196, 204
Brosius, Scott 35–36
Brown, Bobby 73, 75
Brown, Joe 11, 121
Brown, Kevin 193
Brown, Skinny 83
Buck, Joe 70
Buddin, Don 44
Budig, Dr. Gene 33
Buffalo Bisons 206
Buhner, Jay 55
Bunning, Jim 7, 42, 46–47, 64, 83, 88
Burris, Ray 108–109

Cali, Rose 57
California (Los Angeles) Angels 47, 60, 100, 130, 155, 171–172, 174–175, 198, 206
California State League 21

Caminiti, Ken 39
Camden Yards 69
Campaneris, Bert 196
Campanis, Al 108
Canadian Provincial League 204
Can-Am League 40
Candlestick Park 114, 209
Cannon, Robert 7
Carew, Rod 172
Carlton, Steve 31, 68, 123, 176
Carolina League 129
Carolina Textile League 167
Carpenter, Bob 180–181
Carroll, Parke 209
Carter, Amon 105
Cash, Dave 121, 155
Cattrell, Patty 113
Cedeno, Cesar 100
Cepeda, Orlando 117, 119–120
Cerv, Bob 84
Chambliss, Chris 151–152
Chance, Frank 189
Chandler, Spud 23
Chicago Cubs 18, 29, 68, 88, 94, 168, 189
Chicago White Sox 29–30, 42, 60, 78, 142, 169, 173, 195, 204
Chiles, Eddie 105, 141
Christopher, Joe 159, 162
Cincinnati Reds 52, 60, 77–78, 91, 99, 115, 134, 136–137, 154, 178–182, 185, 188–192, 197, 208, 212
Cisco, Galen 94
City College of San Francisco 73
Clayborne, John 198
Clemens, Roger 70, 171, 189
Clemente, Roberto 9–11, 27, 117, 130, 133–134, 145, 153–155, 158–159, 162–163, 182–183, 185–186, 191
Clendenon, Donn 139
Cleveland Indians 1, 2, 15, 32, 35–36, 42, 75–76, 78, 82, 84, 189
Clyde, David 100
Coates, Jim 9–10
Cochrane, Mickey 192
Colborn, Jim 152
Coleman, Jerry 73, 75, 80
Combs, Merrill 22
Comer, Steve 101
Comiskey Park 169, 173
Commodore Hotel 114
Concepcion, Dave 60
Cone, David 36, 49
Conley, Gene 18
Consolo, Billy 26

Consuegra, Sandy 204
Cora, Joey 71
Corrales, Pat 105
Cosell, Howard 78
Costas, Bob 59
Craft, Harry 178, 204
Cronin, Joe 22, 26, 198
Crosetti, Frank 75, 84, 209
Crosley Field 11–12, 179–180
Cy Young Award 66

Daley, Pete 42, 44
Dallas Cowboys 106
Dalton, Harry 198
Darl, Al 16
Davis, Chili 35
Davis, Willie 116
Dawson, Andre 57
Dean, Dizzy 112
DeJesus, Ivan 68
Del Canton, Bruce 94
Delock, Ike 44
Demars, Billy 64
Dempsey, Jack 18
designated hitter 33, 56, 96, 200, 210
Detroit Tigers 20, 25–26, 29, 42, 46, 56, 78, 101, 126, 143, 162–163, 167–169, 175–176, 190, 193, 198–199, 204, 208, 213
Devine, Bing 121
Dickey, Bill 192, 209
Dickson, Murry 22
DiMaggio, Dom 23–26, 72
DiMaggio, Joe 56, 72, 77, 92, 150, 169–170, 177
Dobson, Pat 149
Doby, Larry 35, 57
Dodger Stadium 91
Doerr, Bobby 24–25, 27, 47
Donnelly, Rich 104
Donovan, Dick 47
Doyle, Denny 64
Dressen, Charlie (Chuck) 16
Dropo, Walt 26
Drysdale, Don 45, 70, 117, 171
Duncan, Dave 196
Duren, Ryne 46, 90
Durocher, Leo 13, 15, 18, 53, 88, 194

Eastern League 204
Eastern Shore League 40
Ebbets Field 9,12
Elizabethtown College 87
Embry, Wayne 118

Ennis, Del 90
Erskine, Carl 8
Escalera, Nino 182
Evans, Darrell 173
Evers, Johnny 189
expansion 33, 70
Face, Elroy 157, 164
Fairly, Ron 116
Fantasy Camp 176
Feezle, Stan 8
Feller, Bob 35, 78
Fenway Park 36, 39, 41, 43, 46–47, 117, 169
Figeroa, Ed 152
Finch, Steve 101
Fingers, Rollie 196
Finley, Charles 147, 197–198, 200
Firestone, Roy 2
Fisk, Carlton 187
Flood, Curt 117, 120
Florence, Paul 190
Florida Marlins 35
Florida State League 86, 190
Foli, Tim 52, 55
Forbes Field 9, 11, 88, 163
Ford, Whitey 30, 44, 189, 206, 208, 210
Foster, George 197
Fowler, Dick 25
Fox, Nellie 30
Fregosi, Jim 130–132
Friend, Bob 7–19, 156–157, 184
Friends of Yogi 57
From Here to Eternity 40
Furillo, Carl 17

Game-of-the-Week 61, 112
Garber, Dick 86
Garber, Gene 85–97
Garber, Karen 96
Garcia, Dave 175
Garcia, Mike (Indians) 42, 78, 206
Garcia, Mike (Mariners) 59
Garciaparra, Nomar 60
Gardner, Billy 43–44
Garner, Phil 53
Garrett, Wayne 138
Gehrig, Lou 49, 67, 150
Gentry, Gary 132
Gernert, Dick 26
Gibson, Bob 33, 70, 116–119, 123, 154, 195
Gibson, Kirk 190, 199
Girardi, Joe 49
Glavine, Tom 95

Gold Glove Award 30, 38, 45, 60, 160, 189, 202
Gomez, Lefty 21–22, 178
Gomez, Preston 191
Goosetree, Eddie 167
Gorbous, Glen 180
Gordon, Joe 22
Gordon, Sid 15
Grammas, Alex 193
Gray, Jim 138
The Greatest Generation 79
Green, Dick 196
Greenberg, Hank 49, 168
Greengrass, Jimmy 177–183
Greenwade, Tom 26
Greer, Rusty 35–36
Grieve, Tom 106
Griffey, Ken 60
Griffey, Ken, Jr. 60
Griffith, Cal 200
Griffith Stadium 74
Grimm, Charlie 168
Grissom, Marv 9
Groat, Dick 10–11, 158, 185–186
Grove, Lefty 29
Grubb, John 104
Guidry, Ron 152
Guiliani, Mayor Rudolph 36
Guinness, Alec 56
Gulf Coast League 206
Gulf Oilers 14
Gullett, Don 136
Gwynn, Tony 71

Haddix, Harvey 30, 181–182
Hagen, Paul 102
Hall of Fame 10, 24–25, 29, 31, 35, 42, 48, 66–67, 77–78, 82, 92–94, 119, 122, 124, 137, 147, 150, 160, 181, 190, 192, 197, 207, 209
Hamey, Roy 209
Hamner, Granny 90
Haney, Fred 78
Hankin, Buddy 8
Harder, Mel 80
Harrelson, Bud 51, 137, 139
Harvard University 191
Hatfield, Freddy 26
Hayes, Charlie 103
Hegan, Jim 212
Helling, Rick 34–35
Henderson, Rickey 103
Henrich, Tommy 23
Herman, Billy 45

Hernandez, Orlando "El Duque" 34, 59
Herndon, Larry 173
Herrmann, Ed 149
Hershiser, Orel 164
Herzog, Whitey 31
Higgins, Pinky 25, 27, 45
Hoak, Don 157, 185
Hodges, Gil 8, 15, 131, 164
Hodges, Russ 13
Holland, Al 103
Holtzman, Ken 138, 196
Honeycutt, Rick 102–103
Hornsby, Rogers 74–75, 178–179, 182
Houk, Ralph 26, 41, 79, 198, 205, 208–214
Houston Astrodome 186, 188
Houston Astros 39, 43, 56, 66, 159, 173, 187–188, 190
Howard, Elston 32, 77, 201–205, 208, 214
Hubbell, Carl 156–157
Hunter, Billy 104–105
Hunter, Jim "Catfish" 147–150, 189, 196–197, 213
Hyatt Hotel 114

I'm Glad You Didn't Take It Personally 203
Industrial League 14
Instructional League 114
International League 204

Jackson, Grant 151
Jackson, Larry 9, 45
Jackson, Michael 103
Jackson, Milt 117
Jackson, Reggie 18, 56, 147, 152, 189, 196–197, 213
James, Mick 143
James Madison University 98, 100–101
Jansen, Larry 79
Javier, Julian 116, 120
Jenkins, Ferguson 142
Jensen, Jackie 43–44, 48
Jeter, Derek 32, 35–36, 54, 59–60, 81
Johns Hopkins Medical Center 150, 181
Johnson, Billy 75–76
Johnson, Bob 122
Johnson, Darryl 105
Johnson, Ernie 21
Johnson, Tom 12
Johnson, Walter 171
Jones, Cleon 139
Jones, K. C. 118
Jones, Willie 90

Joost, Eddie 73, 81
Jordan, Michael 78
Joss, Addie 35

Kaat, Jim 2, 28–37
Kaline, Al 208
Kansas City A's 81, 147, 202, 204–205, 209
Kansas City Royals 66, 90–91, 94, 96, 100–101, 151–153, 155, 172
Kauffman, Ewing 100
Keane, Johnny 115–116, 210
Kell, George 45
Kelly, Tom 213
Kemp, Steve 55
Kessinger, Don 89
Key, Jimmy 173
Killebrew, Harmon 32, 47–48
King, Clyde 55
Klein, Joe 101
Kluszewski, Ted 181–182
Knepper, Bob 173
Knothole Gang 61
Knowles, Darold 197
Koosman, Jerry 128–129, 132, 139
Korean War 40
Kosko, Andy 136
Koufax, Sandy 9, 116–117, 171
Kranepool, Ed 50
Krichell, Paul 177
Kroc, Joan 70, 199
Kroc, Ray 70, 198–199
Kruk, John 71
Kubek, Tony 9, 44, 210

Labine, Clem 161–165, 184
Labratich, Steve 143
Lafayette Red Sox 8
Lanier, Hal 56
Larsen, Don 49
Lary, Frank 42, 83
Lasher, Fred 1
Lasorda, Tom 86, 194, 214
Laver, Rod 18
Law, Vern "Deacon" 88–89, 156–160
Lemon, Bob 35, 42, 78
Lemon, Jim 30
Lenhardt, Don 26
Leonard, Dennis 152
Lepcio, Ted 26
Lextano, Sixto 104
Littell, Mark 151–152
Little League 29, 63, 96, 112, 126–127
Lockman, Whitey 16

Lolich, Mickey 20, 171, 176
Long, Dale 8
Lopez, Al 8, 76
Lopez, Hector 201–207, 210
Los Angeles Coliseum 45
Los Angeles Dodgers 9, 73, 93, 108, 113, 116, 190, 193, 198
Lucchesi, Frank 63–64
Luisetti, Hank 78
Lumpe, Jerry 204
Luzinski, Greg 57, 67
Lyle, Sparky 149, 152, 212

MacArthur, John D. 198
Mack, Connie 29, 190
MacPhail, Lee 26, 213
Maddox, Garry 188
Maddux, Greg 95, 170
Madlock, Bill 52
Maglie, Sal 162
Major League Baseball Players Association (MLBPA) 7, 98, 101–103
Malzone, Amy 38, 40, 42, 44
Malzone, Frank 2, 38–48
Mantle, Mickey 13, 31–33, 43–44, 50, 74–76, 80, 161, 169–170, 189, 205, 208–211, 214
Manush, Heinie 22, 120
Marichal, Juan 122
Marion, Red 30
Maris, Roger 119–120, 189, 208–210, 214
Markusen, Bruce 133
Marquard, Rube 157
Marquis, Bob 179
Marshall, Max 22
Martin, Billy 53, 56, 75, 80, 105, 149, 187, 194, 204, 214
Martinez, Buck 152
Martinez, Edgar 59
Martinez, Jose 101
Martinez, Tino 29, 35–36, 59
Masterson, Walt 75
Mathews, Eddie 9, 78
Matlack, Diane 142–144
Matlack, Jennifer 144
Matlack, Jon 3, 102, 125–144
Matlack, Jonathan Daniel 144
Matlack, Kristen 144
Maugham, Somerset 5
Maxville, Dal 120
Mays, Willie 17, 53, 158, 161, 169, 191–192, 196, 209
Mazeroski, Bill 8, 10, 12, 25, 84, 121, 153, 157, 160, 163, 185

220 Index

McCarver, Tim 70, 116, 119
McCovey, Willie 209
McDonald, Joe 140
McDougald, Gil 72–84
McDowell, Sam 1, 42
McGraw, John 190
McGraw, Tug 130
McGwire, Mark 18, 54, 69, 170, 189, 200, 209–210
McHale, John 26
McKeon, Jack 90, 199
McLemore, Mark 34, 36
McRae, Hal 185
McWilliams, Larry 91
Memorial Stadium 173
Merritt, Jim 48
Messiah College 85
Michael, Gene 148
Millan, Felix 138
Miller, Marvin 7
Miller Huggins Field 131
Milwaukee Braves 9, 17, 77–78, 158
Milwaukee Brewers 104, 156
Milwaukee County Stadium 104
Minnesota Twins 30, 47–48, 174, 213
Mizell, "Vinegar Bend" 164
Modern Jazz Quartet 117
Monroe, Marilyn 72
Montanez, Willie 140
Montclair State University 49, 57
Montreal Expos 64, 68, 188, 198–199
Montreal Royals 14
Moose, Bob 87–88, 145, 154, 159–160, 185
Morgan, Joe (Red Sox) 114
Morgan, Joe (Reds) 189, 197
Mossi, Don 42, 78, 206
Most Valuable Player Award 10, 74, 81, 100, 158, 173, 186, 195, 202
Mueller, Don 16
Mullaney, Jack 23
Municipal Stadium (Cleveland) 75
Municipal Stadium (Kansas City) 204–205
Munson, Thurman 145, 147–148, 150, 152–153, 173–174, 187, 191–192, 212
Murcer, Bobby 1–2, 94, 148, 211–212, 214
Murtaugh, Danny 10, 121, 156–159, 162–163, 185–186
Musial, Stan 9, 58
Myer, Billy 8
My Turn at Bat 25

Namath, Joe 18
Narleski, Ray 78, 206

National Basketball Association (NBA) 36, 73, 108
National Hockey League (NHL) 21
National League 9, 13, 45–46, 59, 71, 77, 100, 107, 124, 140, 164, 169, 180, 186–187, 190, 196–197
National League Championship Series (NLCS) 52, 121, 136, 154, 185, 190, 198
Nettles, Graig 148, 152, 212
Nevell, Bob 179
New England Patriots 18
New Jersey Jackals 49, 58
New York Daily News 98
New York Giants 13–18, 39, 77, 79, 161, 163
New York Giants (football) 18
New York Jets 18
New York Knicks 36
New York Mets 50–51, 56, 59–60, 68, 70, 115, 127–132, 136–140, 154, 164, 172, 175
New York-Penn League 51
New York Times 98, 132
New York University 98
New York Yankees 1, 8–10, 12, 24, 26, 28–29, 31, 33–36, 39, 44, 50, 53–56, 59, 61, 71–74, 76–78, 80–81, 105, 113, 118–119, 131, 147, 151–152, 162–163, 169, 177–179, 184, 186, 189–192, 195, 197–198, 200–201, 203–213
Newcombe, Don 16
Newell, Pete 73
Newhouser, Hal 78, 168
Newsom, Bobo 168
Niekro, Phil 92–94
Nolan, Joe 91
Norman, Nelson 103
Northern League 49

Oakland A's 118, 134, 138, 189, 196–198
O'Brien, Harry 14
O'Connell, Dick 47, 196
Odom, Blue Moon 196
Old Timers' Game 37, 44, 55, 131, 178
Oliver, Al 105, 155
O'Malley, Walter 196
O'Neill, Paul 29, 35–36
O'Neill, Steve 168–169
Ordonez, Rey 81
Otis, Amos 151
Ott, Mel 15
Owens, Jesse 18
Ozark, Danny 90

Index

Pacific Coast League 22–23, 38, 73, 113, 181
Palmeiro, Rafael 28
Pankovits, Jim 100
Parcells, Bill 18–19
Parker, Dave 57
Patek, Fred 151–155
Paul Gabe 178-18
Pearson, Albie 43
Pellagrini, Eddie 22
Pepitone, Joe 50, 202, 211–212
Perez, Marty 134
Perez, Tony 78, 130, 189, 197
Perrone, Charles 127
Perry Como Show 16
Pesky, Johnny 2, 20–27, 45, 90
Pesky, Vinnie 21
Pete Rose—My Life 91
Peterson, Pete 52
Phelps, Ken 101
Philadelphia A's 25, 29, 81, 89
Philadelphia Daily News 102
Philadelphia Phillies 15, 31, 52, 60, 62–63, 65–67, 71, 89–91, 93–94, 103, 113, 115, 180–181, 188, 190, 198
Phillips, Cy 39
Phillips, Richie 32
Piazza, Mike 54, 70, 180
Pierce, Billy 42
Piersall, Jimmy 26, 44
Piniella, Lou 53, 60, 152
Pittsburgh Pirates 8–12, 27, 45, 51–55, 84, 86–88, 90, 94, 104, 113, 117, 121–122, 133, 153–157, 159, 162–163, 184–186, 199, 209
Pittsburgh Pirates Alumni Association 111, 123
PNC Stadium 11, 123
Polo Grounds 12, 16, 18, 39, 183
Pony League 177
Portland Beavers 113
Posada, Jorge 36, 49
Power, Vic 201–202, 204
Pride of the Yankees 49–50
Prince, Bob 158
Puckett, Kirby 103

Radatz, Dick 206
Rader, Doug 105
Raines, Tim 100
Ramos, Pedro 30
Reynolds, Allie 166
Richards, Gene 100
Richards, Paul 169

Richardson, Bobby 8, 44, 50, 209–210
Rickey, Branch 8–9, 196
Riessenger, Grover 114–115
Rivera, Mariano 59
Riverfront Stadium 129, 136, 179, 185
Rivers, Mickey 152, 192
Rizzuto, Phil 61, 75, 80–81
Roberts, Curt 180
Roberts, Robin 7, 90
Robertson, Oscar 78
Robinson, Aaron 208
Robinson, Brooks 48
Robinson, Don 103
Robinson, Frank 70, 94–95, 108, 212
Robinson, Jackie 13–14, 162, 196
Rocker, John 137, 207
Rodriguez, Alex 59, 81
Roe, Preacher 22
Rogers, Dr. Harry 180
Rohr, Les 128
Rohrke, Jack 15
Rolfe, Red 23
Rooker, Jim 90
Rookie-of-the-Year Award 132
Rosar, Buddy 25
Rose, Pete 66–67, 91–93, 136–138, 189–190, 192, 197, 207
Rowe, "Schoolboy" 168
Royals Stadium 152
Rudi, Joe 196
Runnels, Pete 43–44, 48
Russell, Bill (Celtics) 117–118
Rutgers University 98, 110
Ruth, Babe 39, 189, 208–209
Ryan, Nolan 62, 106, 128, 130–132, 166, 171, 173, 176, 187

Sadecki, Ray 116
Safety, Joe 55
Sain, Johnny 27
St. Louis Browns 169
St. Louis Cardinals 9, 12, 22, 25, 31, 45, 50, 76, 99, 113–119, 181, 195, 210
Sample, Billy 2, 98–110
San Antonio Spurs 36
Sanders, Ray 22
San Diego Padres 51, 68, 70–71, 93, 142–143, 190–191, 193, 198–199
San Francisco Giants 42, 73, 94, 113, 119, 121–122, 209
San Francisco Seals 72
Santa Clara University 112–113
Santiago, Benito 71
Santo, Ron 89

Sayles, Bill 113
Schaal, Paul 47
Schmelz, Al 128
Schmidt, Mike 57, 66–67
Schoendienst, Red 116–117, 120, 123
Scioscia, Mike 109
Score, Herb 42, 82–84, 135, 206
Scott, George 202
Scurry, Rod 103
Seattle Kingdome 69
Seattle Mariners 59–60, 64, 71, 73, 173
Seaver, Tom 50, 70, 123, 129–130, 132–133, 136, 138–139, 143
Selig, Bud 207
Seminick Andy 180
Seymour, Cy 180
Shannon, Mike 116, 118, 120
Shantz, Bobby 81
Shaughnessy, Frank 167
Shea Stadium 51, 57, 114–115, 140, 149, 198
Sheehy, Pete 76
Shenandoah Valley League
Shephard, Larry 89
Sheppard, Bob 150
Sherry, Norm 175
Shibe Park (Connie Mack Stadium) 64, 89
Shirley, Bob 51
Silvera, Frank 73
Simmons, Ted 109
Simpson, Harry "Suitcase" 204
Singleton, Ken 28
Skinner, Bob 63, 185
Skowron, Bill "Moose" 30, 44, 77, 210
Slaughter, Enos 25
Smith, Al 30
Smith, Ballard 199
Smith, Hal 10
Smith, Ozzie 60, 192
Smith, Randy 143
Smith, Willie 89
Snider, Duke 16
Soar, Hank 212
Sojo, Luis 36
Sosa, Sammy 69, 162, 189, 200, 209
South Carolina State University 100
Spahn, Warren 9, 179
Speaker, Tris 35
Spencer, Shane 36
Splittorff, Paul 152
Sporting News 180
Sports Data Network 134
Sports Illustrated 98, 207

Sportsman's Park 115
Stanky, Eddie 13, 114, 195
Stanley, Fred 149
Stargell, Willie 57, 108
Staub, Rusty 136–137
Steinbrenner, George 36–37, 55–56, 148, 187, 213
Stengel, Casey 45, 50–51, 75–76, 79–83, 169, 178, 192, 194, 205, 208–209
Stennett, Rennie 51
Stephens, Gene 26
Stephens, Vern 26
Stevens, Lee 35
Stobbs, Chuck 74
Stoffer, Blair 104
Stone, Mike 105
Stoneman, Bill 64
Stottlemyre, Mel 50
Strawberry, Darryl 211–212
Stuart, Dick 9, 185
Sullivan, Haywood 47, 213
Sutter, Bruce 91
Swoboda, Ron 50

Tampa Bay Devil Rays 195
Tanana, Frank 171–176
Tanner, Chuck 52–53, 105
Tebbetts, Birdie 180
Tenace, Gene 196
Terry, Ralph 8, 209–210
Texas League 74, 104, 114
Texas Rangers 28, 34, 36, 98–102, 104–106, 122, 131, 140–142, 152, 175, 189
Thomas, Dr. C. I. 82
Thompson, Jim 76
Thomson, Bobby 13–19
Thornball, Roger 183
Three Rivers Stadium 111, 123, 133
Throneberry, Faye 26
Tiant, Luis 42
Tidrow, Dick 151
Tiger Stadium 36, 169, 173, 193–194
Tinker, Joe 189
Tobik, Dave 100
Topping, Dan 77
Toronto Blue Jays 141, 172–173
Torre, Joe 105, 150, 197
Torrez, Mike 152
Triandos, Gus 74
Triple Crown 48, 195, 212
Trout, Dizzy 78
Trucks, Virgil 78, 166–170
Tufts University 191
Tunney, Gene 18

Turley, Bob 206
Turner, Jim 80, 169, 209

Ueberroth, Peter 55
University of Massachusetts 50
University of Minnesota 101
University of Pittsburgh 128
University of San Francisco 73
University of South Alabama 195
University of Texas 104
USA Today 98
USA Today Baseball Weekly 98

Valentine, Bobby 106
Valo, Elmer 25
Vander Meer, Johnny 166
Vaughn, Mo 60
Vernon, Mickey 44
Veterans Stadium 64, 89
Vietnam War 87
Virdon, Bill 9, 130, 148–149, 184–188

Wakefield, Dick 169–170
Waldman, Suzyn 34
Walker, Harry 22, 25
Walker, Rube 132
Warwick, Carl 115
Washington, Denzel 99
Washington, U. L. 100
Washington Senators 26, 30, 43, 168, 206
Weaver, Earl 122, 194, 214
Weidman, Abe 86
Weiss, George 83
Wellman, Bob 62
Wells, David 36, 49
Welsh, Bob 103–104
West Chester Teacher's College 125, 128–129
Western Hockey League 21
Western International League 74

White, Bill 116
White, Frank 100
White, Roy 152, 212
White, Sammy 26, 44
Wight, Bill 26, 41
Wildrick, Paul 177
Williams, Bernie 35–36
Williams, Billy 89, 134
Williams, Dick 47, 195–200, 214
Williams, Ted 2, 16, 20, 22–27, 42–45, 48, 58, 169–170, 206
Williams, Walt "No-Neck" 148–149
Willis, Vic 31
Wills, Bump 104
Wilson, Don 145, 153–154, 187
Woodling, Gene 77, 164
World Series 8–10, 12, 18, 25, 31, 35–36, 50, 52, 56, 59–60, 65–66, 68, 70, 77–80, 84, 92, 96, 103, 115, 117–118, 120, 122, 129, 138, 151–153, 155, 157–158, 161–163, 168, 172, 184, 189–192, 195, 197–199, 205, 207–209
World War One 20
World War Two 32, 79
Wright, Teresa 49
Wrigley Field 64
Wynn, Early 42, 47, 78, 206
Wyse, Hooks 168

Yankee Stadium 1, 28–30, 32–33, 36–37, 39, 44, 55, 59, 77, 94, 149–151, 155, 198, 205
Yastrzemski, Carl 27, 44, 48, 118, 195
Yawkey, Tom 27, 47–48, 196, 213
Yogi Berra Museum 49–50, 55, 57
Yogi Berra Stadium 49

Zauchin, Norm 43
Zimmer, Don 105–106, 164
Zisk, Richie 104

www.ingramcontent.com/pod-product-compliance
Ingram Content Group UK Ltd.
Pitfield, Milton Keynes, MK11 3LW, UK
UKHW041949140426
5217IPUK00014B/720